Donated to
Taylor Historical Society
by
Reginald "Reggie" Fields
1116 Marsh Lane, Apt. 805
Carrolltown, TX 75006-4997
May 17, 2002

THE LOUISIANA AND ARKANSAS RAILWAY

James R. Fair

THE LOUISIANA
— and —
ARKANSAS RAILWAY

The Story of a Regional Line

NORTHERN ILLINOIS UNIVERSITY PRESS

DeKalb 1997

© 1997 by Northern Illinois University Press
Published by Northern Illinois University Press
DeKalb, Illinois 60115
Manufactured in the United States
using acid-free paper ♲ ∞
Design by Julia Fauci

Library of Congress
Cataloging-in-Publication Data
Fair, James R., 1920–
The Louisiana and Arkansas Railway : the story
of a regional line / James R. Fair
        p.   cm.
Includes bibliographical references and index.
ISBN 0-87580-219-2 (alk. paper)
1. Louisiana and Arkansas Railway Co.
2. Railroads—Louisiana. 3. Railroads—Texas.
I. Title.
TF25.L77F35   1997
385'.09763—dc21
96-53960
CIP

James Rutherford Fair

10-14-1920 / 10-11-2010

To Merle and the children

CONTENTS

Preface   *ix*

Introduction   *xi*

Abbreviations   *xiii*

1   William Edenborn, Steel Industry Captain   *3*

2   Edenborn Builds His Personal Railroad   *11*

3   Operation of the LR&N   *21*

4   The Earliest L&A Antecedent: The Texas Line   *41*

5   William Buchanan and the Original L&A   *53*

6   Harvey Couch and the New L&A   *69*

7   A Big Little Railroad   *99*

8   Submerged in the Holding Company: The Final Dissolution   *113*

Afterword   *123*

Appendix A: New Orleans Operations, 1944   *125*

Appendix B: Locomotives of the L&A   *127*

Notes   *129*

Works Cited   *145*

Index   *151*

SHORT LINE
THROUGH THE HEART
OF
LOUISIANA

The research on which this book is based began in late 1970. I had just completed a book, *The North Arkansas Line,* and was casting about for another railroad-history project, on a subject with which I had some familiarity. In collaboration with Harold Vollrath, then with the Kansas City Southern, I embarked on a study of the Kansas City Southern/Louisiana and Arkansas (KCS/L&A) system. While he dealt primarily with the KCS, I tackled the L&A.

My interest in the Louisiana and Arkansas dated back to a 1930 L&A public timetable my father brought to me. I recall with fondness waiting in the summer of 1934 at the Barlow Hotel, in Hope, Arkansas, which fronted on the Missouri Pacific depot plaza, for the arrival of the northbound *Shreveporter.* I was impressed by the clean, glistening locomotive and by the nameplate on the smokebox cover! I watched the train as its through Pullman was switched to the northbound MoPac and then saw the remainder of the train back down to the L&A yards and wye. In the morning it would make its return trip to Shreveport. On that same trip my father—who had more than a casual interest in trains—and I followed the former Louisiana Railway and Navigation Company main line between Shreveport and Alexandria, as well as the branch line from Packton to Ferriday. These were veritable "streaks of rust," dirt ballasted and overgrown with weeds, as was the rule for branch lines during the Great Depression. Later I had many encounters with the L&A, including working at the ordnance plant at Karnack, Texas, and watching an assortment of engines pulling wartime freight past the town's small depot.

During the course of work on our joint project, Harold and I found ourselves so busy earning a living that we were forced to abandon our venture. By then, however, I had written several chapters on the L&A and had conducted a considerable amount of research on the life of William Edenborn, a fascinating but little-known personality who built the LR&N. After moving from industry to academia in 1979, I began to think about completing the L&A portion of the project. Not until 1991, however, did I find time to dust off the old manuscript, update and expand it, gather additional illustrations, and transfer it all to my trusty computer.

As is always the case in endeavors of this type, many people have generously provided assistance. Foremost among them is Harold Vollrath of Kansas City, internationally known for his huge collection of excellent railroad photographs and now retired from the KCS. Harold gave me much of the "inside scoop" about railroad operations without betraying any confidences or deprecating the railroad in any way. The reader will note many references to his collection and his near-encyclopedic knowledge of the L&A/KCS. He is the epitome of "a scholar and a gentleman," and I acknowledge my utmost gratitude to him.

Other key people who made contributions are Hamric Holloway, former president of the Louisiana Midland; L. B. Williams, now deceased, who is quoted frequently in the book; Louis Saillard, a true railroad-history scholar, especially regarding lines in the Louisiana and Mississippi regions; Martha Street, archivist at Louisiana State University–Shreveport; and John W. Barriger III, now deceased, who opened his extensive files to me and provided several of the photographs in this book. Finally, I would like to acknowledge the support of my wife, Merle, who accompanied me on field trips and genially endured my absences from the family circle while I was absorbed in research.

At the beginning of 1992 the Louisiana and Arkansas, a profitable and well-maintained southern railroad line, connected Dallas to New Orleans. By the end of the year, however, the L&A, as it is known, had lost its corporate identity through a merger with its long-time parent company, the Kansas City Southern Railway. Like some other railroads of the region—namely, the Cotton Belt and the Texas and Pacific—the L&A had long endured complete control by a larger entity without losing its individuality of operation. With the merger, though, this independence was finally, and irrevocably, lost. It seems appropriate, therefore, that the story of the L&A be told at this time.

The modern L&A owed its existence to the work of three individuals—William Edenborn, William Buchanan, and Harvey Couch. They were men with wisdom, foresight, and a propensity for hard work, and each would be known today as a railfan. The story of the L&A is largely the story of these men and their longtime interests in trains as well as in the business and physical structures that supported those trains.

William Edenborn was an indigent immigrant from Germany whose rise to success in the American business world in the post–Civil War era could rival the accomplishments of any of Horatio Alger's heroes. Edenborn moved to the top of the steel-wire industry through technical genius, an ability to extract productivity and loyalty from his workers, and shrewd business management. His many patents gave him an edge in the technology of wire making as well as in products such as barbed wire. After selling his company, American Steel and Wire, to the newly formed United States Steel Corporation, Edenborn remained a key official of the new corporation. At the same time, he began to indulge a long-standing interest in railroads and embarked on a second business career, this time in the construction and operation of his own railroad.

Edenborn built and operated a rail line between Shreveport and New Orleans in Louisiana. He did this without a single dollar being provided by holders of stock or bonds or by loans from banks. Later, he purchased an extension that connected Shreveport with the Dallas, Texas, area. He owned it all, and he operated it autonomously. He gave the company the name Louisiana Railway and Navigation Company, and his trains ran over 541 miles of track. This was the route that formed the main line of the L&A until its dissolution in 1992.

At the turn of the century, when Edenborn was beginning his second career, William Buchanan was also beginning his venture into railroading. A native of Tennessee, Buchanan became wealthy in the lumber business and was credited as being the first mill operator to build a railroad to bring in logs. The railfan in Buchanan, however, urged him to extend his logging road and make it a common carrier. By 1917 he was operating some 300 miles of line in southern Arkansas and central Louisiana.

His railroad was well built and enormously profitable. As testimony to its success, it survived the Great Depression without a single deficit year. Unlike Edenborn, Buchanan chose to have others contribute to his enterprise, though he and his family always maintained financial control. He named his line the Louisiana and Arkansas Railway and connected it with Edenborn's line at Shreveport, Winnfield, and Alexandria in Louisiana.

The third member of the triumvirate was Harvey Couch, who appeared on the railroad scene in the 1920s. He made his fortune in the utilities business in Arkansas, Louisiana, and Mississippi. Always fascinated by trains, he purchased the properties built and developed by Edenborn and Buchanan in mid-1929. After the purchase, he indulged himself with frequent trips in the locomotive cabs and even learned to take over the controls himself. His combined system of 843 route-miles retained the name Louisiana and Arkansas Railway.

Couch's involvement with railroading continued beyond the L&A. With associates, he gained control of the larger Kansas City Southern Railway, a profitable road linking Kansas City with the Gulf Coast at Port Arthur, Texas, and Lake Charles, Louisiana. This maneuver was accomplished by the mid-1930s, and it was only natural that he would then ally his L&A with the KCS and take advantage of the common connection of the roads at Shreveport. For many years the combination was known as the KCS/L&A Lines.

In its last fifty years of existence, the L&A maintained a separate identity corporately if not operationally. When the railroads were taken into a holding company, Kansas City Southern Industries, in the 1970s, there began the end of the L&A that would have the inevitable outcome of dissolution.

This, then, is the story of the L&A—the "better way," as Harvey Couch wanted it to be known. Its history has been one of great interest, if not glamour. It is a case study of foresight by people who planned well and built things to last.

ABBREVIATIONS

EMC	Electro-Motive Corporation, later Electromotive Divisions of General Motors
ICC	Interstate Commerce Commission
KCS	Kansas City Southern Railway
L&A	Louisiana and Arkansas Railway
LR&N	Louisiana Railway and Navigation Company
T&P	Texas and Pacific Railroad
VS&P	Vicksburg, Shreveport and Pacific Railroad

THE LOUISIANA AND ARKANSAS RAILWAY

WILLIAM EDENBORN, STEEL INDUSTRY CAPTAIN

Between the Louisiana cities of Shreveport and New Orleans, the proverbial crow flies 280 miles. The shortest rail length between these cities measures 309 miles, a reasonable distance considering the presence of natural barriers such as rolling hills and major watersheds as well as the basic necessity of serving traffic-producing localities. The railroad that runs this stretch is the Louisiana and Arkansas, currently part of the Kansas City Southern system and formerly known as the Louisiana Railway and Navigation Company.

Three major personalities were involved in the development of the L&A system—William Buchanan, William Edenborn, and Harvey Couch—but the company was initially built, designed, financed, and operated by one person, William Edenborn. Biographies have been written for Buchanan and Couch, but little has been recorded about Edenborn, perhaps the most interesting character of the three.[1] Accordingly, this first chapter illuminates the career of William Edenborn, showing how his early years in business strongly influenced the L&A system[2] and covering important events that contributed to Edenborn's personality and business style. In particular, his propensity for succeeding without advice from—or obligation to—others is perhaps the key attribute that led to the unique development of the Shreveport–New Orleans segment of the L&A.

Edenborn was one of Louisiana's great benefactors. At the time of his death in 1926 he was said to be the state's wealthiest resident. His single-handed development and management of a major railroad has few, if any, parallels in history. His contributions to the state of Louisiana extended far beyond the domain of transportation. The *New Orleans Times-Picayune* characterized Edenborn as "one of the most colorful and picturesque,

and at the same time one of the least known, of the Louisiana captains of industry."[3] Few people realize, however, that Edenborn's career in Louisiana was his second significant corporate enterprise, his earlier achievements in the iron and steel industry in time gaining him recognition as "the father of the American wire industry."

William Edenborn was born on March 20, 1848, in Westphalia, Germany, to Jacob and Antoinette (Hessmer) Edenborn. His parents were affluent enough to place him in a private school, but when he was twelve years old, both of them died, a circumstance that left him and a younger sister, Lena, without continuing financial resources. They were taken into the home of relatives named Kayser, where William became a close companion of a cousin, Herman Kayser, two years his senior. Although William was an extremely bright student, deserving of continued formal education, he had to drop his studies and go to work as an apprentice in a nearby steel-wire plant at Plettenberg, in an industrial area later known as the Ruhr District of Germany. This turn of events provided Edenborn with the start of a rewarding career in the steel-wire industry.[4]

At Plettenberg, and later in nearby mills at Altena and Hamm, Edenborn obtained a basic knowledge of wire-production technology. He learned not only about the technology—for example, how to draw wire of a given diameter from metal rods—but also about the fabrication of nails, fencing, dress hoops, and other items from wire. By the time he was nineteen years old, he decided to seek his fortune in America, as so many Europeans were doing at the time. Making the journey with him was his friend and cousin, Herman Kayser, whom he persuaded to join him.[5]

Thus it was that in 1867 Edenborn and Kayser emigrated to the United States, arriving in New York to find that the post–Civil War reconstruction activity had created a great demand for steel-wire and wire products. The two young men easily found work with a small wire company in Frankstown, Pennsylvania, near Pittsburgh. A year later, Edenborn, impatient to find better opportunities, left Kayser behind and moved down the Ohio River to Cincinnati, Ohio, to take a job with another wire manufacturer, Globe Rolling Mill.

In 1869 Edenborn moved farther west, this time to St. Louis, where he assisted a local businessman, F. M. Ludlow, with the design of a new wire mill. This move reflected Edenborn's basic ambition as well as his growing reputation and expertise in the area of wire making. It is clear that he had already established himself as a knowledgeable and clever technician, and these skills were essential to the building of what would become the first wire factory in St. Louis. Because his arrangement with Ludlow seems to have been on a futures basis, whereby he would eventually obtain a share of the company, his needs for subsistence were satisfied by a part-time job as a laborer in the St. Louis Stamping Company plant.[6]

St. Louis seemed to suit Edenborn's taste for working opportunities as well as for living conditions, for he remained there for twenty-five years. Known to his friends as "Bill," Edenborn was not especially gregarious, though he seemed to meet people easily. He took room and board at various places, usually near his workplace, and participated in several activities at the Salem Methodist Church. In 1872 he met a young woman, Fida Dettly, a Swiss immigrant and household servant, with whom he attended social occasions, some related to the church. (Years later, after Edenborn's death, unsuccessful claims against his estate were made by an alleged offspring of this relationship, an individual who was born in 1874.) In 1876 Edenborn met Miss Sarah Drain, the attractive twenty-year-old daughter of John Drain, a prominent local merchant. After a brief romance, they became engaged and were married on October 4, 1876. During the course of their marriage, Sarah acted also as his helpmate and business

confidant, a partnership that continued until his death fifty years later.[7]

Edenborn was a hard worker and tended to be thrifty if not frugal. Keenly ambitious to succeed in the business world, he worked tirelessly to improve his knowledge of business-management methods. To support this effort, he took a business course at Jones's Commercial College in St. Louis. He always impressed his employers with a quickness of mind, an ingenuity with mechanical devices, a general knowledge of wire technology, and an unusual ability to produce a great deal of work over long hours.

These were the characteristics that helped Edenborn to succeed from the start. The wire enterprise that Edenborn created with Ludlow began production in late 1869; he personally drew the first piece of wire ever made west of Cincinnati.[8] He remained with Ludlow for several years, overseeing manufacturing operations until 1874, when he shifted into sales work with an affiliated company, the Ludlow-Saylor Wire Company. This new activity offered Edenborn more flexibility of schedule, giving him the opportunity the next year to take a brief leave of absence in order to travel to Europe, where he assessed state-of-the-art wire technology in Germany, France, and England. By 1877, feeling prepared technically and financially to go into business for himself, in partnership with Oliver P. Saylor, he leased the works originally built by F. M. Ludlow in 1869.[9]

The company formed by the Saylor-Edenborn partnership was named the St. Louis Wire Mills. Elation turned to dejection, however, after only a brief period of operation. Approximately sixty days after start-up, the plant was completely destroyed by fire, and there was no insurance to cover the loss. Edenborn had invested all his funds in the enterprise and was therefore forced on an interim basis to resort to such lower-level production tasks as making wire loops for soda bottles, an undertaking requiring very little capital investment. By the end of 1877, he was able to reactivate the Saylor association, this time bringing in a third partner, Daniel T. Wright. Each partner contributed $1,000, an

Sarah Edenborn, supportive
wife of William, in her forties.

William Edenborn in his for-
ties, still identified by the
trade journal as a "magnate
of the steel-wire industry"
(The Iron Age, *March 23,*
1899, 15).

John W. "Bet-a-Million" Gates has been described variously as Falstaffian and comical—but also as a shrewd businessman and salesman par excellence. He teamed up with Edenborn in the steel-wire business, handling financial and marketing matters while Edenborn took care of production and research. Gates was one of the founders of the Texas Company (Texaco) and also one of the principals of the KCS.

amount sufficient to rebuild the plant on a temporary basis and to bring it back into production.[10]

Still titled St. Louis Wire Mills, the new partnership was, in Edenborn's words, "exceedingly successful." Though within a year the partners lost the lease on their building, in early 1879 they were able to finance the construction of their own building, located at the corner of Twenty-first and Papin Streets. It was at this time that Edenborn bought out the other partners for a total of $11,400 and soon acquired a new partner, Thomas W. Fitch, president of Harrison Wire Company of St. Louis.[11]

Barbs on wire fencing had been introduced in 1874, an innovation that proved indispensable for the containment of cattle on ranches in the American Southwest. The initial patent for barbed wire was granted to Joseph Glidden, of DeKalb, Illinois, and to Isaac L. "Ike" Ellwood, also of DeKalb, who had joined forces with Glidden to promote the use of barbed wire. The success of this pair contributed to a rapidly growing demand for steel wire. In 1879, to accommodate de-

mand, Edenborn founded yet another company, the Missouri Barbed Fence Company, for which he served as both president and general manager. His recent associates contributed financially to this venture. Now the prime mover and principal owner of two concerns, one to draw wire from steel rods and the other to use a portion of the wire output to make barbed wire, Edenborn was clearly moving along in the business world in true Horatio Alger fashion.

Both of Edenborn's enterprises prospered, but in 1881 his barbed-wire company ran into problems of patent infringement. This led Edenborn to form yet another company, the Western Union Barbed Wire Fence Company, which apparently produced fencing material under patent agreements or licensing.[12] Edenborn was poised to move into larger ventures, and his first such move was to form the St. Louis Wire Mills Company, which was incorporated on November 27, 1882, under Missouri laws. Authorized capital stock was $500,000, with $100,000 paid in by Edenborn and Fitch, the former owning 51.1 percent of the stock. In early 1883 Fitch sold his stock to a local banker and moved to the Pittsburgh, Pennsylvania, area. Soon afterward, Edenborn bought the stock from the banker and became the sole owner of the company, a status he seemed to prefer during most of his business career.[13]

Later in 1882, Edenborn entered into business relations with John Warne Gates, one of the original barbed-wire salesmen for Glidden and Ellwood. Much has been written about Gates, including two full-length biographies. An aggressive and clever salesman and an opportunistic financial operator, he was, according to some, not adverse to poaching patents if it served his business needs. His career in steel, railroads, and petroleum was remarkably successful. Later he became known as a "notorious promoter" and a "speculative plunger" with the sobriquet "Bet-a-Million-Gates." For twenty years Gates and Edenborn worked together closely, their complementary talents making a team difficult for others to challenge. Edenborn's role was as manufacturer-technologist and friend of the employees, and Gates excelled as the super salesman and financial wizard.[14]

Gates had formed the Southern Barbed Wire Company in St. Louis around 1878, after employing now legendary methods for convincing ranchers in the Southwest that barbed-wire fencing was essential for containing their herds of cattle—and that they should buy their fencing from him. For his manufacture of barbed wire, he purchased wire stock from Edenborn. After an 1883 fire destroyed his plant, Gates convinced Edenborn that the two of them should join forces. As a result, St. Louis Wire Mills increased its paid-in capital to $250,000, with Edenborn holding 49 percent of the capital stock and the remainder divided between Gates, an associate of Gates named Alfred Clifford, and several other individuals.[15]

The Edenborn-Gates team seemed unbeatable. The expanded corporation acquired and absorbed a number of companies, including Southern Barbed Wire and Western Union Barbed Wire. Mills outside the St. Louis area were purchased or built. The business prospered greatly, almost to the bewilderment of Edenborn. In later years he commented, "After I got a start, I just went ahead in leaps and bounds. Everything I touched made money for me."[16] Edenborn put his mechanical cleverness to work to the financial advantage of the corporation. His first patent, issued December 13, 1881, covered a machine that put the point on wire nails. Three other patents in early 1883, on devices for making barbed wire, not only permitted the corporation to cut production costs but also provided a great competitive advantage in product pricing. In 1884 and 1885, more Edenborn patents followed, and more profits accrued.

With their corporation growing and their patent estate secure, Edenborn and Gates turned their attention to another problem. To obtain adequate raw material for wire making, they had to import special steel rods from Germany. They decided to build their own facility for producing the rods, and on November 20, 1885, they incorporated the Braddock Wire Company, which had headquarters in Pittsburgh and a manufacturing plant in nearby Rankin. This plant also produced vari-

ous forms of wire. Involved in this undertaking was Thomas Fitch, an earlier associate of Edenborn and the first superintendent of the Rankin mill. Initial production capacity was 100,000 pounds of rods per day.[17]

The culmination of this phase of Edenborn's career occurred in 1892 with the formation of the Consolidated Steel and Wire Company. Gates was the prime mover behind this merger of several companies, which generated a total paid-in capital of $4 million, but Edenborn was the largest shareholder. It is likely that by this time Edenborn's personal wealth exceeded $1 million. In addition to St. Louis Wire Mills and Braddock Wire, three other companies were absorbed: Lambert and Bishop Wire Fence Company, in Joliet, Illinois; Iowa Barb Wire Company, in Allentown, Pennsylvania; and Baker Wire Company, in Chicago. Total production of wire reached 560,000 tons per year, and *The Iron Age* states that the corporation combined "the largest drawers of plain wire, and also the largest makers of both barbed wire and wire nails, in the world."[18]

Consolidated Steel and Wire was incorporated under Illinois laws on September 21, 1892, and headquarters were set up in prestigious offices in Chicago in a building known as The Rookery. Edenborn became president; other principals were John Lambert, vice president, Alfred Clifford, treasurer, and F. E. Patterson, secretary. Gates was the general manager, a position that suggests he made a relatively low financial contribution to the enterprise.[19]

The company prospered. It seems to have been little troubled by the stock-market panic of 1893 and the depression that followed. *The Iron Age* notes in 1895 that the stock price for the company increased 40 percent in three years of business and that handsome dividends were paid. Edenborn's good fortune continued, and he began to diversify his investments. He established a working relationship with the Illinois Steel Company, for which Gates also served as an officer, to ensure the supply of raw material for Consolidated Steel and Wire. At this time he shifted his principal place of business from St. Louis to Chicago, and in 1895 he and his family moved to the Chicago area.[20]

Beyond indicating where he was residing, the record reveals little about Edenborn's personal life during this period of business success. His marriage appears to have been a happy one, judging from all accounts. Sarah Edenborn took care of domestic responsibilities and supported her husband's efforts by adjusting to the intense business demands on his time. He traveled a great deal, and Sarah often accompanied him on business trips. After St. Louis Wire Mills was formed, the Edenborns moved into a home in the fashionable LaFayette Park district of St. Louis. Edenborn's cousin and boyhood friend, Herman Kayser, moved from Pittsburgh in 1884 and rejoined him, and his sister, Lena, who had remained in Germany and married a man named Frederick Mann, came to St. Louis with six children in the mid-1880s after her husband's premature death. The Edenborns had a child, a daughter named Antoinette, who was born about 1880. A few years later, they adopted another child, Lilly, the granddaughter of Lena and Frederick, whose father had died shortly after coming to America.[21]

Misfortune struck the Edenborns in January 1895. At the age of fifteen, Antoinette, whom they adored and upon whom they lavished their attention, was killed by a trolley car near their Park Avenue home when she fell from a horse frightened by the trolley. The child apparently died instantly. The Edenborns buried her on property they had acquired west of St. Louis, near the town of Gumbo, marking the grave only by a cedar tree. Soon thereafter the bereaved Edenborns moved to Chicago, but tragedy seemed to pursue them. Three years after the move, their adopted daughter, Lilly, contracted diphtheria at the age of six and died after a short illness. In response to these personal misfortunes, Edenborn immersed himself in the problems of Consolidated Steel and Wire.[22]

The next business move by Edenborn and his associates was to form a large firm, American Steel and Wire Company. This firm, with a total capital stock of $24 million, resulted from the merging of Consolidated Steel and Wire with six other companies. Known as the "wire trust" and incorporated under Illinois laws on March 21, 1898, American Steel and Wire began business on April 3. John Lambert, who in 1879 had formed the Lambert and Bishop Wire Fence Company of Joliet, Illinois, served as president of this company. Edenborn settled for the positions of first vice president and member of the Executive Committee of the Board of Directors. Later, "Ike" Ellwood, who owned two of the merged companies, became the second vice president. Gates, who served as chairman, secured as general counsel for the new company the services of Judge Elbert Gary, who subsequently acted as the guiding genius in assembling the United States Steel Corporation.[23] Though New York banker J. P. Morgan had initially been involved in planning the new enterprise, he backed out in February, reportedly because he did not like the financial showing of "one of the companies." Morgan's biographer, Frederick Allen, speculates that an important motive for Morgan's withdrawal was his personal dislike and distrust of Gates, whose speculative methods he did not appreciate.[24]

Having combined seven plants of Consolidated Steel and Wire with seven plants of the six merged companies, American Steel and Wire had nearly a monopoly on the nation's steel-wire business. American Steel and Wire had a total capacity of up to 800,000 annual tons of wire and wire rods, used for the manufacture of "wire nails; barbed wire; woven wire fencing; plain, galvanized, 'bright' and other varieties of wire; together with sundry products." Production represented almost 75 percent of the total manufacture of steel wire in the United States.[25]

In March 1899, because Illinois law prohibits a company from purchasing the stock of another company, a new charter for American Steel and Wire was granted by the state of Delaware. This new entity began business on April 1. Capital stock of the new corporation was authorized at $90 million. The officers remained essentially the same as for the Illinois corporation chartered one year earlier.[26]

As he had always done, Edenborn continued to invent wire-processing machinery. All his patents were taken out in his name rather than in the name of his corporations, and *The Iron Age* notes that they were licensed extensively throughout the world. Royalties for these patents probably accrued directly to Edenborn, with his own companies being granted royalty-free licensing privileges. Records show that he applied for his sixteenth and final patent, for a wire-fencing machine, on November 13, 1899.[27]

The final chapter of Edenborn's career in steel came with the formation of the United States Steel Corporation in March 1901. The force behind the creation of "Big Steel" was J. P. Morgan, who had backed out of the earlier wire trust. The negotiation and planning of the enterprise extended over many months, with lawyer Elbert Gary acting as the chief architect. American Steel and Wire became a major component of U.S. Steel (the largest component was Carnegie Steel Company), and holders of its securities received $98.3 million in U.S. Steel common stock. Illinois Steel was another component, and in negotiations over management control, John Gates lost out to Morgan, who did not trust Gates. "I don't think the property is safe in his hands," the serious-countenanced Morgan was quoted as saying. Biographers have observed that this was the toughest encounter of Gates's career.[28]

Although Morgan emphatically refused Gates a place on the Big Steel Board of Directors, "faithful and stolid" Edenborn was eminently acceptable. After all, Big Wire had been merged into Big Steel, and wire know-how on the board was essential. Thus Edenborn, concerned about protecting his sizable investment, though now feeling some reluctance to continue in the steel business, agreed to become a member of the Big Steel board and a member of its Executive Committee. The latter body, chaired by Gary, was all-powerful in the operation of the corporation; the president, Charles Schwab, reported directly to it. Shortly after this merger, Edenborn opened an office in New York City. His initial appointment to the board was for two years. As things turned out, however, he accepted two subsequent three-year terms before finally resigning

from the board on November 30, 1909.[29]

During the period in which Edenborn founded American Steel and Wire, three years before U.S. Steel was formed, he had contemplated business ventures in other directions. Though he was working diligently to form American Steel and Wire, he had grown weary of the wire business. Through business connections, Edenborn had become interested in railroads, and he decided to indulge himself in this interest by building his own. Edenborn and his wife had visited Shreveport, the key business city in northern Louisiana as well as an important port on the Red River. There they had become charmed with the gardenlike river valley and decided on that locale for a "second career." Edenborn had perceived a need for improved transportation in the valley, especially for moving cotton, timber, and wood products to market. In his characteristic straightforward manner, he elected to build a railroad that would run southeastward from Shreveport and serve the cotton-growing regions along the river. Thus it was that on July 23, 1897, using his own finances, Edenborn obtained a charter for the Shreveport and Red River Valley Railway Company, under the general laws of the State of Louisiana.[30] With his Louisiana enterprise uppermost in his mind, Edenborn remained active in American Steel and Wire only because his partners prevailed upon him to do so.

The initiation and early development of U.S. Steel coincided with an active period of diversification of Edenborn's business interests. Because he was living in New York City and could not directly oversee progress on his Louisiana railroad venture, he was forced to rely heavily on two lieutenants who operated out of a Shreveport office. This required much in the way of letter and telegram communication, a situation Edenborn disfavored, because he disliked relinquishing control of the railroad venture by delegating too heavily. Another railroad venture with which Edenborn became involved was the Kansas City, Pittsburg and Gulf Railroad—recently completed between Kansas City and a new terminal, Port Arthur, Texas—which, in collaboration with

Gates, he reorganized. The reorganized enterprise was named the Kansas City Southern Railway Company. In March 1900 Edenborn was elected to its Board of Directors and shortly afterward was appointed first vice president. He remained on the board until 1902, when the troubled company could stand on its own again.

Yet further diversification of Edenborn's business interests occurred. During this period Edenborn became involved, as officer or as board member, in several St. Louis firms: Sheffield Coal and Iron Company, Superior Pressed Brick Company, and St. Louis Iron and Machine Works. He was also involved with the White Cliffs Cement Company in southwestern Arkansas. He had made large investments in the Vache Grasse coal fields of Sebastian County, Arkansas, and through his agents had begun buying vast acreages of timberlands in Louisiana, strategically located to serve his railroad or to divert other lines that might pose serious competition.[31]

As Edenborn turned away from the steel-wire business, he left behind a legacy of concepts and practices that had been instrumental in lowering the cost of wire production. One example is related in his words:

> I claim that by natural instincts or talent I made improvements in systems of manufacture, in tools and machines, by which a workman with the same muscular exertions as formerly could produce many times the daily output. F. M. Ludlow paid for drawing wire rods to No. 12, the size used for barb fencing, 66 cents per 100 [pounds], and when I ceased to manage the mills, the company paid 6 cents per 100. . . . I am entitled to considerable credit for improving the economical production of wire.[32]

Another of Edenborn's legacies was his attention to employee needs, a sensitivity that demonstrated his perceptiveness in human relations. At American Steel and Wire, for example, he organized the Employees' Benefit and Insurance Association for mill workers, with contributions made solely by the company. As Edenborn stated,

> I had [always] been in sole charge of machinery appliances of all kinds, and of labor. I had originated and succeeded in getting adopted . . . the formation of the scheme for the benefit of the sick or otherwise unfortunate employees and for a pension fund, and my successors found an organization of harmony between employees and officials which prevents strikes, lockouts and troubles, and I am convinced that the favorable results have continued and, under wise management, extended.[33]

Although not unique in industry and although suggesting paternalism, Edenborn's ideas about employee relations, recognized by the management of U.S. Steel, were particularly important during the gradual assimilation of employment practices of the several companies that became a part of the merger.[34]

William Edenborn had become wealthy in the steel business. He had achieved success through a combination of diligence, financial acumen, and the fortunes of the wire industry in a booming post–Civil War America. He was able to enter the railroad business in a relatively carefree fashion with the formation of the Shreveport and Red River Valley Railway Company and through his participation on the Board of Directors for the Kansas City Southern Railway Company. He certainly had the financial resources to undertake this new field. But could he conquer it?

EDENBORN BUILDS HIS PERSONAL RAILROAD

When William Edenborn's business interests shifted from wire and steel making to the construction and operation of railroads, he used the wealth he had amassed in steel to build a railroad in Louisiana. A state far removed from his familiar territory, it was nevertheless attractive both to him and to his wife. Extricating himself from his steel responsibilities took much longer than he had planned, and in the interim he managed his railroad at a distance through others, delegating to them the everyday tasks of construction and operation. Though he communicated largely through letters and telegrams, he was also able to visit occasionally, and the work progressed remarkably smoothly, considering Edenborn's innate desire to supervise directly.

Clarence Ellerbe became the "man on location" and the prime contact for Edenborn. A native of Alabama, Ellerbe was twenty-three years old and living in New Orleans when Edenborn hired him. How the two men became acquainted is not known. Though Ellerbe had no previous railroad experience, he presumably knew the territory. It is surprising that Edenborn did not seek out a more mature person, one with some railroad construction or operation experience, but Ellerbe evidently convinced him that he could handle the problem of absentee management—never an easy task.[1]

Edenborn planned for the Shreveport and Red River Valley Railroad to run through the Louisiana parishes of Red River and Bossier, along the left bank of the river, to a point at or near the town of Coushatta, some 44 miles southeast of Shreveport. There was no direct rail competition for the planned route, but across and removed a few miles from the river the Texas and Pacific had its main line between Shreveport and Alexandria. In addition, to the north, an individual named William Buchanan, of Stamps, Arkansas, soon began a southward extension of his Louisiana and Arkansas Railway from Sibley, Louisiana, 27 miles east of Shreveport, along a route roughly parallel with Edenborn's projected road. Edenborn clearly had no intention of stopping construction at Coushatta—a quiet, 44-mile feeder line would hardly be a worthy challenge for a second business career.

When the Shreveport and Red River Valley Railroad was chartered in 1897, it was authorized to issue capital stock at a rate of $20,000 per mile of road constructed and to sell first mortgage bonds at the same rate. Edenborn served as president of the railroad and Ellerbe as secretary. Directors were George Fouke and Ben Collins, of Texarkana; W. F. Taylor, a Shreveport businessman; and Edenborn's brother-in-law, Edgar Drain, of Chicago.[2] Fouke and Collins, who had just completed a railroad between Texarkana and Shreveport, brought experience to the fledgling line and provided insights into Edenborn's venture. Furthermore, it was hoped that their railroad, the Texarkana–Shreveport Railway, would offer an important connection for freight to and from the Iron Mountain and Cotton Belt lines at Texarkana. Unfortunately for the Shreveport and Red River Valley Railroad, its competitor, the Texas and Pacific, acquired the Fouke-Collins line shortly after the latter was re-chartered in 1899, thus removing a convenient northern outlet.[3]

Edenborn formed a separate company to serve as prime contractor for all procurement and construction work on the line. The Louisiana Central Construction Company, chartered on January 6, 1898, was convenient for accounting and legal purposes, and it enjoyed a limited liability. Serving as president of the construction company, Ellerbe

This American-type (4-4-0 wheel arrangement) was the first motive power owned by the Shreveport and Red River Valley. A product of Baldwin Locomotive Works, it was purchased secondhand from the New York, Pennsylvania and Ohio line in December 1897. (Courtesy of Harold K. Vollrath)

was responsible for obtaining right-of-way, persuading citizens of the communities involved to provide cash bonuses and free land, overseeing location surveys, ordering equipment, and arranging subcontracts for grading and bridging. Though almost all of Ellerbe's duties pertained to the railroad, he did occasionally purchase land for Edenborn. These were considerable responsibilities for a young man, but records show that Edenborn was in almost constant contact with Ellerbe and made all decisions of any consequence.[4]

Grading of the roadbed commenced in October 1897. By December it was complete to Coushatta, with forty carloads of sixty-five-pound rails on hand in the town of Bossier (across the Red River from Shreveport), the initial point of tracklaying. By this time Red River and Bossier Parishes, plus the communities of Shreveport and Coushatta, had approved cash bonuses that ultimately amounted to almost $81,000. Edenborn did not intend to share ownership with the public through stock subscriptions, but he was eager to augment his personal funds through community largess. Construction was not diffi-

cult, for the route followed the broad valley of the Red River and thus had few curves and a maximum grade of 0.3 percent. Edenborn insisted that the line run as straight as possible and that rot-resistant cypress crossties be used in the alluvial soils. The only significant obstacle was the bridging of Loggy Bayou, considered a navigable stream; this was handled with a temporary frame trestle, which was later replaced with a steel turn span.[5]

The first locomotive arrived in December 1897, just in time for tracklaying. To conserve capital, Edenborn purchased the engine secondhand from the New York, Pennsylvania and Ohio Railroad, part of the Erie system. He gave it the number 49, because he was forty-nine years old at the time. (He never used the numbers one through forty-eight for locomotives on his railroad.) On April 4, mixed freight and passenger service was established to Des Arc, 27.3 miles from Bossier; on April 14, service began to Loggy Bayou, 29.1 miles from Bossier. In July 1898, in Grand Rapids, Michigan, Edenborn purchased another secondhand engine for $2,000, to which he assigned the number 50.[6]

Through traffic was established on July 23 over the 44.2 miles to Coushatta. The local press noted,

> Coushatta is now on the railroad. Trains reached us today. Quite a number of persons came in on the train, including Mr. Edenborn and several other celebrities. Two trains in town at once. A considerable pow-wow between them as they tooted away. They have got the tackiest whistles we ever heard blow. Coushatta feels big now. She can take a train for Shreveport. Hurrah for Edenborn![7]

Edenborn himself dealt with the matter of procuring rolling stock and steel rails. When he discovered that boxcars he obtained from Missouri Car and Foundry contained unseasoned lumber, he refused to make the final payment for them. When the manufacturer suggested that he return the cars for inspection and possible correction, Edenborn responded pointedly to vice president W. K. Bixby:

> Your request to return the cars after we have paid you over $28,000.00 is about as sappy as most of the lumber in those cars. No, the cars are needed, but they are in evidence; they tell the tale as to quality of lumber; the specifications are also in evidence. We shall not pay the $1,400.00 you claim because our claim against you now being formulated will be much in excess of that figure.[8]

How they resolved the matter is not clear, but it is likely that Edenborn continued to use the cars and refuse to make the final payment.

Though Edenborn had set up the operating and construction offices of the railroad in Shreveport, the railroad had not yet obtained full right-of-way directly into the city. The two impediments were the high cost of using the only existing railroad bridge, that of the Vicksburg, Shreveport and Pacific Railroad, which wanted $2.50 per car, and securing permission to cross a portion of real estate belonging to the St. Louis and Southwestern Railroad. The latter obstacle proved to be the more difficult of the two, and this situation was not settled until the Louisiana Supreme Court ruled favorably on it in June 1898.

Six months later, on January 1, 1899, the completed line to Coushatta was transferred from the construction company to the operating company of the Shreveport and Red River Valley Railroad, and the first train of the line crossed into Shreveport. Initially, Edenborn chose not to use the recently completed Union Station in Shreveport; instead, he constructed a small frame depot on the riverfront that was adequate for the relatively small amount of traffic generated between Shreveport and Coushatta.[9]

In April 1898 Edenborn hired an additional lieutenant, Peter McIlvried, previously superintendent of his Rankin, Pennsylvania, wire plant, to manage the affairs of his railroad. Curiously, as he had done before, Edenborn brought in a person without previous railroad experience. He appointed McIlvried as vice president and general manager of the railroad, and he assigned Ellerbe to the combined positions of secretary/treasurer/general freight and passenger agent. These assignments favored an old acquaintance, but Ellerbe retained his responsibilities as president of the construction company. Indeed, reflecting the equality of their positions, Edenborn's letters to Shreveport were addressed jointly to the two men. It is clear, however, that Ellerbe remained fully in charge of obtaining land for the expansion of the railroad; he knew the territory and already had several landmen in the field.[10]

Edenborn was understandably concerned about competitive railroads. One of them, the Louisiana and North West, the "Beardsley road," was headed south from Gibsland, Louisiana, with the intention of intersecting a section of his road, now referred to as the "Valley Line." Another competitive railroad was the Arkansas Southern, which was being built south from the Arkansas–Louisiana state line at Junction City; this "Henderson–Brown road" was targeting Winnfield as part of an ambitious plan to extend to the Gulf of Mexico. But Edenborn's primary concern was the L&A, being built by William Buchanan, a line whose plans were to extend southeastward from Minden to Winnfield and Alexandria.

Edenborn's concern over these matters is expressed in a letter to Ellerbe and McIlvried:

> We must put a stop to Buchanan's encroaching on that territory so necessary to us while he can so easily work 10 to 20 miles eastward . . . I trust you will succeed in corralling sufficient timberlands to put us in a commanding position in that territory ahead of Buchanan and Beardsley.[11]

Shortly after the start of construction, to the surprise of no one, Edenborn announced that he would not terminate his railroad at Coushatta but would instead push on toward the Mississippi River. He called a stockholders' meeting on January 6, 1898, and proposed to amend the charter accordingly. (He had no difficulty in getting the proposal passed, for he owned almost all the stock—the other officers held a few qualifying shares.) He directed Ellerbe to have surveys made to the town of Campti, 17 miles beyond Coushatta, and by August he began clearing and grading operations for the extension. Edenborn was noncommittal about the destination of the line; he wanted to play one community against another and so let it be known that he could build the road either to Natchez or to New Orleans, or to some point in between them on the Mississippi River. He particularly wanted concessions from Winnfield and Alexandria, but the citizens of those towns were reluctant to pass bond issues to raise the money. For the time being, the only certainty was that Campti would be the immediate destination.[12]

When Edenborn attempted to join the cotton pool of Shreveport in order to share more equitably in cotton shipments in the Red River valley, he encountered other logistical problems. To transport cotton he needed to provide coordinated boat and rail service to New Orleans from points south of Coushatta. After an extensive search for a suitable river steamer, he purchased a sternwheeler he named *U&I*, built at Jeffersonville, Indiana, and placed it into operation in September 1898. Advertisements for this coordinated service show that it transferred southbound shipments of various commodities at Coushatta and took them downriver to Alexandria or, in some cases, depending on the water level at the Alexandria rapids, all the way to New Orleans. After the *U&I* burned at Coushatta on February 23, 1899, Edenborn worked out an arrangement with the Red River line to use the steamer *William Scovell*.[13]

During this period, Edenborn oversaw little of the railroad project. He wrote letters to Ellerbe and McIlvried frequently, often enclosing personal drafts of $5,000 and encouraging them:

> Now boys, I am trying to get into a financially strong position and I am working hard to that end! You must not lose heart if things don't always come our way. Some day they will. Don't worry about high water coming. Go right on and push your grading and do as if everything down to Alex. had to be done within 18 months and as if the Winnfield branch was only a side issue. The harder we push, the sooner our compet. will lay down.

Edenborn stressed frugality but also alertness to good investment opportunities. Importantly, he did not want Ellerbe and McIlvried to discuss specific plans for extending the railroad beyond Campti. He was anxious about the need for the railroad to generate more business, and he was concerned that too few sawmills were being built along the line. He was also concerned about whether the city of Alexandria would provide financial inducements for him to build to that point. In November 1898 Edenborn traveled to New Orleans and from there to Alexandria, where F. M. Welch, a prominent local businessman, showed him the city and apparently convinced him that even without concessions Alexandria was the logical immediate destination for the Valley Road. Certainly it would provide important rail connections. On November 11, Edenborn initiated surveys from Campti to Alexandria, and the news spread quickly about the immediate destination of the road. But construction proceeded at a slow pace, commensurate with funds that Edenborn made available.[14]

Service of the Valley Line to Campti began in April 1899 and to St. Maurice, milepost 75.0, on June 30. Machen, milepost 82.9, was reached in late 1900, with service beginning on January 8 of the next year. By this time, Edenborn was counting on freight and passenger revenues to relieve some of the pressure on his personal expenditures. The route had now left the immediate valley of the river, but Edenborn insisted on low grades—a grade of 0.5 percent was to be the upper limit—and approved as much earthmoving as might be required. This foresight would pay handsome dividends in the future when the line became a heavy traffic artery of the Kansas City Southern Lines.[15]

To reach Alexandria it was necessary to cross the Red River, and to this end construction began in March 1901 on a large steel bridge between Pineville and Alexandria. For the remainder of the year, as the local press reported, there was slow but steady progress on the line. For some time Edenborn had wanted to tap the timberlands in the vicinity of Winnfield, and on July 10, 1901, he chartered a branch line to that community. The branch, known as the Colfax and Northern Railway Company, connected with the main line at a point about 5 miles south of Machen.[16]

In connection with this branch line Edenborn incurred the long-time enmity of Huey Long, who later become a prominent, and controversial, Louisiana governor and U.S. senator. In keeping with his usual mode of operation, Edenborn sought partial financial support from the citizens of Winnfield, one of whom was Huey Long's father. The senior Long, a local politician, was incensed at the idea of public support. He led a campaign to defeat a proposed local tax, saying that Edenborn would build the branch line anyway, for the sole purpose of shipping out timber—and when the timber was gone he would tear up the tracks. When Long's campaign succeeded, Edenborn built the branch line anyway: he wanted to get at that timber. Young Huey never forgot the name of Edenborn and in later life never missed an opportunity to place obstacles in the path of the railroad.[17]

Extension of the main line continued in

1901, with service to Colfax, at milepost 98.0, being opened on August 4. Four days later, tracklayers reached the important destination of Pineville, a community that lay opposite Alexandria on the Red River and a key location for rail connections. Need for surfacing the Colfax–Pineville segment, together with the untimely death of U.S. President William McKinley on September 14, delayed the grand inauguration of the Shreveport–Pineville line until October 2. On opening day a welcoming parade and other special events were staged on a grand scale, and a special train bearing officials of the railroad (including Ellerbe and McIlvried), regional dignitaries, and friends arrived from Shreveport at about noon. Local business people paid their respects by closing stores from noon until 2:00 P.M. and blowing all available steam whistles. With the establishment of regular service to Pineville, along with a passenger and freight ferry transfer to Alexandria, the interim river-steamer service between St. Maurice and Alexandria came to an end.[18]

Construction of the bridge across the Red River at Alexandria was a major undertaking that delayed service into Alexandria for several months. Work on the bridge, estimated to cost $300,000, had started the previous March. The design called for four through-truss steel spans totaling 941 feet in length, including a turn span measuring 300 feet.

The Valley Road occupied this new frame office building and depot in August 1900. The lower floor served as the depot; the upper floor contained offices and a directors' conference room. After the line to New Orleans was completed, passenger trains shifted to the Union Station in 1909. This building continued to serve a variety of operating purposes for some years. (Shreveport Times, August 30, 1900)

Approach trestles would measure some 4,000 feet. Designed for heavy loadings with a Cooper's rating of E–60, the bridge would prove serviceable for all future traffic demands; this was another tribute to Edenborn's technological foresight. When Buchanan's L&A line reached the Alexandria area, in 1906, Edenborn denied it use of the Edenborn bridge, ostensibly because he believed that Buchanan was invading his territory. He did, however, permit the Rock Island, which had trackage rights over the L&A, to use the bridge. It was thus necessary for the L&A to use the Iron Mountain bridge and to follow a less direct route into Alexandria.[19]

The opening of the Alexandria bridge was celebrated on April 28, 1902. (Coincidentally, on the same day a new highway bridge near the Edenborn bridge was dedicated.) The celebration included short rides on the new rails in and around Alexandria. On the following day the first through train from Shreveport arrived at precisely 1:00 P.M., carrying seven coaches filled with passengers, a brass band, and William Edenborn. Cannons were fired when the train pulled up to the station platform, and a "last spike" ceremony took place, with Edenborn swinging the spike maul. Following this ceremony, a barbecue was held under the auspices of Welch, the businessman who had worked hard to arrange for the Edenborn line to come to Alexandria and who was now mayor of the city.[20]

With the rails across the river, Edenborn announced that freight service to the south would be coordinated with the Southern Pacific system, assuring shippers of through service between Shreveport and New Orleans. But this did not dampen his enthusiasm for pushing on to New Orleans, a city now identified as the southern terminus. Operations into Alexandria were taken over from the construction company on July 1, 1902. By this time, tracklaying was proceeding toward the next objective, the old town of Mansura, some 30 miles to the southeast. In August contracts were awarded for grading 20 miles beyond Mansura, to a town called Water Valley (this was later changed to the station name of Sarto). The tracklayers spiked rails to

Mansura in September, but official service to that community did not begin until November 25, 1902. A little more than a month later, on January 1, 1903, the Alexandria–Mansura segment was transferred formally to the Valley Line.[21]

The route south and east of Mansura was projected to cross the Mississippi River in the vicinity of Angola Plantation, on the east bank opposite the old river port of Red River Landing. The southernmost bridge crossing of the river was at Memphis, Tennessee, too far north to serve the Valley Line, but building a bridge across the Mississippi was deemed out of the question. The deterrent was not simply the cost, which would be prohibitively high, but also the physical limitations. Engineers questioned whether a bridge at this point would be technologically feasible because of the great width of the river and the need for very long approach structures. After deliberation, Edenborn decided in favor of a ferry transfer arrangement.

Meanwhile, Edenborn worked on plans for a direct route to the Mississippi River. One route required bridging the Atchafalaya River, a swift-flowing and treacherous stream that represented a Mississippi River water shortcut to the Gulf of Mexico (which tended to rob New Orleans of some of its river flow). Because erecting a bridge over the Atchafalaya would be expensive in terms of both money and time, Edenborn elected to deviate from the regular survey and to run east and north to a point on the Red River just above its confluence with the Mississippi River, a point where the Atchafalaya left the Mississippi for its quick flow to the gulf. The landing location was given the name of Naples, and the ferry route of some 8.3 miles followed first the Red River and then the Old River, and finally crossed the Mississippi River to Angola Plantation (see the map in chapter 3). The decision concerning location turned out to be a bad one because of the long time of ferry transit. Though the originally planned route, including the bridge over the Atchafalaya River, was eventually constructed, the line used the "temporary" service for more than twenty years, paying a rather stiff operating penalty.[22]

Edenborn built the Colfax and Northern Railway Company branch line to Winnfield as planned, with service beginning December 20, 1903. Winnfield, deep in the pine forest, had been a destination of the Arkansas Southern (which was, by this time, part of the Rock Island system) as well as the L&A and was expected to contribute to the LR&N in several ways. But another reason for the branch line was that it would serve a tract of one thousand acres of cypress timber that had been procured by Edenborn's agents. In an article on the cypress lumber industry that featured the tract, Rachael Norgress made the following comments:

> The famous Edenborn brake of cypress in Winn Parish is probably the most widely known tract of timber that grew in the south. . . . It was jokingly said that during the first decade of the twentieth century the Edenborn tract "kept up" the livery stable and the hotel in the little town of Atlanta by attracting so many estimators and prospective buyers . . . the timber was without a doubt the largest and oldest cypress timber standing anywhere in the United States.[23]

As Norgress indicates, Atlanta was a station on the branch line, and in time, more than sixty million board feet of cypress lumber were cut from the Edenborn brake and shipped out over the LR&N.

Because of his planned river operations, as well as other aspirations, Edenborn formed a new corporation, the Louisiana Railway and Navigation Company, chartered under the general laws of Louisiana on May 9, 1903. The charter empowered the company to purchase the Shreveport and Red River Valley Railroad, to extend the road northward from Shreveport, and to operate ocean-going vessels. The Valley Line was purchased on June 22, 1903, for $600,000 cash and $2,529,000 par value stock. The LR&N also assumed $2,760,000 par value of first-mortgage bonds. In effect, Edenborn provided all the cash and took possession of all the securities; he still was not ready to go public with his railroad enterprise. Officially, the LR&N ac-quired 196.12 miles of railroad and all associated fixed property, including 10 locomotives, 12 passenger cars, and 274 freight cars.[24]

Surveys for the newly formed LR&N were completed all the way to New Orleans in 1903, and during the year work proceeded vigorously on both sides of the Mississippi. Grading was completed on the short, 4.5 mile stretch between Sarto and Naples, with operation awaiting completion of a truss bridge over Bayou des Glaises. In April contracts were awarded for construction from Baton Rouge north to Angola. The segments between Mansura and Sarto, and from Baton Rouge 18 miles north to Port Hudson, were opened for business on December 19. As usual, the Louisiana Construction Company operated the trains until each segment was turned over to the LR&N. As 1903 ended, there was work in progress on the Naples and Angola yards and on the inclines that connected the ferry-boat tracks with those at the higher-level yards. Grading continued north of Port Hud-son, where deep cuts were required to main-tain alignment in the Tunica Hills.[25]

In contrast to the feverish activity in 1903, the following year showed little progress in further construction of the line. There ap-peared to be no big rush to complete trackage to the ferry landings, for Edenborn had not yet contracted for the transfer vessels. On the Angola side of the river, work proceeded slowly north of Port Hudson, where earth-moving was extensive. In April 1904 an-nouncements were made that clearing and grading contracts for work between Baton Rouge and New Orleans had been awarded, but this turned out not to be the case. In gen-eral, Edenborn seemed more interested in di-gesting the accomplishments in hand than in taking on new burdens, especially financial ones. During the course of the year McIlvried left the organization, apparently for health reasons, and Ellerbe continued to oversee ac-tivities in Louisiana while Edenborn contin-ued his attempts to disencumber himself from steel-industry responsibilities in New York.[26]

Contracts for construction of the line into New Orleans were awarded in February 1905, and on the west side of the river the

This rush-hour scene on Canal Street in New Orleans is graphic evidence of why Edenborn wanted his southern terminus to be the Crescent City. It was indeed a vibrant business city, one very much on the move. The photograph dates from 1904, when the LR&N was building toward the city.

line from Sarto to Naples was opened on March 10. Work continued at Naples and Angola in preparation for the ferry-transfer operation. Edenborn contracted for the construction of a towboat at Jeffersonville, Indiana, a sternwheeler he named the *William Edenborn*. He also ordered a transfer barge, the *Angola*, which could hold twelve freight cars on two parallel tracks.[27]

The work between Baton Rouge and New Orleans moved slowly because a survey for a direct line between the two cities traversed the McElroy, St. Charles, and Harahan swamps, an area that required a considerable amount of clearing, draining, filling, and bridging. The line needed more than two miles of trestlework through the swamps, and for several miles it was laid over a corduroy of large cypress trunks. Topping this support structure were large quantities of dirt, sand, and gravel. One section ran absolutely straight for 14 miles, and the completed route was about 10 miles shorter than the competitive Yazoo and Mississippi Valley Line.[28]

During this time Edenborn leaked news to the press that he was considering running a

branch line from Pineville to Jena, an important lumbering center in Catahoula Parish. William Buchanan's L&A had already reached Jena, with service beginning in February 1905, yet the *Railroad Gazette* reported in mid-1905 that surveys were in progress. Was Edenborn just taunting Buchanan? It is likely that he was, for, except for a short 7-mile segment to Ems, the branch was never built.[29]

In 1906 Edenborn completed his line into New Orleans. On June 3, the first locomotive ran the stretch from Angola to the station of Edenborn, 21 miles south of Baton Rouge. The Angola Transfer Company was organized early in the year (but not chartered until October 13, 1921) to handle the river-transfer operations. The track work into New Orleans was completed on October 25, and on October 27 the first "train," a small motorcar, was run into the city with Edenborn and Ellerbe aboard. The *New Orleans Daily Picayune* of October 28 announced that the *William Edenborn* was on its way down the Mississippi to begin ferry operations. On December 12, through freight service began between Shreveport and New Orleans, the *William* being on hand to push a twelve-car bargeload across the Mississippi. (Locomotives were not normally carried on the barges.)[30]

Preparations for regular service into New Orleans took some additional time. In September 1903 a cooperative New Orleans City Council had granted Edenborn a right-of-way that followed the New Basin Canal into the heart of the business district. Among the other concessions granted was land for freight and passenger facilities. A temporary frame depot was erected at the Carrollton Avenue crossing while the groundwork was laid for regular service; this depot was a little more than two miles from the downtown area but was conveniently located on the Tulane Avenue trolley line.[31]

In anticipation of a large surge in mainline business, Edenborn ordered a number of new engines from Baldwin Locomotive Works and two secondhand engines. Over the next few years, between January 1904 and October 1906, the new motive power arrived and began service. The order delivered from Baldwin included twelve mogul (2-6-0), three American (4-4-0), one six-wheel switcher (0-6-0), and two eight-wheel switcher (0-8-0) types; the two used engines were of the mogul type. These engines, numbered 60 through 80, represented a 33 percent increase in the total number of locomotives owned by the railroad.[32]

Local passenger service north to Angola from New Orleans began on February 8, 1907, and not long afterward, on Sunday, April 14, the first passenger trains ran between Shreveport and New Orleans. This was cause for celebration all along the line. Under the headline "Red River Valley Road Runs First Train Through," the *Daily Picayune* described the trip of the northbound train (comprising 4-4-0–type engine number 51, a baggage-mail car, and three passenger cars) that left Carrollton Avenue early in the morning:

> The conductor, with a majestic sweep of the hand, signalled to the engineer, and the first through train of the Louisiana Railway and Navigation Company was off. Promptly at 7 A.M. the official party, with their friends, boarded the palatial parlor car St. Lawrence. . . . The train was in charge of conductor A. T. Waycott, engineer W. T. Lipton and fireman S. L. McCants. . . . Although a new line, its [the railroad's] roadbed is in almost perfect condition and its equipment and appliances are of the latest and most approved patterns. . . . At Angola the entire train was run on a large and commodious barge, capable of carrying eight passenger coaches and [or] 12 freight cars. The barge was in tow of the powerful steamboat William Edenborn, Captain McClelland commanding, which had flags flying from the bow and stern. On board the boat an elegant dinner was served.[33]

Because Edenborn was the sole owner of the property, he indulged himself from time to time. For example, he named some of the new stations after places and people in his German homeland: Hessmer, Zimmer, Wilhelm, Plettenberg, Manheim, Bonn, and Essen, among others. In an uncharacteristic move, he even named a station after himself—though after a short time Edenborn station was renamed Gonzales station, which reflected the name of the locality. One activity Edenborn distinctly enjoyed was the ferry-transfer operation; it seemed to satisfy an urge of his to "go to sea," and he spent much of his spare time riding back and forth on the *William Edenborn*, or, after its 1908 arrival, the *Sarah Edenborn*. As he had done in his earlier career in the steel business, he made it a point to become acquainted with many of his employees, who affectionately called him and his wife "Uncle Billy" and "Aunt Sarah." What remained to be seen was whether Edenborn intended to operate the railroad company as a hobby or to make it into a money-making enterprise.[34]

Thus Edenborn had at last completed his personal railroad, and now it was time for him to separate himself from the steel business, move to Louisiana, and begin to enjoy what he often called his "hobby." He and Sarah moved from New York to New Orleans in early 1907 to be closer to his just-completed project. They occupied a modest dwelling on Hampson Street, in the Crescent area of the

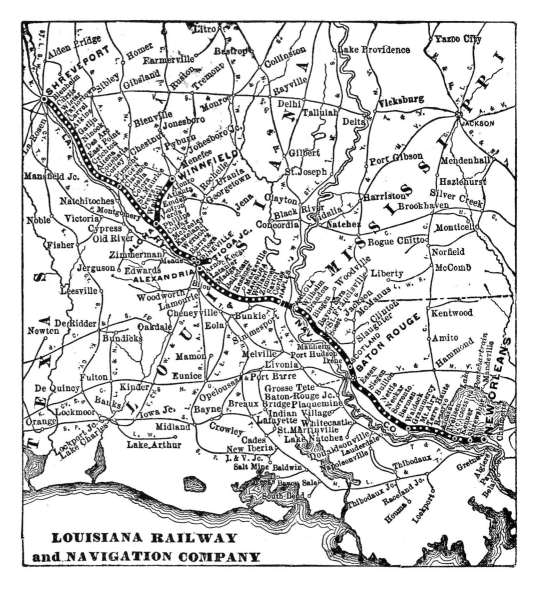

Map of the completed LR&N circa 1912. The short branch to Tioga Junction (later called Ems) was built in 1906 to serve the needs of a large lumber mill.

LOUISIANA RAILWAY and NAVIGATION COMPANY

city. This residence was much less pretentious than the one they had occupied in St. Louis; the Edenborns experienced a stage of frugality in lifestyle while they devoted their full energies to making the railroad project a success. Edenborn resigned from the Board of Directors of U.S. Steel in November 1909 and opened an office in the Hibernia Bank Building on Carondelet Street. The operating headquarters of the railroad were kept at Shreveport; the reasons for this separation between offices are not clear, but one may speculate

that in addition to the railroad the riverboat operation was one of Edenborn's favorites, and New Orleans was a good deal closer to Angola and Naples than was Shreveport.[35]

Edenborn had built a complete, well-located railroad with personal funds and little advice from outsiders. Now he faced the challenge of proving to himself and to others that the investment was a good one and that he could be as successful in railroads as he had been in wire making.

With the task of building his railroad between Shreveport and New Orleans, the two largest cities of Louisiana, at last completed, William Edenborn had achieved a unique personal feat. It had taken him almost ten years to create the 306-mile-long main line of the LR&N and to equip it for operations, but during the process he had written personal checks for all expenditures—and had borrowed no money. His route was 20 miles shorter than that of the competing T&P—and it served Baton Rouge as well as Alexandria (the T&P missed Baton Rouge). The well-engineered railroad had low grades and a minimum of curves. The bridge across the Red River at Alexandria was a first-class structure, designed for the heavy loads of the future. If there was a problem with the alignment of the route, it was at the Mississippi River crossing, a distance of more than 8 miles, much of which coincided with the treacherous Old River. Though a shorter and more convenient crossing had been part of the original survey, Edenborn had economized. The less expensive crossing took about two hours for passenger trains, and much longer for freight trains. In contrast, the crossing of the T&P at New Orleans was simple and for passenger trains took less than an hour. All in all, though, Edenborn could take pride in a job well done—and a job of a type not previously attempted by any other individual.

Building the LR&N had been expensive. The charter for the railroad allowed capital stock and first mortgage bonds to be issued to Edenborn based on the mileage of construction. When the main line and the Winnfield branch were completed, Edenborn held $8,131,000 in capital stock and $10,545,000 in 4½ percent first-mortgage bonds, which were due in 1953. Edenborn's total outlay of

money is unknown, but, according to Interstate Commerce Commission records, he spent at least $8,907,000. This amount covered not only the acquisition of the right-of-way and construction of the trackage but also the erection of various buildings, the procurement of locomotives and rolling stock, and the establishment of a fleet that soon consisted of two sternwheel steamboats and two transfer barges capable of handling ten to twelve freight cars each.[1]

The challenge of completing the road had been considerable; the challenge of making it economically viable was even greater. It was incumbent upon Edenborn to justify his enormous outlay of personal funds in order to bring the railroad to completion, and it was in his character to do just that. He saw the need not only to attract business to the railroad but also to provide a service that within a growing territory would reinforce demand. In addition to the passenger traffic Edenborn anticipated, he recognized that the region's agricultural crops were important. He had seen for himself the potential for traffic in cotton, corn, and forest products while the line was still under construction.

The LR&N immediately established through freight and passenger service between New Orleans and Shreveport. With its direct line, Edenborn expected the LR&N to compete with the T&P for both passenger traffic and interline freight. At the Shreveport end, the T&P had its own line plus the resources of its ally, the Missouri Pacific system, for connections to the north and west. By 1891, however, the Missouri, Kansas and Texas had separated from the Missouri Pacific system and could become a working partner with the LR&N for the interchange of traffic at Shreveport. At the New Orleans end, the

LR&N and the T&P were competitors on a more equitable basis. Moreover, the LR&N had an advantage over the T&P and the Southern Pacific, in that its tonnage did not require a New Orleans river transfer for connections to and from the East.[2]

From the start, Edenborn set out to upgrade passenger facilities at each end of the line. The first through passenger trains, which began operation on April 14, 1907, ran only during the day. These trains carried Pullman Parlor Buffet cars, and the *William Edenborn* provided midday lunch during the two-hour ferry ride across the Mississippi River. At Shreveport Edenborn made arrangements to use the Union Station, which had opened in August 1897. This move allowed Edenborn to use the two-story frame structure, which had served as a passenger station, as an operating headquarters building. The first LR&N trains arrived at the Union Station on February 1, 1909; because all other railroads entering Shreveport were already using the facility, transfers of passenger and express were simpler than they had been. In another move intended in part to increase passenger comfort,

on November 30, 1907, Edenborn shifted from using the T&P bridge at Shreveport to using the relatively new Cotton Belt bridge.[3]

At New Orleans Edenborn arranged to use the handsome new Terminal Station, just opened on June 1, 1908, and well located on Canal Street. The architect of the building was D. H. Burnham, famous for his design of the new Union Station at Washington, D.C. Owned by the New Orleans Terminal Company, the Terminal Station was a subsidiary of the Southern Railway. Terminal trackage extended west to a connection with the LR&N at Shrewsbury, near the city limits of New Orleans, where Edenborn had purchased land for a freight yard. This made it convenient for LR&N passenger trains to move to the Terminal Station using trackage rights, and the LR&N trains moved out of the temporary depot at the Carrollton Avenue crossing and began to use this station on January 31, 1909.[4]

With inauguration of service into first-class stations at both ends of the line, Edenborn changed the through passenger trains to overnight schedules on January 31, 1909. He placed broiler-buffet sleeping cars in service

The Union Station at Shreveport was owned by the Kansas City, Shreveport and Gulf Terminal Co., a subsidiary of the KCS. It opened in August 1897, and Edenborn's LR&N began using it in February 1909. Under Couch management it was modernized in the early 1940s, when touches of art deco were added. The last passenger train to use the station was the Southern Belle, *on November 4, 1967; a few days later the building was severely damaged by fire. The photograph dates from the mid-1930s. (Photograph courtesy of Archives and Special Collections, Noel Memorial Library, Louisiana State University–Shreveport)*

and made arrangements with the Missouri, Kansas and Texas (the "Katy") to run them through to Dallas; this provided direct competition with the T&P service between New Orleans, Shreveport, and Dallas. The running time on the LR&N between New Orleans and Shreveport was about one hour longer than that of the T&P because of the prolonged ferry transfer between Angola and Naples.[5]

Edenborn set out to develop the interline business, both freight and passenger. Toward that end, he opened sales offices in Dallas, Oklahoma City, Kansas City, and Little Rock and began to build what would eventually be eight large warehouses in New Orleans. Located near Liberty Street and the New Basin Canal, the first two warehouses were constructed in 1907, one with 18,000 square feet and the other with 22,500 square feet. Later, in 1911 and 1914, he erected much larger, three-story brick buildings. He bought land along the river with the intent of building a

grain elevator for storage and export purposes. The city blocked this plan, however, so he put his efforts into constructing a large, public grain elevator, which opened in 1916.[6]

Shop facilities were established at New Orleans and Shreveport, with small engine houses at each city. At New Orleans the shops, located near the intersection of Hagan Avenue and the New Basin Canal, did not include a turntable, so it was necessary to turn engines on the wye at the Shrewsbury yards. The location of the Shreveport shops just south of Cross Creek required transfer movements across the VS&P, an operation that was cumbersome at times.[7]

Edenborn provided for the convenient transfer of freight cars at Shreveport between his small yard near the river and that of the VS&P (also used by the Katy). The overnight passenger-train schedules, in contrast, were not particularly convenient. There were scheduled stops at most of the towns along

The Terminal Station was considered one of the more elegant structures on Canal Street in New Orleans. It was designed by well-known architect D. H. Burnham, of Chicago. The LR&N began to use it in 1909, a year after it opened, but moved out in 1923 to occupy its own station on Rampart Street. The photograph was taken not long before the building was razed in 1954. (Photograph courtesy of Tulane University)

the line, and this undoubtedly made sleeping difficult for the Pullman passengers. During the transfer time between Angola and Naples, the dining room on the *William Edenborn* was kept open for those not able to sleep through the river-crossing operations. (The barges were lashed tightly to the sides of the towboats to allow for ease of passenger movement during the river ride)[8]

Edenborn was taking the proper actions for an aggressive businessman. He was concerned with terminals and interline traffic, but he was also concerned about generating on-line freight. As one of his first maneuvers, while he was still on the board of directors of U.S. Steel, he laid the groundwork for the construction of a large oil refinery north of Baton Rouge. Edenborn convinced H. H. Rogers, a vice president of Standard Oil, of the advantages of a site about two miles north of the Baton Rouge station. With deepwater dockage on the river as well as an alternate railroad connection, that of the Yazoo and Mississippi Valley, it was indeed a good location for a refinery. After the refinery was built, Edenborn commented, "Yes, that's a fine plant. I had the privilege of bringing it there. When I was on the executive committee of the steel corporation H. H. Rogers was one of the directors of the . . . corporation, though not on the executive committee."[9]

The refinery began operations on November 15, 1909. Identified initially as part of the Standard Oil Company of Louisiana, through the years it provided a great deal of business for the railroad. At first it proved highly profitable for the LR&N, not only with shipments of construction materials but also with tank-car transport of crude oil from Oklahoma (up to forty cars per day) and outward movement of refined products. Six months after start-up, however, the refinery began to receive much of its crude oil by pipeline. Though that aspect of the business dropped off dramatically for the railroad, the business of transporting products continued. Today a part of the Exxon Corporation, the refinery is one of the largest refining and petrochemical complexes in the world.[10]

Another source of income for the railroad derived from the sugar business. The route between Baton Rouge and New Orleans passed through the towns of Gramercy, where Colonial Sugars Company built a large refinery in 1896, and Reserve, where Godchaux Sugars, Incorporated, erected a large refinery in 1919. The companies welcomed the Edenborn line as an alternate carrier to the Y&MV. The LR&N apparently competed well with the older line; in 1915 it was said to be the second largest handler of refined sugar in the South.[11]

Yet another opportunity for revenue presented itself when the Colorado Southern, New Orleans and Pacific Railroad, completed between Houston and Baton Rouge in early 1909, arranged with Edenborn for trackage rights into New Orleans. The contract with the CSNO&P was signed on February 15, 1909, and Houston–New Orleans passenger service began on September 1, 1909, with trains crossing the Mississippi River at Baton Rouge by ferry. The CSNO&P, part of what was known as the "Gulf Coast Lines," was controlled by the Rock Island–Frisco system. On March 21, 1910, its name was changed to the New Orleans, Texas and Mexico Railway. In later years, the route came under the control of the Missouri Pacific.[12]

Edenborn built a short branch line of the LR&N in 1909 to serve lumbering operations in the Alexandria area. This line extended 7.1 miles from Pineville to a station called Ems (earlier known as Tioga Junction). At Ems, a connection was made with the Tioga Southeastern Railroad, which served the Lee Lumber Company at Tioga. The LR&N shared in the shipment of finished lumber as well as logs to the mill. The branch also provided passenger service, with passengers riding in the caboose. At one time, the branch was regarded as the first segment of a line eastward to Natchez, but later maneuvering by William Buchanan and his L&A put a stop to that idea. Eventually, in 1916, the branch line was abandoned.[13]

Overall operations of the LR&N settled into something of a routine, but occasional problems did arise. The sleeper service to

Dallas did not prove profitable and was discontinued in 1910. The use of the LR&N by the Gulf Coast Lines turned out to be an irritant to Edenborn; when he discovered that the tenant was violating the trackage rights agreement by conducting local business between Baton Rouge and New Orleans, he ended the arrangement on March 17, 1913, forcing the Gulf Coast Lines to begin using the circuitous Y&MV tracks.[14]

Upkeep of the tracks and the right-of-way was particularly troublesome for the railroad and posed a threat to its future. Though Edenborn seems to have spent money as needed on equipment and rolling stock, he was somewhat reluctant to spend money on track maintenance. The rail was relatively light (sixty-five and seventy pounds per yard), and much of the line was ballasted with dirt only, which provided poor drainage and subsequently caused the track structure to become uneven. As the years went by and the track deteriorated, the Louisiana Railroad Commission eventually stepped in to pressure the line to improve its track.[15]

At about this time, Edenborn had a falling-out with Clarence Ellerbe, who had worked as his right-hand man since he began to build his railroad. When Edenborn terminated his affiliation with Ellerbe, apparently because of a problem that arose between the two over land purchases, a young nephew by the name of Paul Sippel, not long off the boat from Germany, began to assist Edenborn with some of the managerial tasks. Also during this time, Henry B. Helm, an auditor with railroad experience, moved into the first vice presidency in January 1913. Both these men provided crucial support to both William and Sarah Edenborn for many years.[16]

In 1915, the year after oil was discovered in the Crichton area of Caddo Parish, 36 miles south of Shreveport on the LR&N, the railroad began a program of converting its locomotives to oil-burners. Land owned by Edenborn produced high-quality petroleum that required only modest refining and provided a satisfactory fuel oil for his locomotives. The oil was nearby and cheap; coal, which had to be hauled in from Oklahoma or Arkansas, was comparatively expensive. Moreover, for passenger trains, which had windows that opened, problems with cinders and soot could be averted. Other railroads in the region had recognized the advantages of oil-burning locomotives, and they too were converting, at least in part, to oil.

In 1915 a group of investors bought 360 acres of land across the Mississippi River from Sellers, Louisiana, and adjacent to the LR&N tracks, for the purpose of building an oil refinery to process crude oil shipped in by water from Mexico. Eventually, the installation of the Good Hope Refinery of the New Orleans Refining Company led to considerable freight traffic for the railroad. The name of a new station, Norco, derived from the name of the refining company. In later years this venture became a property of Shell Oil Company, and its expanded operations in chemicals provided important revenue for the railroad.[17]

Though there was a great deal of activity on the LR&N, required reports by the railroad to the ICC every year showed a deficit. Evaluations of a property by the ICC reflect a record of profit and loss for the line during its early years. Such evaluations, performed on every railroad for the purpose of rate making, cover the period from the date of initial operations to June 30, 1917. A summary for the LR&N is found in Table 1. Running a deficit every year, the railroad failed to cover full payment of interest on bonded indebtedness and to pay dividends on capital stock. For a conventional operation with publicly owned stocks and bonds, such a situation would have led to a receivership and a reorganization of the line. The LR&N, however, was not a conventional operation. William Edenborn owned all the stocks and bonds. As long as the cash flow met the needs for operations and Edenborn remained unconcerned about receiving interest on his investment, there was no problem. Table 1 indicates that the 4.5 percent bonds were earning an average of about 1.5 percent interest and that any surplus was being used for operating purposes. As Edenborn later spent large amounts of his own money on behalf of the railroad, it is possible that the earnings available for fixed charges were transferred directly to Edenborn's personal accounts. And so it went—Edenborn enjoyed his railroad and his transfer boats, performed a useful service, and did not worry about accumulating a large estate for others to enjoy.[18]

TABLE 1

Cumulative Financial Results for LR&N

July 1, 1903, to June 30, 1917

Net revenue from rail operations	$4,420,236
Railway operating income	3,597,212
Other income	1,340,057
Other costs	2,364,060
Earnings available for fixed charges	$2,573,208
Fixed charges	5,578,242
Deficit	**$3,005,034**

Source: ICC *Reports* 106 (1925).

When World War I erupted in 1914, business for the LR&N boomed, as it did for most other railroads in the country. Edenborn claimed a profit at the end of 1917, the only year the railroad ever operated in the black. Passenger business was good enough to justify two daily through trains between New Orleans and Shreveport, each with first-class accommodations. On the broader front, as the nation's railroad system became bogged down with freight traffic, the government felt compelled to form the U.S. Railroad Administration, which took over the operation of all major railroads at noon on December 28, 1917. This arrangement effectively speeded up wartime transportation, but it led to extended controversy over the issue of just compensation of railroad owners by the federal government. Even after the government returned the railroads to their owners in 1920, the controversy continued.

Because the LR&N had annual revenues of between $100,000 and $1,000,000, the government considered it a Class II railroad in the "short line" category. The government initially assigned the railroad to the Southwestern Region. Most short lines taken over by the government were returned to their owners by mid-1918, because they did not contribute in a significant way to the national traffic problem and represented more trouble than they were worth to the government. Owners of many of the returned lines objected to such action, believing that there would be much less financial risk in having the government absorb the increased costs of operation during wartime while still guaranteeing the owners a profit. The government returned the LR&N to Edenborn on August 9, 1918, but he appears not to have objected, perhaps influenced by its excellent performance in 1917.[19]

On the personal front, wartime pressures on German natives in the United States affected Edenborn. Though there is no evidence whatsoever that Edenborn was in any way supportive of the German movement during the war, his German background plus his slight accent created suspicion among patriotic zealots. In an extreme move, the prominent Pickwick Club of New Orleans, of which Edenborn was a member, asked him to resign. Declining to contest the action, he willingly left the organization on May 1, 1918, and in characteristic fashion forged ahead with his business and work. He continued to be involved with the German Old Folk's Home and the German Protestant Orphans' Home, and he retained his membership in the New Orleans Country Club.[20]

Another force of opposition, in the person of Huey Long, was not as easy for Edenborn to dispel. During the building of the Winnfield branch, Huey Long Sr. had spoken out against Edenborn and his railroad, and his son had taken up the crusade. By 1918, the younger Huey had become a well-known lawyer and opponent of big business, which he believed discriminated against the "common people" of Louisiana. One of his primary targets had been the Standard Oil Company of Louisiana (the company with the large refinery at North Baton Rouge). According to his biographer, T. Harry Williams, Long "was drawn to the great art of politics as if by an irresistible magnet, and even at his first political experience he acted with the instinctive skill of the natural politician." In 1918, after Long had succeeded in the role of lawyer and friend of the common man, he decided to run for his first political office, that of railroad commissioner. That year he was elected to serve a six-year term on the three-person Louisiana Railroad Commission, an achievement that proved to be the first rung on a ladder that eventually led to the U.S. Senate. Long had not forgotten the Winnfield incident, and his new position gave him the opportunity to refresh himself about the activities of William Edenborn.[21]

Shortly after Long was elected to the commission, on March 25, 1919, the LR&N was ordered to improve its tracks. Compliance with this order was difficult because of excessive rainfall over several months; nonetheless, twelve months after the order, the railroad was able to report:

> Gravel ballast was distributed in larger quantities than ordinary maintenance required. Over 170,000 ties were placed . . . under the track, which amount is more than double the number ever placed in one year. Bridges and trestles were repaired and painted, stations were also repaired and painted and several new structures were erected where it was deemed necessary. The motive power was given a general and thorough repair, as well as the coaches and freight cars. . . . The statement that the tracks of the company are not in safe condition is not well founded. The [LR&N] has a record second to none in the matter of safety. During 22 years of operation not a passenger was killed, and none of them hurt, unless very slightly, and in 22 years not one trestle collapsed under the traffic, which at times was very heavy.[22]

Despite the railroad's effort, the commission remained dissatisfied with the appearance of the property, and in March 1920 it reissued the order for the LR&N to improve its track.

The commission fined the railroad $1,000 for noncompliance and threatened to compound the amount $100 per day after March 30. Edenborn had the fine waived by demonstrating his willingness to comply with the order, but he certainly did not have the help of Long, who chose not to sign the commission's waiver agreement.

Further opposition to Edenborn occurred after Long became chairman of the Louisiana Railroad Commission, renamed the Public Service Commission. Pointing out that since 1909 the citizens of Mansura had complained that coach 100, used south of Alexandria on trains 15 and 16, was "not good enough to haul coal in, let alone to put women and children in," Long signed another order in March 1922. It contained the following passage:

> [The LR&N] is unstable, unfinished, lacking in power, equipment and track facilities of every kind; and a deplorable state of affairs exists along its line, so far as service to the public

Huey Long, prominent politician in Louisiana and longtime adversary of William Edenborn and his railroad. While on the Louisiana Public Service Commission, Long rarely missed an opportunity to call the LR&N to task for inefficient operation, unsafe conditions, or poor maintenance.

This LR&N public timetable shows the peak in passenger train service: double daily trains between Shreveport and New Orleans, all with first-class accommodations. The timetable is not dated but appears to match the schedules in the December 1918 issue of the Official Guide. *(Courtesy of Franklin Garrett, Atlanta Historical Society)*

LOUISIANA RAILWAY & NAVIGATION COMPANY

SHREVEPORT TO BATON ROUGE
and Vice Versa

No. 15 Daily Read Down	No. 3 Daily Read Down	No. 1 Daily Read Down	STATIONS	No. 2 Daily Read Up	No. 4 Daily Read Up	No. 16 Daily Read Up
	6:01AM	5:00PM	Lv......Shreveport......Ar (Union Station)	7:25AM	7:30PM	
		f 5:30PM	Ar......Blenheim......Lv		f	
			Ar......Curtis......Lv	f		
	f 6:41AM	s 5:41PM	Ar......Taylortown......Lv	s 6:41AM	f 6:46PM	
			Ar......Curvel......Lv			
	f 6:50AM	f 5:50PM	Ar......Elm Grove......Lv	f 6:28AM	f 6:38PM	
			Ar......McDade......Lv			
	f 6:57AM	s 5:59PM	Ar......Atkins......Lv	f 6:20AM	f 6:31PM	
		f 6:04PM	Ar......Poole......Lv	f 6:15AM		
	f 7:09AM	f 6:11PM	Ar......Ninock......Lv	f 6:05AM	f 6:18PM	
			Ar......Des Arc......Lv			
		f	Ar......Loggy Bayou......Lv			
	f 7:22AM	s 6:26PM	Ar......East Point......Lv	s 5:49AM	s 5:58PM	
	s 7:30AM	s 6:33PM	Ar......Crichton......Lv	s 5:39AM	s 5:50PM	
	f 7:33AM	s 6:36PM	Ar......Lenzburg......Lv	s 5:36AM	s 5:46PM	
	f 7:35AM	f 6:43PM	Ar......Carroll......Lv	f 5:30AM	f 5:40PM	
	s 7:51AM	s 6:54PM	Ar......Coushatta......Lv	s 5:16AM	s 5:27PM	
			Ar......Steuben......Lv	f		
			Ar......Pirmont......Lv			
		f 7:18PM	Ar......Grappes Bluff......Lv	f 4:55AM		
	s 8:27AM	s 7:32PM	Ar......Campti......Lv	s 4:40AM	s 4:51PM	
	f 8:34AM	s 7:39PM	Ar......Hagen......Lv	s 4:32AM	s 4:45PM	
	s 8:41AM	f 7:47PM	Ar......Clarence......Lv	f 4:23AM	f 4:37PM	
			Ar......Irma......Lv			
			Ar......Luella......Lv	f		
	f 8:54AM	s 8:00PM	Ar......St. Maurice......Lv	f 4:09AM	s 4:25PM	
			Ar......Crews......Lv			
	s 9:12AM	s 8:19PM	Ar......Montgomery......Lv	s 3:50AM	s 4:06PM	
			Ar......Billis......Lv			
	s 9:31AM	s 8:37PM	Ar......Aloha......Lv	s 3:28AM	s 3:45PM	
	s 9:45AM	s 8:51PM	Ar......Colfax......Lv	s 3:14AM	s 3:32PM	
			Ar......McNeeley......Lv			
			Ar......Ravencamp......Lv			
	f 9:56AM	f 9:03PM	Ar......Kateland......Lv	f 3:01AM	f 3:20PM	
			Ar......Werdohl......Lv			
	f10:09AM	f 9:16PM	Ar......Meade......Lv	f 2:47AM	f 3:07PM	
		f	Ar......Tyrawley......Lv		f	
			Ar......Barrett......Lv			
	s10:37AM	s 9:45PM	Ar......Pineville......Lv	f 2:20AM	s 2:40PM	
	s10:47AM	s 9:55PM	Ar......Alexandria......Lv	2:10AM	2:30PM	
	11:00AM	10:05PM	Ar......Alexandria......An	2:00AM	2:20PM	
			Ar......Arno......Lv		f	
		f10:24PM	Ar......Latanier......Lv	f 1:36AM		
			Ar......Whittington......Lv		f	
			Ar......Richland......Lv		f	
			Ar......Magda......Lv			
f11:34AM	f10:44PM		Ar......Bijou......Lv	f 1:16AM	f 1:44PM	
			Ar......Belledeau......Lv			
f11:49AM	f11:02PM		Ar......Hessmer......Lv	f12:58AM	f 1:29PM	
s11:57AM	s11:11PM		Ar......Mansura......Lv	s12:49AM	s 1:22PM	
f12:06PM	f11:20PM		Ar......Moreauville......Lv	f12:40AM	f 1:14PM	
			Ar......Willard......Lv			
f12:14PM	f11:31PM		Ar......Bordelonville......Lv	f12:28AM	f 1:04PM	
			Ar......Rexmere......Lv		f	
			Ar......Kleinwood......Lv		f	
f12:27PM	f11:46PM		Ar......Sarto......Lv	f12:14AM	f12:51PM	
			Ar......Cordes......Lv			
s12:40PM	s12:01AM		Lv......Naples......Lv	s12:01AM	s12:40PM	
s12:40PM	s12:01AM		Lv......Naples......An	s12:01AM	s12:40PM	
s 2:30PM	s 2:15AM		Lv......Angola......Lv	s10:00PM	s11:00AM	
f 2:42PM	f 2:27AM		Ar......Wilhelm......Lv	f 9:48PM	f10:43AM	
			Ar......Brandon......Lv			
f 2:52PM	f 2:39AM		Ar......Plettenberg......Lv	f 9:37PM	f10:32AM	
			Ar......Bingen......Lv			
			Ar......Fulda......Lv			
s 3:12PM	s 3:02AM		Ar......Bayou Sara......Lv	s 9:16PM	s10:13AM	
			Ar......Manheim......Lv		f	
			Ar......Paloma......Lv			
f 3:32PM	f 3:25AM		Ar......Port Hudson......Lv	s 8:50PM	f 9:53AM	
f 3:36PM	f 3:29AM		Ar......Bonn......Lv	f 8:46PM	f 9:50AM	
			Ar......Irene......Lv		f	
f 3:56PM	f 3:51AM		Ar......Scotland......Lv	s 8:22PM	f 9:30AM	
s 4:01PM	s 3:57AM		Ar......North Baton Rouge......Lv	s 8:15PM	s 9:24AM	
s 4:20PM	4:10AM		Ar......Baton Rouge......Lv	s 8:05PM	s 9:15AM	

BATON ROUGE TO NEW ORLEANS
and Vice Versa

No. 3 Daily Read Down	No. 1 Daily Read Down	STATIONS	No. 2 Daily Read Up	No. 4 Daily Read Up
s 4:20PM	s 4:10AM	Lv......Baton Rouge......Ar	s 8:05PM	9:15AM
f	f 4:20AM	Ar......Essen......Lv	f 7:46PM	
		Ar......Siegen......Lv		
f 4:42PM	f 4:32AM	Ar......Kleinpeter......Lv	f 7:34PM	f 8:47AM
f 4:47PM	f 4:37AM	Ar......Bullion......Lv	f 7:28PM	f 8:42AM
f 4:52PM	f 4:42AM	Ar......Nettie......Lv	f 7:22PM	f 8:37AM
		Ar......Witten......Lv		
s 5:01PM	s 4:51AM	Ar......Gonzales......Lv	s 7:12PM	s 8:28AM
		Ar......Brittany......Lv	f	
s 5:13PM	s 5:03AM	Ar......Sorento......Lv	s 7:00PM	s 8:16AM
		Ar......Barmen......Lv		
s 5:23PM	s 5:13AM	Ar......McElroy......Lv	s 6:50PM	s 8:05AM
	f 5:25AM	Ar......Waldeck......Lv	f 6:37PM	
s 5:40PM	s 5:29AM	Ar......Gramercy......Lv	s 6:32PM	f 7:49AM
f 5:50PM	s 5:39AM	Ar......Garyville......Lv	s 6:23PM	f 7:41AM
		Ar......Terre Haute......Lv		
s 5:57PM	s 5:46AM	Ar......Reserve......Lv	f 6:16PM	f 7:35AM
f 6:08PM	f 5:54AM	Ar......Montegut......Lv	f 6:08PM	f 7:28AM
	f	Ar......Ory......Lv		f
	f 6:01AM	Ar......Elvina......Lv		
f 6:24PM	f 6:10AM	Ar......Alcazar......Lv	f 5:57PM	
f 6:40PM	f 6:23AM	Ar......Kassel......Lv	f 5:51PM	f 7:13AM
f 6:46PM	f 6:30AM	Ar......Frellsen......Lv	f 5:37PM	f 7:00AM
s 6:59PM	s 6:46AM	Ar......Kenner......Lv	s 5:31PM	s 6:56AM
		Ar......Shrewsbury......Lv	s 5:21PM	s 6:46AM
s 7:20PM	s 7:10AM	Ar......New Orleans......Lv (Terminal Station)	s 5:00PM	6:25AM

WINNFIELD TO ALOHA
and Vice Versa

No. 19 Daily Read Down	STATIONS	No. 20 Daily Read Up
6:30AM	Lv......Winnfield......Ar	5:30PM
f	Lv......Alonzo......Lv	f
f	Lv......Whitford......Lv	f
s 7:20AM	Lv......Atlanta......Lv	s 4:45PM
f	Lv......Emden......Lv	f
s 7:50AM	Lv......Verda......Lv	s 4:15PM
s 9:00AM	Ar......Aloha......Lv	3:50PM

f—Trains stop on signal.
s—Trains will stop.
Trains do not stop where no time is shown.

Pullman Service

Between Shreveport and New Orleans
In Trains 1 and 2

Between Alexandria and New Orleans
In Trains 1 and 2

Cars at Alexandria ready for occupancy at 9:00 p. m.
Cars at Alexandria can be occupied until 7:00 a. m.

Observation Buffet Parlor Cars
Are operated in Trains 3 and 4
Between Shreveport and New Orleans

can apply. Wrecks, derailments, delays, tie-ups, congestions, and various other occurrences of like character, is the common rule and report which this commission receives constantly. It is in no position to supply service . . . and shippers and travelers avail themselves of the use of its railway only as a last resort.[23]

Evidence suggests that some of the commission's concerns about the LR&N were well founded. Lax about the appearance of the LR&N, Edenborn failed to keep his rail-

road neat and well trimmed for the public, as befitted a first-class operation. Though he was willing to make proper capital investments during road construction, he cut corners to keep operating costs low. One local operation reflected particularly poorly on the line. Shortly after the Baton Rouge refinery began its operations in 1909, Edenborn started a shuttle service between the Baton Rouge depot and the Standard Oil plant for the convenience of the workers. Because the ride took only a few minutes, Edenborn fashioned pas-

TABLE 2

Watercraft of the Louisiana Railway & Navigation Company

Name	Year acquired		Cost	Length (in feet)	Width (in feet)	Gross Weight (in tons)	Draft (in feet)	Type
William Edenborn	1906	New	$12,835	143	33	267	6.5	Sternwheel towboat
Sarah Edenborn	1908	New	50,094[a]	143	33	259	6.5	Sternwheel towboat
J. B. Lewis	1908	Used[b]	15,059	?	?	?	?	Sternwheel towboat
William Edenborn II	1914	New	52,344	143	33	267	6.5	Sternwheel towboat
Kellogg [c]	1924	Used	30,000	303	46	?	9.8	Sidewheel carrier
Angola	1906	New	32,000	256	37	645	6.5	Barge
Naples	1908	New	33,000	296	37	716	6.5	Barge

[a]   See chapter 3, note 29.

[b]   Rebuilt in 1911.

[c]   The *Kellogg*, built in 1898 as a four-track, twenty-eight-car barge named *Halbrook*, was renamed and converted to a sidewheel steamer in 1918, with two tracks removed.

Sources: ICC *Reports* 97 (1925): 406; *Way's Packet Directory, 1848–1983*; L. B. Williams interview.

senger service from his flatcars by fitting benches on them. Even though the average annual rainfall in Baton Rouge is about sixty inches, it was 1915 before he was coerced into covering the flatcars with canvas roofs.

For a prolonged period of time the commission skirmished with the LR&N, and Long continued to prod Edenborn about what he perceived to be substandard performance. In one notable example of the commission's disfavor toward Edenborn, it denied a request made by the LR&N on January 27, 1927, to discontinue service of overnight trains between New Orleans and Shreveport. Overnight service was given to an average of only 1.5 southbound sleeper passengers and 0.5 northbound passengers each train, and the railroad wanted to shift entirely to day trains. Despite overwhelming evidence that day trains would more efficiently serve the public, Long commented, "I decline to sign or concur in this order. I respectfully dissent." Evidence shows that the Public Service Commission was behind the overly stringent requirement that the river-transfer operation be realigned, at great expense to Edenborn, in order to improve service to shippers and pas-

sengers.[24] During his final years on the commission, Long managed to send these words to Edenborn:

> You haven't a decent coach on the railroad that I have seen. To us it seems that Providence has indeed been with the passengers who ride your road. Why more people have not been killed is not only due to the slow schedules which you have maintained, which is [*sic*] none too fast at that, but to the most fortunate of circumstances.[25]

Not until 1928, when Long moved to the governor's office, did the commission abandon its vendetta against Edenborn.

The river-transfer operations of the LR&N fascinated many people—shippers, passengers, and Edenborn himself. He had founded the Angola Transfer Company in 1906, but he did not incorporate it under a state charter until much later, in 1916. Locomotives were not transferred; switch engines and locomotive-servicing facilities, as well as storage tracks, were maintained on each side of the river. The sole purpose of the company was to provide transfer services for the railroad cars

The Hagan Avenue shops of the LR&N at New Orleans, circa 1925. Left to right: engine number 122, a former MK&T 2-6-0; and numbers 103 and 106, Russian decapods purchased from the U.S. government in 1921. These shops were always considered too cramped, but not until the 1950s were more commodious accommodations provided at Shrewsbury.

over a difficult 8.3-mile course from Naples, on the Red River a few miles west of the Mississippi, to Angola, on the east side. Eastward from Naples the route followed a former course of the Mississippi River, now called the Old River, which, because of slow currents, silted significantly. It was the railroad's responsibility to keep its channel clear, and this required constant dredging in order for the towboats and their barges to remain on schedule. Moreover, frequent fog along the river made navigation difficult. Foundering occurred regularly—and so did calls to the landing for assistance. In contrast to the treacherous passage through the Old River, the actual crossing of the Mississippi River, constituting a distance of about one mile, was handled simply and expeditiously.[26]

Throughout its history, Angola Transfer had a modest fleet of watercraft (see Table 2).[27] The *J. B. Lewis* was used primarily for dredging. The barges could hold ten to twelve cars, and after 1908 the two towboats with barges could handle an average-sized freight train in a single crossing. The *Kellogg,*

purchased from the river-transfer operation of the Missouri–Illinois Railroad near Ste. Genevieve, Missouri, could handle twelve cars without a barge. Edenborn used this boat until it sank in 1928. When the first *William Edenborn* sank in the Old River in 1914, Edenborn immediately ordered another ferry of identical design.

Misfortune, however, continued to hound the river operation during the building of the ferry. While supervising construction of the *William Edenborn II,* the captain of the boat, William McClelland, suffered a fatal illness. A steamboat captain for thirty years, he had been one of the most popular people on the river and a particular favorite of Edenborn. His understudy, a colorful character by the name of William Dippel, took over from McClelland and became equally popular among the rivermen.[28] The *William Edenborn II,* along with the *Sarah Edenborn,* survived to the end of ferry operations, when the trains began to use the Baton Rouge bridge in 1940.[29]

In the early 1920s Edenborn began to tire of the leasing arrangement for passenger-terminal facilities in New Orleans. Planning studies for an independent passenger station in the vicinity of his warehouses proved favorable, and he applied to the City of New Orleans for permission to build a new depot at the corner of Rampart and Girod Streets, a few blocks north of Union Station, which served the Southern Pacific and the Illinois Central lines. On March 1, 1922, the city council passed an ordinance that granted Edenborn the right-of-way he needed and permitted him to begin construction, though it imposed the restriction that he spend at least $125,000 in building a first-class facility. After some negotiations, Edenborn agreed to the restriction and proceeded to build a brick-and-concrete building covering an area of 200,000 square feet. Owned outright by Edenborn, its final cost was reportedly $150,000. The station initially had two passenger tracks divided by a single platform with an umbrella shed. There was space to add more tracks, although this was never done. The last LR&N train departed from the Terminal Station on May 10, 1924, and the next day regular service began at the new Rampart Street Station. With the new depot, reactivation of the Carrollton Avenue Station to provide service for west-end passengers became a feasible venture.[30] The Rampart Street Station adequately served the needs of the railroad until the new Union Passenger Terminal opened in New Orleans in May 1954.[31]

Another of Edenborn's projects in the early 1920s was the acquisition of the Sherman, Shreveport and Southern Railroad, which connected Shreveport with Greenville and McKinney in East Texas (using trackage rights over the VS&P between Shreveport and the Texas state line, a distance of 17 miles). Part of the Missouri, Kansas and Texas (Katy) system, it was the line with which the LR&N collaborated in the movement of freight between Dallas and Shreveport. The Katy had gone into receivership in 1915, and under a 1923 reorganization plan the SS&S had come to be considered surplus. Edenborn made a bid for the property, which comprised 179.04 miles of railroad, 13 locomotives, as-

sorted rolling stock, and a number of trackside structures. The operating headquarters of the SS&S was in Greenville, 171 miles west of Shreveport. Also included in the deal was Richard R. Farmer, general manager of the SS&S, whom Edenborn believed was one of the strongest assets of the purchase.[32]

The sale of the SS&S took place on Stonewall Street in Greenville at 1:00 P.M. on December 16, 1922. Judge Robert Milling, representing Edenborn, made the "highest, best—and only" bid of $700,000. The SS&S, purchased for approximately $4,000 per mile of railroad and fully equipped, was a bargain. The transfer of the railroad assets to Edenborn occurred on April 1, 1923. It was a rare situation for the recipient of assets of this kind to be an individual and not a corporation, but this soon changed when Edenborn delivered the title to the property to the Louisiana Railway and Navigation Company of Texas. The working arrangement with the VS&P continued at the east end of the line. At the west end, three different railroads vied to move freight into Dallas—the Katy and the Cotton Belt in Greenville and the Santa Fe in Farmersville. Although not truly competitive with the LR&N, the Southern Pacific route through McKinney also occasionally competed for service.[33]

Edenborn immediately began to integrate the Texas property into the LR&N system. In part due to his new line, he started a monthly house organ entitled *Edenborn Lines*. He incorporated the LR&N of Texas on March 27, 1923, and requested permission of the ICC to issue $200,000 in capital stock and $2,963,000 in first-mortgage bonds at 6 percent in the name of the railroad. The ICC did not approve this apparent overcapitalization, but on June 20 it approved the issuance of $400,000 in capital stock and $750,000 in bonds, an amount that still exceeded the purchase price of $700,000.[34]

Unfortunately, the Katy receivers had allowed the property to deteriorate, and the bargain price paid by Edenborn begged the loosening of additional funds for a complete renovation. This was not, however, Edenborn's way, and his ultimate solution brings to mind his conflicts with the Public Service Commission. Instead of renovating the line, he spent a minimal amount for necessary items and trusted that good employees who were fairly paid would bring operations to a proper level without significant capital expenditures. Well past Edenborn's time, the Texas line remained an unballasted, light-rail branch line and was not upgraded until the advent of World War II.[35]

To celebrate the acquisition of the Texas line, in mid-April a "Goodwill Special" train ran from New Orleans to McKinney carrying more than one hundred guests. One of them was Meigs Frost, a reporter for the *New Orleans States*. When the train crossed into Texas, Edenborn invited Frost to his business car at the rear of the train for an interview. The story of the interview ran on April 29 under the headline "Who's This Man Bill Edenborn Anyhow?" It provides some interesting insights into Edenborn:

> He was dressed in a baggy grey serge suit. His shoes hadn't been blacked for several days. His collar was low and comfortable. His hat was a soft and battered felt. His necktie must have cost all of fifty cents—his shirt fully a dollar. His big, capable hands rested on the ancient horn handle of a walking stick of twisted wood. Every thing he wore, from feet to crown, could have been bought in open market for something less than fifty dollars.
>
> Stretched comfortably in a worn armchair in the observation section in the rear of his private car, he was looking at the green and rolling Texas country. . . . That private car, by the way, was the pinnacle of simplicity. You've seen more luxurious ones housing the manager of a traveling circus.

The car that Frost describes was an old observation–sleeping car purchased secondhand from the Pullman Company. Edenborn rejected the usual fittings of the railroad business car—such amenities as cook-attendant, private dining room, and special bedrooms—a preference that further revealed his character. Though Edenborn rejected this kind of lux-

ury, he permitted Farmer, the general manager, to use the only true business car owned by the railroad—a car acquired along with other rolling stock from the Katy. Frost illuminates other aspects of Edenborn's personality:

> Sundays you'll find William Edenborn riding back and forth on that train ferry—a water trip of a couple of hours. He owns the ferry and the railroad it carries. It's his amusement and his wife's. Side by side with him you'll find Mrs. William Edenborn, usually in black skirt and white shirtwaist, her whitening hair neatly brushed back and simply knotted.
>
> "You see that the pay-car rolls on schedule" were his orders . . . and he [once] drew his personal check for one million dollars, dedicating it to that one task—to make sure that the pay car rolled on schedule. . . . Is it any wonder that the employees of the Louisiana Railway and Navigation will fight for him?
>
> A big man is William Edenborn. Big physically. For all his seventy five years and the slight stoop they give to his shoulders, he bulks huge today; not fat, but huge and broad-shouldered, passing the six-foot mark. His close-cropped white hair, his close-cropped moustache, his eagle-keen blue eyes throw all thoughts of his wrinkled, baggy clothes and his carelessness in wearing them far into the background. . . . He sits quietly, a good listener, a man who talks rarely. But when he talks! In simple words and few he goes directly to the point at issue.[36]

The tour party stopped overnight at Greenville. While Farmer entertained the guests with a special showing of the movie *Doctor Jack*, Edenborn went down to the railroad shops and became acquainted with the workers there.

Although advanced in years, Edenborn took on what was perhaps his greatest challenge in 1925. With the possibility of added business from Texas, and with some persuasion from the Public Service Commission, Edenborn began to consider seriously the need to relocate the LR&N on the west side of the Mississippi crossing. He had diverged from the original survey in order to avoid the

The Sarah Edenborn *moving across the Mississippi River, lashed together with a light-loaded barge of freight cars, in June 1940. (L&A photograph, courtesy of Louis Saillard)*

View of the dining area of the William Edenborn in June 1940, little changed from the earlier days of the stern-wheeler. To the left, Captain William Dippel; above the door, a portrait of William Edenborn; through the doorway, a view of the incline at Filston. (L&A photograph, courtesy of Louis Saillard)

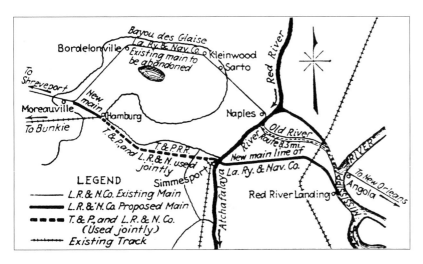

William Edenborn's last construction project—one of tremendous interest to him—
was the erection of a new bridge across the Atchafalaya River at Simmesport,
Louisiana. Coupled with this project was the relocation of part of the main line and
the development of a new west-bank incline on the Mississippi. This map shows how
the bridge, new trackage, and relocated incline tie together. Trackage rights over the
T&P were involved, and the ferry transfer distance was reduced greatly. The map
was published in Engineering News-Record, October 6, 1927.

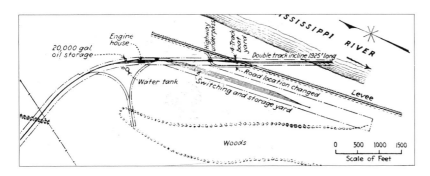

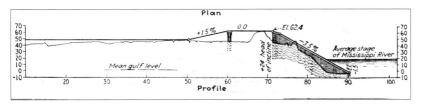

Layout of the new terminal facilities at Filston, which included a boatyard, a storage
yard, an engine house, and a double-track incline. The map was published in Engineering News-Record, October 6, 1927.

expensive bridging of the Atchafalaya River; it
was this diversion that had led to the Naples
landing location and the problem-riddled
transfer through the Old River. Edenborn
had attempted some homemade remedies,
such as cutting through an arm of Turnbull's
Island to speed up the movements, but with
no success. Freight traffic had increased to an
average of 170 to 180 cars per day, and these
had to be moved between the shores. Considering the lengthy time for a round-trip freight
transfer in addition to the needs for the passenger trains, the two towboat-barge combi-
nations seemed to have reached their limits.[37]

Another matter associated with the river
transfer was pressing. In late 1924 or early
1925 Edenborn invited executives of the
Kansas City Southern to consider purchasing
the railroad. Their analysis showed that Edenborn's arrangement for river transfer chal-
lenged the economic viability of the railroad.
Because others who were interested in buying
the property had also made this observation,
Edenborn was finally forced to confront the
transfer problem head-on.[38]

In 1925 Edenborn began to plan the relocation of the west shore landing as well as the
railroad line that led to it. He found that he
could avoid some tracklaying by using the rails
of a T&P branch line. The survey, placing the
new landing directly opposite the existing
landing at Angola, cut the transfer time for a
passenger train from about two hours to
about one hour. Edenborn applied to the
Public Service Commission and to the ICC
for authorization to relocate the main line, negotiated with the T&P for trackage rights, had
the Hedrick and Frost engineering firm, of
Kansas City, develop a design for the bridge,
and requested permission from the War Department to cross the Atchafalaya River at the
town of Simmesport. In due course the various agencies granted their approval, and work
on the project began in 1925.[39]

From the start, construction of the bridge
over the Atchafalaya River was plagued by difficulties. The design specified five through-
truss spans totaling 1,200 feet, one of them a
300-foot turn span. Arrangements called for

joint use with vehicular traffic, and because of this the State of Louisiana absorbed a portion of the cost. Edenborn, however, elected to do much of the construction work with his own forces, which tended to prolong the time it took to complete the project. A new yard and a set of inclines were installed, and the station was given the name Phillipston, presumably for a Phillips family that sold portions of the land to the railroad. Later the name was contracted to Filston.[40]

The Great Mississippi Flood of 1927, which stopped progress on the bridge, dealt severe blows to the LR&N. Flooding in Arkansas and Mississippi was extensive, and by June the crest approached the railroad's territory. Locally, authorities patrolled the districts of the Atchafalaya and Mississippi Rivers and added sandbags to the levees to resist the unprecedented high-water levels. But the insubstantial levees in the Bayou des Glaises district gave way in many places between Moreauville and Sarto, washing out miles of LR&N track. During the crisis, the government commandeered the *William Edenborn II* and the *Sarah Edenborn* to carry people as well as animals between Natchez and Baton Rouge. Paul Sippel, who had become a vice president of the LR&N, moved his business car to Mansura, where a camp of four to five thousand people had been located temporarily. The car served as a headquarters unit for the Louisiana National Guard, of which Robert Kennon, later governor of Louisiana, was in charge.[41]

President Coolidge appointed Herbert Hoover, who was then serving as secretary of commerce, to coordinate all flood-relief operations. At one point Sippel escorted him by special train into the flooded areas south of Alexandria so he could have a firsthand look at the destruction. Sippel describes the inspection:

> We got as far as Hessmer, where there was some water over the track, and [Hoover] . . . wanted to turn back, and remarked that he had seen everything he wanted to see. I told him he hadn't seen everything, and had to go

on down to Mansura where, if he wanted to, he could have someone take him into the flooded district. He finally consented to go that far . . . we got to Grande Ecore south of Mansura, and he could see all right because the entire country for hundreds of miles was just one big ocean. The water over the Grande Ecore fill was from 12 to 20 feet deep . . . deep enough that our steam boats could run across it and clear the telephone wires.[42]

The LR&N was out of service in this part of Louisiana for weeks due to the floodwaters, and construction on the Atchafalaya bridge at Simmesport was halted. The economic impact on the railroad was severe.

Other factors also slowed progress on construction of the bridge over the Atchafalaya, known to be one of the deepest and swiftest rivers in the country. After being placed, the center pier, the one that would support the rotating center span, was moved by the impact of the swift-flowing water. No longer in a vertical alignment, it was unsuitable for supporting the turn span. It was necessary to sink lateral piers and connect them to support the span. High water persisted through much of 1927, making it difficult to erect a temporary wooden structure ("falsework") on which to support the span as it was being assembled. This was the final span to be put in place, and was a 300-foot-long riveted truss weighing approximately 600 tons. As an almost desperation measure, the LR&N engineers decided to assemble the span in shallow water near the south bank and then float it out into place. This was finally accomplished and received national attention as an innovative approach.[43]

The methodology of this maneuver was described by L. B. Williams, a long-time key employee of the railroad, who was stationed at Naples at the time:

> At Simmesport they built the last span along the bank on some piling, figuring when the water rose that they would run the barges up under there and pick the span up and set it in place, which would save a lot of time. As the water came on up, it was decided to put the

William Edenborn was especially interested in the planning and construction of this 1,200-foot-long truss bridge across the Atchafalaya River at Simmesport, Louisiana, and it is regrettable that he did not live to see it completed. The project began in 1925, but the bridge was not opened until 1928. The mammoth Mississippi River flood of spring 1927 delayed progress, and floodwaters were still high when the last span was put in place with the aid of the William Edenborn *and two transfer barges lashed together, as shown in the photograph. The 300-foot-long span was assembled by the riverbank and then shifted into place astride the barges. The final lifting was done by pumping water out of the barges. The bridge was still in service in the mid-1990s. The photograph appeared in* Railway Age, *April 27, 1929.*

span in place. We sent the *William* and the *Sarah* down to Simmesport [with the barges]. . . .

[T]he two boats filled the barges [with water], got up under the span and pumped the water out, raised the span and I believe it took about an hour and a half (the barges were well lashed together with piling) to get the span in place and begin pumping the water back into the barges, lowering the span into place. Immediately thereafter, the water was pumped out and both boats were sent to Naples to begin the transfer work which had been left undone by the *Kellogg*.[44]

While work proceeded on the span, the *Kellogg*, a sidewheeler used by the LR&N for pumping sand and gravel, and sometimes for commercial trips, sank in the Old River. It was running heavy loads in place of the *William Edenborn II* and the *Sarah Edenborn*, both of which were occupied with construction. Records show that it sank on March 21, 1928, at 2:15 A.M., with Captain C. M. Guess in command. The wreck was not removed from the mud until 1945—by the U.S. Army Corps of Engineers.[45]

Edenborn did not live to see his bridge completed. When, in early 1926, he was invited to become a director of the Louisiana Development Association, he responded, "I am 78 years old and am busy building a bridge across the Atchafalaya River for my railroad. This work is taking all my time and you can see that at my age I already have my hands full." Not long afterward, Williams heard him comment at the construction site, "If I could just see trains go across this bridge I will be satisfied and ready to go. You know I'm getting pretty old."[46] On May 6, 1926, while working near the town of Emden (on

the Winnfield branch of the LR&N) on a farm he had purchased, he suffered a stroke. A special train transported him to Schumpert Sanatarium in Shreveport, where he and Sarah had moved after the purchase of the Texas line in 1923. He died there, on May 14, at 1:30 A.M.[47]

The news of Edenborn's death was telegraphed throughout the LR&N system, and special trains brought employees to the funeral. Burial was at 3:00 P.M. on May 16 at Forest Park Cemetery in Shreveport, and all the trains on the line stopped running for ten minutes to show the railroad employees' respect for their "benevolent boss." At its meeting on May 19, 1926, the Board of Directors of the LR&N passed a resolution that stated, in part:

> We knew him as a great creative genius and as a man equally great in his simplicity and modesty. He was the last man who would desire any fulsome adulation of his life achievement and such he does not need as his career spoke for itself and his works do live after him. . . . Other men have done great things for Louisiana in industry, but William Edenborn wrote his name large in the history of Louisiana, and whatever record leaps to light, his never can be shamed.[48]

The *Times-Picayune* had these final words about the line and its builder: "Other railroad men were inclined to smile at the Edenborn line. They regarded it as a rich man's hobby, and it was a hobby for Edenborn—more than that it was an absorbing interest, both for him and his wife."[49]

The widow was left without the consolation of children but with the strong support of her brother and sisters. Unfortunately for Sarah, Edenborn died intestate, and she was immediately faced with a difficult settlement of the estate. Lawyer Robert Milling, confidant of Edenborn and chief solicitor from the inception of the LR&N, provided assistance in this matter. Milling described the situation during testimony before the Interstate Commerce Commission.

. . . . A year and a half before Mr. Edenborn's death, negotiations started between him and the Kansas City Southern Railway Company for the purpose of trying to sell the road to that company. I sat in on those conferences, and the principal objection occurring at that time was the long river transfer; you could not make any time over the road [and] that the road could not make money as long as that [river transfer] existed.

He became convinced of that, so he decided to relocate about 20 miles of the line and bridge the Atchafalaya so as to give him a bank-to-bank crossing. He applied to the Interstate Commerce Commission for permission to do so and for authority to issue a couple of millions of short term notes which it was stated in the petition he would take at par, bearing six percent interest.

He started this construction, and when he had invested about $750,000 in the construction, he died, left no ascendants or descendants, and his wife, Mrs. Edenborn, became heir to this estate; that is, all of the community property existing in the state of Louisiana. Of course she did not inherit his separate estate of a few properties in other states.[50]

By June 1926 the estate appears to have been settled, with the court making Sarah the sole benefactor. (The award was later contested.) The value of the estate at the time was estimated to be $12 million. As evolving events later disclosed, this figure was on the low side.[51]

In addition to the difficulties of settling the estate, Sarah was left with the burden of

Car number 1000, of the LR&N of Texas, was the only property of the Edenborn Lines that could properly be called a business car. It was used by R. R. Farmer, general manager of the Texas line. William Edenborn preferred the use of an old Pullman car for his travels. In this photograph, taken at the Shreveport station in 1927, the car is serving needs of the "Edenborn Line Boosters." (Courtesy of Harold K. Vollrath)

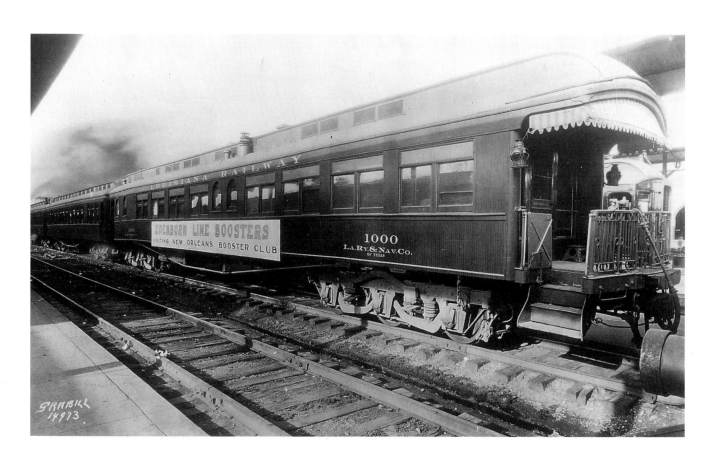

administering the railroad and finishing construction of the bridge. A week after the funeral, on May 23, she was elected president of the LR&N. She had no particular zeal for this responsibility, but she had little choice. Assisting in both business and personal capacities were Sippel, the nephew who by this time had the official title of assistant to the president, and Edward Staman, a long-time official of the railroad; along with Sarah they were trustees of the estate. Responsibility for the operations of the LR&N fell to the capable hands of Staman and Henry Helm, another long-time official of the railroad. Milling continued to provide legal counsel. Conduct of the day-to-day enterprise went on as usual.[52]

As president of the LR&N, Sarah confronted two immediate challenges. One was completion of the Simmesport bridge, along with its associated line relocation (the flood of 1927 occurred the following year). To complete the construction work, Sarah borrowed $1.5 million. Although she took out a loan, records indicate that her personal financial situation was excellent, because William's many investments provided considerable cash flow.[53] On Sunday, April 15, 1928, southbound passenger train number 1, which left Alexandria at 11:24 A.M, became the first through train to cross both the bridge at Simmesport and the ferry from Phillipston to Angola. If William Edenborn had lived, he undoubtedly would have been aboard that train. The press reported that the new crossing arrangements would cut the passenger-train schedules by eighty minutes and the freight-train schedules by more than seven hours. The new, first-class facilities were sufficient to meet the requirements of the future, as history has shown. The opening of the highway portion of the bridge was celebrated in August 1928. At Phillipston there was a 400-car classification and storage yard, a 28-car "boat yard," an engine house, a wye, and a double-track incline with a 3.5 percent grade. The railroad's investment in the bridge, ferry landing, and new right-of-way trackage was well over $2 million. A reasonable return on the investment was expected, but predictions did not take into account the

unprecedented downturn in the economy that occurred soon afterward.[54]

Sarah's other challenge was to find a buyer for the property. By happy circumstance, a potential purchaser appeared in mid-1926. William Edenborn had devised a rail link between the most important cities in the state, one that later became a key traffic artery in the region, but it would take the ingenuity of Harvey Couch to assure this ultimate success. Couch, a successful utilities magnate from Pine Bluff, Arkansas, had a lifelong interest in railroads and in trains. He had already negotiated for the purchase of the L&A, a line familiar to him since its earliest days (it ran close to his home in Calhoun, Arkansas[55]). Like the LR&N, the L&A had been developed by a businessman, William Buchanan, a competitor of Edenborn, with a style suggesting that the line was a hobby as well as a business. There was one big difference between the ventures of Buchanan and Edenborn, however: Buchanan's railroad had turned a profit since its inception. When Buchanan died in late 1923, his heirs, lacking his enthusiasm for the railroad, offered the line for sale. To purchase the L&A, Couch astutely put together a syndicate of private investors and investment bankers, people who had supported him in his successful development of the Arkansas Power and Light Company. It was his personal assessment of the opportunity, however, that guided the investment plans. In the LR&N Couch saw an important adjunct to the L&A, particularly in regard to its line into New Orleans and its potential for export freight business. The maneuvers of Couch turned out to be a critical factor in the continued viability of the Edenborn line.[56]

Couch entered into negotiations with Staman and Milling on the basis of Sarah's offer to sell the LR&N for $16 million. According to her figures, Sarah's heavily discounted price appears to have been reasonable (see Table 3). The Couch group, however, based its counteroffer on a valuation of the property by the ICC at $15.13 million, an assessment that was made available to them prior to its publication in 1928. Negotiations for the LR&N continued through 1927, and on November 1 Couch and Sarah, through their attorneys Hamilton Moses and Robert Milling, respectively, finally settled on a price that was lower than the ICC valuation.[57]

On May 1, 1928, the following agreement was announced: Sarah would receive $8 million in 5 percent first-mortgage bonds and $4 million in 5.5 percent second-mortgage bonds, all in the name of the reorganized L&A. In a generous gesture, she agreed to turn over all the LR&N stock (including that of the Texas line), to transfer the bonds, to cancel the notes, and to forgive the unpaid interest and general indebtedness. She was not interested, however, in tying up her money in bonds—she wanted cash. To this end the Couch group agreed to purchase the first-mortgage bonds for $7.5 million cash. Furthermore, the second-mortgage bonds were exchanged for a negotiable note from the L&A for $2.5 million, an amount representing a short-term loan that would be repaid no later than May 1, 1929. The Couch group raised $10 million in cash over a brief period of time; fortunately, the climate for this was good in the months before the October 1929 stock-market crash.[58]

TABLE 3

Valuation of the LR&N

According to Sarah Edenborn

Par value, capital stock of the LR&N	$ 8,131,000
First mortgage bonds of LR&N	10,361,000
Accumulated unpaid interest on bonds	6,151,000
Two-year notes, at 6 percent	1,500,000
Short-term notes, at 5 percent	375,000
Demand notes, at 5 percent	150,000
General indebtedness	500,000
Total	**$27,168,000**

The ICC endorsed the settlement arrangements effective February 23, 1929. This included approval of the request by the L&A to lease the LR&N for 999 years, effective the same date as a cash conservation measure.

During the ICC deliberations, Edenborn's old nemesis, Huey Long, was heard from again, but he had a somewhat different attitude. Now governor of Louisiana, he wrote the following to the ICC:

> As you likely know, one of the greatest problems of this State during the past several years has been with the Louisiana Railway & Navigation Company. It is in reality one of the, if not the, most important railway lines that we have, but its financial condition and its lack of interchanges and through line connections have been such as to materially handicap it and to cause great loss and inconvenience to the territory which the line has been serving. The proposition to merge this line with the Louisiana & Arkansas is one upon which our State looks with great favor.[59]

Sarah retired at the age of sixty-two with a considerable net worth. Fortunately, the $10 million cash she received from the Couch group was not affected by the October 1929 stock-market crash. Estimates of the value of Edenborn's estate are as high as $76 million, though the probate court used the figure of $12 million when it named Sarah as William's sole heir. Moreover, Sarah retained interests in valuable timber and oil properties in Louisiana, and perhaps many other satellite investments made by William during his business career.[60]

Soon after the sale of the LR&N, people began to come forward to claim a part of Sarah's inheritance. The first to appear was Sophie Meier, wife of William Meier, a farmer from Gumbo, Missouri. Sophie claimed that she was the illegitimate daughter of William Edenborn and Fida Dettly, the girlfriend he had dated before he met Sarah. Sophie sued the Edenborn estate in July 1926, claiming a daughter's share of the total legacy. Litigation dragged on until Sarah settled with Sophie in April 1928 for $300,000, much less than the $2 million Sophie was demanding. She received only half of the award after lawyers deducted their share for fees.[61] Other people who came forward to claim money were

The William Edenborn *and its barge are at the Filston landing, and ten-wheeler 511 is in the process of unloading the cargo. After the cars are pulled up the 3.5% incline they will be shunted into a storage yard. Then the engine will take cars from the holding yard and move them down to the barge for transport across the Mississippi to Angola. This picture was taken in October 1937; in less than three years the watercraft and the incline will be replaced by a new bridge at Baton Rouge. (Photograph courtesy of L. B. Williams)*

William's four nieces and nephews, the daughters and sons of his sister, Lena, whom he had befriended when she became a widow at an early age. In July 1926, shortly after William's death, Sarah had given them some real estate in St. Louis, where they resided. Eventually Sarah settled with them also, giving them each $34,750, a tidy sum in the late 1920s.[62]

In 1934 Sarah moved from Shreveport to St. Louis to be closer to her sisters, Malvina and Henrietta Drain, and her brother, Edgar Drain. When Sarah died on August 9, 1944, her property in Louisiana was valued at $9,499,964. Her money was left to her sisters and to Edgar's children. (Edgar's death came shortly after Sarah's.)[63]

Sarah's passing severed the final link between the Edenborns and the "Short Line Through Louisiana," as the LR&N advertised itself. No Edenborn heir has ever been associated with the railroad. By the time of her death, the Couch group had taken control of the LR&N and a new, "entirely management" philosophy prevailed. William and Sarah made a positive contribution to the State of Louisiana and to the railroad industry, one that was significant in their time and continues to be so today.

For the history of the Louisiana and Arkansas to be complete, it is now necessary to go back in time and pick up another of its predecessors, the Texas line.

The Texas line that William Edenborn acquired in 1922 became an integral part of the LR&N and subsequently a key segment of the L&A. He purchased the SS&S from the receivers of the Missouri, Kansas and Texas Railroad of Texas. Representing the earliest antecedent of the L&A system, it has a long, rich history and predates all other components of the L&A by twenty years. Initially incorporated by the Texas legislature as the East Line and Red River Railroad Company on March 22, 1871, the line was originally conceived and built by the citizens of Jefferson, Texas, to protect their business interests in the region.

A prominent port on a tributary of the Red River, Jefferson was a flourishing economic center in eastern Texas 50 miles northwest of Shreveport, Louisiana. By 1870 it had become one of Texas's largest cities and its most prominent inland port. The founding of the line by Jefferson's citizens was a long-delayed response to a cry in 1847 by the *Jefferson Democrat* for a "railroad to the prairies," with the purpose of expanding a thriving trade between Jefferson and the Texas counties to the west and north.[1] A considerable amount of tonnage moved by riverboat between Jefferson and the Red River via Big Cypress Bayou and Caddo Lake, and much of the cargo unloaded at Jefferson moved west by wagon train.

By 1871, however, some of this business was being lost to the Marshall "gateway," some 30 miles to the south, because of a new railroad that ran from Shreveport to Marshall. First connecting these two communities in 1866, it was part of a planned railroad that would run from Shreveport to Dallas.[2] Furthermore, almost concurrent with the origin of the East Line and Red River was the founding of the Texas and Pacific Railroad Company, chartered on March 3, 1871, by a

special act of the U.S. Congress. Its plan was to build west from Texarkana and Marshall, hopefully to the West Coast. These lines, plus projections by other railroads to move into the region, prompted the Jefferson citizens to build their own railroad.[3]

The charter of the East Line and Red River Railroad called for construction of a "continuous line of railway from the city of Jefferson, in Marion County, Texas, to the city of Sherman, in Grayson County . . . thence in a westerly or northwesterly direction to the western limits of the state of Texas." It granted the railroad a 200-foot right-of-way across any public lands encountered in its route survey.[4] Eventually, the route passed through Mount Pleasant, Sulphur Springs, and Kentucky Town. W. M. Harrison, president of the Jefferson Bank, was named president of the Board of Directors for the line. Other directors included E. W. Taylor (vice president), W. B. Ward (treasurer and general superintendent), T. J. Rogers, J. P. Russell, L. A. Ellis, J. H. Bemis, S. D. Rainey, all of whom resided in Jefferson; and W. S. Ferrell, of Sulphur Springs.[5]

The start of construction on the East Line was delayed for several years. Jefferson encountered problems in raising the needed capital, in part due to the national economic panic in 1873 and 1874. Another factor that delayed construction was the completion of the T&P from Marshall to Texarkana in December 1873, a road that passed through an edge of Jefferson and enabled through service to Dallas by way of Marshall. Yet another delay was imposed on construction when the U.S. government removed massive obstructions in the Red River, which caused the water levels in Caddo Lake and Big Cypress Bayou, the Red River tributary that served Jefferson, to lower significantly. This "Red

River raft" had dammed water to a level at which water transport to Jefferson was feasible year-round; after its removal such transport became seasonal at best. There was also some controversy among the organizers regarding the exact route of the line.

Despite delays on the East line, the Texas legislature continued to support the project. On May 17, 1873, it made a land grant to the East Line, in the amount of sixteen sections (10,240 acres) per mile, payable to the railroad upon completion and operation of each 20-mile segment. Presumably most of the land could be sold readily to provide needed capital. At this time the charter was amended to show a main line from Jefferson to Greenville, about 125 miles. A time limit of four years was specified for completion of the main line.[6]

At this juncture a critical question arose: should the rails be set in a standard gauge (4'8½") or in a gauge smaller than standard? The many advocates of narrow gauge had held a convention in St. Louis in 1872, and reports from that gathering undoubtedly influenced the East Line directors. On one hand, a narrow gauge clearly had the advantage of being less expensive to build and to equip with locomotives and rolling stock. The virtues of "thinking small" were said to be savings of between 20 and 40 percent of the cost of standard gauge, for construction as well as for equipment purchases. Moreover, a narrow gauge could accommodate tighter curves and steeper grades than the standard gauge because of better locomotive-wheel traction. Of the miles of railroad constructed in the United States in 1875, about a quarter were narrow gauge, usually with a measurement of three feet.[7] On the other hand, choosing a narrow gauge would forfeit convenience. The T&P, which served Jefferson, ran on a standard gauge; during interchanges with the East Line, its carloads of merchandise or commodities would have to be reloaded manually, causing time delays and significantly increasing shipping costs. With high levels of interchange, transshipment costs would easily outweigh the capital cost savings of the narrow gauge. In some instances it was possible to install hoisting equipment to lift the large cars onto narrow-gauge trucks, but this led to problems of instability because of the large overhang at the sides of the smaller trucks, and the practice was considered bad.[8]

After weighing the options, the directors of the East Line selected a narrow gauge of three feet. This decision was made on the grounds that construction money was in short supply and relatively little carload freight from the T&P would be forwarded to East Line customers. As many advocates of narrow gauge discovered too late, the selection of this gauge was a mistake, and before the line was completed there were pressures to convert it to standard gauge.

The first construction work on the East Line began during the summer of 1876. A ground-breaking ceremony was held in Jefferson on June 9, and the attending crowd of townspeople was swelled by members of the Texas Press Association, which was holding its annual convention there. As reported in the regional press, "Carriages were provided and accompanied by an excellent band of music . . . flags were floating in the breeze . . . and cannon belched forth a ringing welcome. . . . A temporary stand had been erected for speaking, over which hung three flags" (presumably the flags were those of the Republic of Texas, the Confederate States of America, and the United States). Speeches followed, after which laborers went to work turning earth for the right-of-way.[9]

The Board of Directors of the East Line was busy during the summer of 1876. It authorized the purchase of one thousand tons of iron rails from Vulcan Iron Works, three flatcars and one boxcar from Litchfield Car Company, and a steam locomotive of the 2-6-0 type from Porter, Bell and Company. The board also agreed with L. U. Polk, chief engineer, that a maximum gradient of eighty feet per mile (1.5 percent) would be more realistic than the previously set maximum of sixty-eight feet per mile (1.3 percent).[10]

The road was completed to Hickory Hill, a distance of 20 miles, on November 18, and four days later an excursion party of nearly four hundred people rode the cars to the end of the track. Regular operations began on December 1. The quality of construction of the East Line appears to have been good, as indicated by the first inspection report. To qualify for the first grant of land (which was contingent on completing 20 miles of road), it was necessary for an inspection to be made by the State of Texas; this was done by E. A. Blanch, who dated his report December 2, 1876. Typical of his comments:

> The grading is done in good style, and has a neat and symmetrical appearance . . . the trestle bridges are constructed of the best heart pine throughout . . . the track is laid of a handsome pattern of T rail . . . [and is] laid in most excellent style, and even upon an old road-bed it would be considered in perfect order. . . . I think I may safely add that it is the best new road over which I have ever traveled.[11]

Extension westward was slow, with the line reaching Daingerfield, 33 miles from Jefferson, in time for a Fourth of July celebration. On May 21, 1877, the directors had resolved to proceed immediately with an extension to Pittsburg, 15 miles beyond Daingerfield, with completion targeted for September or October, if the citizens of the town would raise $30,000 for the cause. In June the citizens reported that they had raised only $18,000, but the directors accepted the money without hesitation and went ahead with construction. The railroad reached Pittsburg late in the year and posted the first schedule there on December 11, 1877. The rails entered Sulphur Springs, 93 miles from Jefferson, in April 1878. A May 1879 schedule for the daily train from Jefferson to Sulphur Springs documents a running time of nine hours and fifteen minutes. Rolling stock included three locomotives, four coaches, two mail/express cars, twelve boxcars, one stock car, and forty flatcars. The preponderance of flatcars reflects the lively timber business in the heavily wooded area served by the road. At this time, the railroad halted construction for almost two years to generate income and to consolidate plans. Also in this period of time, records show that

one of the strongest promoters of the road, Ben W. Epperson, an influential lawyer of Jefferson, died on September 6, 1878. Epperson had also been involved in the Memphis, El Paso and Pacific, a forerunner of the T&P.[12]

In December 1879 a special excursion was run between Jefferson and Sulphur Springs. The train left Jefferson at 7:00 A.M. and arrived at Sulphur Springs at 11:00 A.M. With six stops along the way, for breakfast, wood, and water, which together took about an hour, the average speed was about 31 miles

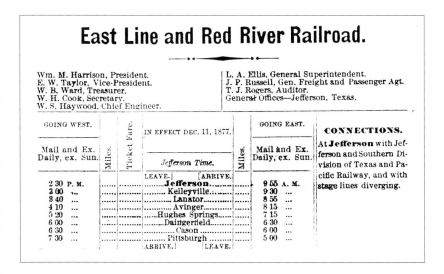

per hour. A feature story on the event published in *Railway Age* reflects the correspondent's positive impression of the line:

> The whole party were enchanted with the smooth, steady, easy motion. . . . The wonder of all is that the East Line is a narrow gauge road . . . this excursion has shown that a speed of over thirty miles an hour may be reached with entire ease, comfort and safety. . . . The track of the road is in splendid condition, and the equipments are first class . . . no accident or damage has ever happened of any consequence during the three years of operation of the road. . . . Its business is already very large, its transportation being cotton, lumber, hides and other productions of the country, and merchandise in large quantities for the interior. . . . Its influence upon the prosperity of this city [Jefferson] is beginning to tell.[13]

This early schedule of the East Line was published in the Texas Railroad Gazetteer for Distribution on Railways, Steamships and Stages in 1878. The mail-and-express train appears to spend its nights at Pittsburgh, perhaps doing extra duty handling supplies for the railroad construction in progress to Greenville. (Courtesy of Barker History Collection, University of Texas at Austin)

Annual pass of the East Line, for 1881, signed by John C. Flynn, general manager.

Advertisement for the East Line as it appeared in The Texas Railroad Gazetteer for Distribution on Railways, Steamships and Stages in 1878. Elsewhere in the book it was pointed out that "This road, when completed, will pour into the lap of Jefferson the inexhaustible wealth of the iron region, and also the farm products of several large counties not now tributary. . . . [S]everal furnaces along the East Line and Red River Railroad are turning out considerable quantities of pig metal." (Courtesy of the Barker History Collection, University of Texas at Austin)

The railroad's immediate objective was to complete the road to Greenville. It accomplished this feat in December 1880 and established regular service on March 14 of the following year. The 124-mile-long road passed through rolling country; minimizing the amount of earthwork had resulted in a number of grades. Because construction ran behind schedule and the road failed to reach Greenville by October 1, 1880, the line forfeited a cash subsidy of $5,000 raised by Greenville citizens. The line was adequately built (with thirty-pound rails), however, and separate freight and passenger trains were placed into operation.[14]

A crucial change in ownership of the East Line and Red River Railroad Company occurred in 1881, when the line caught the attention of railroad tycoon Jay Gould. By this time, the line was running six locomotives and up to ninety-six pieces of rolling stock. It was operating successfully, showing a slight profit for the year ending May 31, 1881. Securities issued included $615,000 in capital stock and $861,000 in first-mortgage bonds. Gould purchased the line from the citizen-promoters for about $1.2 million. When he replaced Harrison with one of his own people, James A. Baker, as president of the Board of Directors on November 28, 1881, he severed any remaining connection between the Jefferson group and management of the East Line and Red River.[15]

Immediately after the purchase of the line, Gould began to plan a 31-mile extension west from Greenville to McKinney, where a connection could be made with the Houston and Texas Central. By October 27, 1881, he had negotiated a contract for the work with the International Railway Improvement Company (a Gould enterprise); he financed the extension with $315,000 in capital stock and $220,000 in first-mortgage bonds. At Greenville, passenger trains began to use the Katy depot instead of the small structure erected earlier on Stonewall Street. Construction on the extension began in February 1882; by late March trains were running to Farmersville, and by mid-May they had arrived in McKinney, 155 miles west of Jefferson. Though Gould retained the three-foot gauge, he installed crossties and bridge members to the standard-gauge width with the expectation that the entire line would be broadened soon. Some technical details of the completed line are shown in Table 4, and a complete roster of locomotives on the East line is given in Table 5.[16]

In connection with the new service to McKinney, the press had this amusing comment:

> A saucy engineer on the Houston and Texas Central railroad hailed a little engine on the East Line yesterday, which was just in sight, and said, "Bring the little thing up and let it suck." The engineer of the proud little engine replied, "wait 'til your grain and cotton comes in, then we will suck you dry."[17]

TABLE 4

Physical Characteristics of the Completed East Line and Red River Railroad

1883

Length of main track in miles	155.3
Length of side track in miles	7
Length of main track laid with iron	155.3
Weight of iron per lineal yard, lbs.	35
Number of miles of main track ballasted with sand	38.5
Length of pile and trestle bridges, ft.	22,480
Length of wood-truss bridges, ft.	280
Length of combination bridges, ft.	100
Length of iron and steel bridges, ft.	60
Maximum grade per mile, ft.	66
Maximum degree of curvature	6
Gauge, ft.	3
Number of locomotives	13
Number of passenger cars	6
Number of mail and express cars	3
Number of box and stock cars	64
Number of flat cars	221

Source: Texas Railroad Gazetteer for Distribution on Railways, Steamships and Stages (based on a report by the State Engineer of Texas).

Under new ownership the East Line and Red River continued to run its routes profitably, but from the start Gould had stirred up controversy. In a fashion typical of him, in November 1881, on the day he had replaced Harrison as president, Gould turned over the line to one of his properties, the Katy. As a subsidiary of the Katy, even though its identity was retained by the Gould group, control of the East Line and Red River went out of state, an arrangement that was counter to the terms of its original charter.[18] Several years after this transfer, the State of Texas protested the sale of the East Line to the Katy on the grounds that the Katy was not incorporated in the state. Heading the protest was James Stephen Hogg, who had been elected attorney general in 1886. In the words of prominent Texas historian T. R. Fehrenbach,

> [Hogg] brought suit after suit to disentangle Texas roads from out-of-state control, no matter where their ownership lay. He was instrumental in getting every company that operated rails in Texas to establish a general office within the state. . . . He asserted state control of every track that lay within Texas' borders.[19]

As one of Hogg's test cases, the East Line achieved a degree of notoriety. On November 1, 1888, Hogg succeeded in having the charter of the East Line forfeited and the road placed in the hands of a federal receiver. The Katy appealed the decision to the Supreme Court of Texas, but the court upheld the decree on February 17, 1890. On April 13, 1891, the receivership was transferred to the state court.[20]

The forfeiture of the East Line and Red River Railroad charter represented a landmark action of the state. Background on the action is best described in Hogg's own words, spoken on April 21, 1892:

> The East Line & Red River Railroad is a narrow gauge road extending from Jefferson to McKinney, a distance of 155 miles. It was well constructed and fully equipped by Texas people living at Jefferson and cost them only $7000 per mile. The owners issued to themselves

TABLE 5

Narrow-Gauge Locomotives of the East Line and Red River Railroad Company

ENGINE NUMBER					Date	Date	Cylinders	Drivers	WEIGHT (in tons)	
Original	Final	MK&T	Type	Builder	built	acquired	(in inches)	(in inches)	Drivers	Total
1[a]	195	408	2-6-0	Porter-Bell 253	1876	1876	9×16	31.5	12	18
2[b]	196	407	2-6-0	Porter-Bell 271	1877	1877	10×16	35.5	13	19
3[c]	197	—	2-6-0	Baldwin 4435	1878	1878	12×16	36	?	?
4[d]	198	409	2-6-0	Baldwin 4821	1879	1879	12×16	36	13	21.5
5	199	410	4-4-0	Pittsburgh 431	1880	1880	11×18	38	12.75	19.75
6	200	411	4-4-0	Pittsburgh 432	1880	1880	11×18	38	12.75	19.75
—	186[e]	401	4-4-0	National	1874	1882	11×16	44	12	18
—	187[e]	—	4-4-0	National	1874	1882	11×16	44	12	18
—	188[e]	402	4-4-0	National	1874	1882	11×16	44	12	18
—	189[e]	403	2-6-0	National	1876	1882	11×16	36	11	17
—	190[e]	404	4-6-0	National	1875	1882	11×16	36	14.5	19
—	191[e]	405	2-6-0	Baldwin 5015	1880	1882	13×16	36	16	20.5
—	192[e]	406	2-6-0	Baldwin 5017	1880	1882	13×16	36	16	20.5

Sources: Interviews, S. R. Wood, Lou Koeppe, J. B. Harper, Robert Brendel, and Harold K. Vollrath; East Line and Red River Railroad, Minutes of the meetings of the Board of Directors, 1876–1881, DeGolyer Library, Southern Methodist University, Dallas, Texas; various published articles.

[a]   Original number 1 cost $4,985, plus $320 freight.

[b]   Original number 2 cost $4,500, delivered to Carondelet, Missouri, and was built for the Columbus, Washington and Cincinnati Railroad. It was named *Pittsburg*.

[c]   Original number 3 was named *Sulphur Springs* and was sold to the J. H. Bentley Lumber Company in about 1883.

[d]   Original number 4 was named *Governor Throckmorton*.

[e]   Numbers 186–192 were transferred from the Kansas City and Eastern Division of the Missouri Pacific when that division was converted to standard gauge on August 20–21, 1882. Their KC&E numbers were 1–7. Of these, numbers 1–5 were earlier Wyandotte, Kansas City and Northwestern numbers 1–5. Apparently number 187 was gone when the Katy renumbering took place in 1889.

bonds in an equal amount to reimburse them for the outlay. They also issued without consideration, but fictitiously, $5000 of stock per mile, making the aggregate of $12,000 in stocks and bonds per mile of road. They received from the State of Texas 10,240 acres of land per mile. The state therefore more than paid for the whole road. Besides the profit made in this way, those gentlemen procured contributions of money, notes, depot grounds and other property along the route. After operating the line for several years successfully and profitably, its owners sold it to Jay Gould for $9500 cash per mile. I proved these facts in court on the trial by the secretary of the road, who was one of the original owners. I also proved in that trial that the road was immedi-

ately mortgaged to pay bonds to the amount of $35,000 per mile, issued without consideration and in violation of the Constitution.

Up to the time of sale to Mr. Gould this property was in splendid condition and operated at cheap rates to the satisfaction of the public. Within a few years, under the new management, the roadbed, rolling stock, depots and general equipment became so out of repair that complaint became general against it. I brought action and produced a forfeiture of its charter and the appointment of a receiver to take charge of the property. It is now and has been in his hands for about twelve months. On the trial of the case, in addition to showing the fictitious issuance of bonds and stocks, I proved by one of the officers of the

road that from McKinney to Greenville at least 30 per cent of the cars ran off the track. *It was absolutely so dangerous that a tramp would hardly ride in its best passenger coach* [italics added].[21]

Hogg goes on to point out that the receiver with whom he had placed the East Line and Red River had set it on a sound operating basis, had made numerous improvements out of earnings, had reduced outstanding indebtedness to $8,000 per mile, and had eliminated $4 million of bonds fictitiously issued by "Mr. Gould's crowd." The most significant improvement made by the receiver to the line, however, was its conversion from narrow gauge to standard gauge. Issuing $400,000 in certificates, the receiver was able to pay the cost of converting the entire line, from Jefferson to McKinney.

Throughout the years, the disparity of gauges within the Katy system had remained a continual source of expense and operating delays, and in some cases it had been the cause of derailments. In August 1882, two loaded standard-gauge boxcars went off the tracks at Scroggins, 6.5 miles east of Winnsboro; passenger L. N. Tetro was killed and his estate was awarded $15,000. In a similar vein, a January 1883 wreck near Winnsboro, attributed to unstable standard-gauge cars, caused the death of a passenger by the name of C. R. Harper. This time the court awarded $7,600 to Harper's father. The McKinney extension was converted to standard gauge in 1887, the remainder of the line being converted in a massive one-day effort on Tuesday, September 13, 1892.[22]

The Gould management came to an end when the East Line was sold under foreclosure at Jefferson on January 25, 1893, to Henry W. Poor, acting on behalf of the Central Trust Company of New York. Payment was $1.4 million. Poor was representing bondholders and stockholders of the Katy, which had emerged from a three-year receivership (and from Gould control) on April 16, 1891.[23]

A new Texas corporation, the Sherman, Shreveport and Southern Railway Company (SS&S) was chartered on February 28, 1893, for the purpose of taking over the rights,

A narrow-gauge mogul engine at the National Locomotive Works, Connellsville, Pennsylvania, in 1876. It began its career as engine number 4 of the Wyandotte, Kansas City and Northwestern; the Gould interests transferred it, along with six other engines, to the East Line in 1882. It served there as EL&RR number 4, and was renumbered Katy 403 in 1889. It ended its days on the East Line when that road was changed to standard gauge in 1892. (Photograph courtesy of Robert Brendel and John B. Harper)

Map of the Katy system for 1891, when the Texas line was operated as the Sherman, Shreveport and Southern. The projected extension from McKinney to Denton was never built.

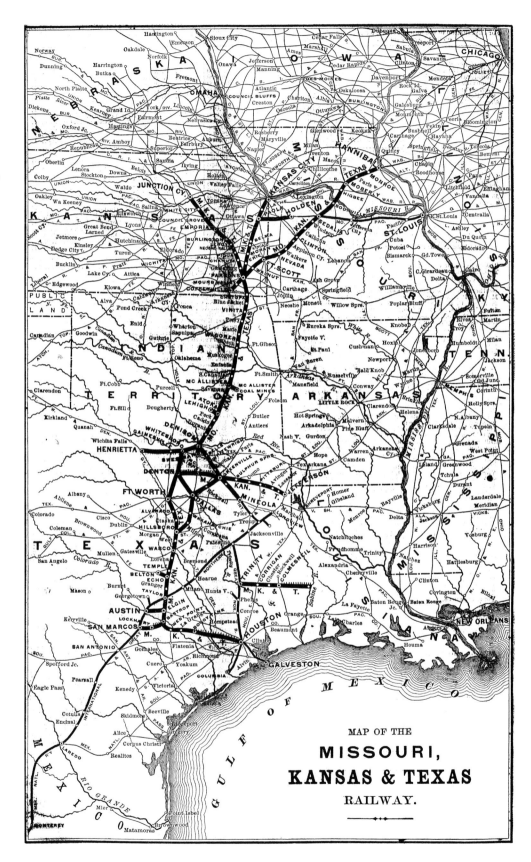

MAP OF THE

MISSOURI,
KANSAS & TEXAS
RAILWAY.

franchises, and properties of the East Line and Red River. Purchase was completed March 2, 1893, and securities of $1.55 million in capital stock (at $10,000 per mile) and $3.1 million in first-mortgage bonds (at $20,000 per mile) were issued. The Katy retained control of the SS&S. Plans were announced to build a branch line northward from Greenville to Whitesboro, a distance of 35 miles, and to extend the other end of the road some fifty miles eastward to Shreveport from Jefferson. Rumors also circulated that the line would be extended westward from McKinney to Decatur, about 50 miles; this extension would provide a connection with the Fort Worth and Denver line and make possible a bypass around Dallas for freight traffic to and from the Panhandle region of Texas.[24]

Only the extension to Shreveport would be built, and serious consideration of that did not begin until 1895. The Katy management held back on this move on the basis that the Vicksburg, Shreveport and Pacific line (part of the Queen and Crescent Route), Shreveport's outlet to the East, would surely need to build to Jefferson and thereby provide itself with a good western connection. Furthermore, the VS&P already owned a 17-mile extension from Shreveport to the Texas state line at Waskom, which it leased to the T&P. In the meantime, the SS&S operated as a separate company but under close control of the Katy. W. B. (Ben) Munson, a former Katy land agent and prominent businessman of Denison, Texas, was president, and F. W. Fratt, a construction engineer from the Katy, was general manager, both with offices at Greenville. The company did $300,000 to $400,000 gross operating business each year, paid interest on its bonds, and steadily accumulated a surplus. On the other hand, the VS&P was not doing well financially and was headed for a foreclosure that would occur in 1901. It would be up to the SS&S to build the link between Jefferson and Shreveport.[25]

In late 1894 general manager Fratt and his party took field trips over the route of the planned extensions and decided to concentrate on the one eastward to Shreveport. In

January 1895 the Shreveport voters passed a bond issue for $75,000 to provide funding for the SS&S facilities; and, in March, Fratt announced that trackage rights would be secured from the VS&P for the entry to Shreveport from Waskom. (The T&P also had rights over this Waskom–Shreveport property of the VS&P.) Thus, the extension would require only 31 miles of new construction, between Jefferson and Waskom. Engineering surveys for this work were completed in July 1895.[26]

Despite these definite plans, the actual construction was delayed for several years. The cat-and-mouse game with the VS&P continued. Over the next few years there were occasional announcements about the extension, but the Katy management did not appropriate the needed funds. Fratt left the road in May 1896, and E. M. Alvord took over operating responsibilities as part of his position as general superintendent. At this time the parent Katy took steps to acquire and to absorb the SS&S. Early in 1899 a bill was introduced into the Texas legislature that would permit the acquisition as well as construction of the Shreveport extension. As finally passed and signed by Governor J. D. Sayers on May 16, 1899, the bill also required completion of a Katy connection between San Marcos and Lockhart in Central Texas, in order to create an entry into San Antonio for the Katy.[27]

Grading for the Shreveport extension began on January 5, 1900, at Jefferson, and connection was made with the VS&P at the Texas–Louisiana state line (near Waskom station) at 6:00 P.M. on June 22. After allowance for surfacing of the track, a new schedule called for through service between Shreveport and Dallas (using the Katy between Greenville and Dallas) beginning July 29, 1900. On the evening of July 28 a special train puffed into Shreveport from the west. It comprised thirteen freight cars, a caboose, and a business car loaded with railroad officials and was pulled by flag-bedecked locomotive 16, a 4-4-0 type. The train was met by the mayor of Shreveport, a brass band, and several hundred citizens. After the welcoming ceremonies the official group took carriages to the Columbia

The original joint Katy–East Line depot at Greenville was replaced by this brick structure in 1896, at a reported cost of $25,000. This photograph was taken in about 1930, when the Texas line still had passenger service to the station. The second story was removed in 1951. In 1992 the building was vacant but intact. (Photograph by Arthur G. Charles, courtesy of Martin Hilton and John B. Charles)

Club for dinner and a speech by a local dignitary, Judge Newton Blanchard.[28]

The next morning train number 1 pulled out of the Shreveport station carrying the business cars of J. W. Maxwell (general superintendent of the Katy) and Edward Ford (superintendent of the VS&P). According to the *Shreveport Times,*

> Conductor B. F. Boydston pulled the bell cord at 7:06 A.M. and the first trip was on. Superintendent Alvord was in the cab of the locomotive to put engineer Maydwell on to the curves of the new track. The equipment of the SS&S is excellent, the chair car being especially good. The track was in good condition for one just completed and the ride was a pleasant one. No dust was flying. The day was fairly cool and the company excellent. Through the mist of the early morning the train made its way past fields of nodding corn and cotton just breaking into bloom, past farms and houses whose people cheered the train as it passed.[29]

The new line measured 31.41 miles; the 17.0 miles of trackage rights were negotiated on a twenty-five-year lease, signed December 22, 1899. Rights were separately negotiated for use of VS&P freight terminals and shops in Shreveport. The new union station would be used by passenger trains. At this same time, the T&P completed its own line from Waskom to Shreveport and shifted away from the VS&P on January 1, 1900.[30]

Operations into Shreveport had a salutary effect on SS&S business. For the year ending June 30, 1900, gross revenues were $398,033 and surplus was $31,349. For the next eleven-plus months (to May 7, 1901), a period including the through service, gross revenues jumped to $721,815 and surplus to $105,811. The Katy seemed to be enjoying the opportunity to compete with the T&P for the lucrative Dallas–Shreveport business. The connection also had a beneficial effect on the VS&P; in its annual report for the year ending June 30, 1901, it attributed a 30 percent increase in business to the opening of the through route with the Katy.[31]

The SS&S was formally assimilated into the Katy system on May 7, 1901, the sale having been made the day before by the Central Trust Company, holder of all outstanding stock. Thus the SS&S became the Shreveport District of the Katy. Through passenger trains between Shreveport and Dallas had been placed in service during the fall of 1900. An overnight train, the "Texas Express" or the "Shreveport Express," depending on direction, carried sleeping cars, covered the 224-mile run in about nine hours, and made direct connections with the VS&P trains to eastern parts of the country. Schedules would later be coordinated with the LR&N for connections to New Orleans, as noted in chapter 3.[32]

The Katy of Texas fell into receivership in 1915 and continued in such a condition until 1923. As part of their reorganization plan, the receivers decided to sell the Shreveport subdivision; the purchaser, as mentioned in the previous chapter, was William Edenborn. As he began to take over the business, Edenborn elected to discontinue the leased-line operation of the T&P property between Waskom and Shreveport, finding a more favorable arrangement with the T&P. The

freight terminal and shop facilities of the VS&P in Shreveport were no longer needed because the LR&N had its own.[33]

Edenborn received from the Katy sixteen locomotives, assorted rolling stock, and 184.4 miles of main-line railroad. The route traversed prosperous farm country and served a number of growing communities. Connections at both ends—that is, at Shreveport and at Greenville-McKinney—were excellent and productive of interchange traffic. The property itself would hardly rate "main-line" status for most larger systems; in fact, it might have trouble even rating a branch-line classification. Rails were fifty-two to sixty-six pounds per yard, some being laid as early as 1893. Ballast had always been dirt, and by the late 1920s was clogged with a profusion of weeds. Inherited shop facilities were available at Greenville and Hughes Springs. The layout of the route was fairly good, a 1895 report showing only

The sawtooth profile of the Texas line is evident, though somewhat accentuated by the scales used in this 1930s chart. The maximum west-bound grade is 1.6 percent, at Veals (milepost 79), and the maximum eastbound grade is 1.2 percent, at Faker (milepost 94). The grade between Veals and Daingerfield was later reduced. (Courtesy of Harold K. Vollrath)

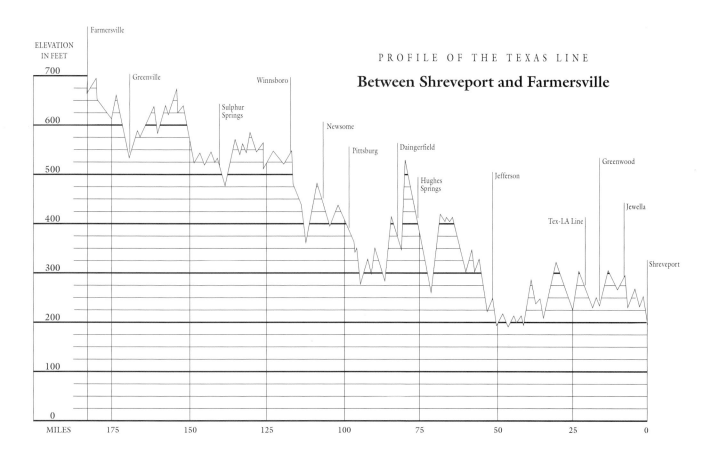

PROFILE OF THE TEXAS LINE

Between Shreveport and Farmersville

19 percent of the Jefferson–McKinney line to be curved. But the undulating countryside and light original construction had resulted in 92 percent of the line being nonlevel. The maximum westbound grade was 1.2 percent at Faker, 94 miles from Shreveport, and the maximum eastbound grade was 1.6 percent at Veals, 79 miles from Shreveport.[34]

Thus, the Texas line became one of the Edenborn lines in 1923 and was operated as part of the LR&N system until being absorbed into the L&A in 1928. In time it would be an important and profitable main line of the Kansas City Southern lines, but it still had a number of lean years ahead of it.

A westbound freight train near Waskom, on the Texas line, in 1932. The light rail and dirt ballast are carryovers from the Edenborn administration. The 673 is former Missouri, Kansas and Texas 673, inherited when Edenborn bought the Texas property from the Katy in 1923. It was built by the American Locomotive Company in 1901 and scrapped in 1942. (Photograph by C. W. Witbeck)

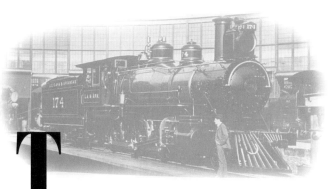

WILLIAM BUCHANAN AND THE ORIGINAL L&A

The origin of the L&A dates back to 1882, when Minden, the seat of Webster Parish in northern Louisiana, was bypassed by the Vicksburg, Shreveport and Pacific Railroad survey. This was indeed unfortunate for Minden; the five-mile separation from the railroad could mean what similar circumstances had meant for many towns across the nation: dying a slow death or moving the town to the railroad. But the residents of Minden exercised another option: building their own railroad to connect with the trunk line. Thus, the Minden Railroad and Compress Company was chartered on August 22, 1882. The line would connect with the VS&P at Lanesville, due south of Minden, when the rails of the latter company were laid to that point.[1]

The VS&P completed its line through Lanesville in the summer of 1884 and established through service between Monroe and Shreveport on August 1 of that year. Grading for the Minden connection (or "Minden Tap") was completed in July 1885, and tracklaying (done under contract by the VS&P) was accomplished by November, when the road was opened. The first locomotive of the Minden Tap was purchased secondhand from the Queen and Crescent Route (of which the VS&P was an entity) and was named the Ross Meehan. It was an inside-connected 4-4-0 type and apparently was able to handle without difficulty the 15-minute shuttle run between Minden and Lanesville (the station name of which was first Minden Junction but by 1887 had become known as Sibley). The driving force behind the Minden Tap was a local resident and community leader, F. H. Drake.[2]

While the above was happening, the Texas and St. Louis (now Cotton Belt) line completed its three-foot-gauge tracks between the Arkansas cities of Pine Bluff and Texarkana in late 1882. This line ran through Lafayette County and served the county seat, Lewisville, in its relocated site on the railroad. The railroad had been cut through an abundant forest of pine and assorted hardwood trees, and, as might be expected, several sawmills were established near the right-of-way. One such operation, set up by a family named Stamps, was located on the railroad about five miles east of Lewisville. The mill town was called Stamps, and a post office with that name was designated.[3]

In 1887 the mill was purchased by Caleb Crowell, and on January 15, 1889, the operation was organized as the Bodcaw Lumber Company, with formal incorporation following on June 14 of the same year. By this time E. A. Frost, G. W. Bottoms, and W. T. Ferguson had bought into the company, each of the three owning 20 percent of the capital stock, with Crowell retaining the other 40 percent. By 1891, William Buchanan had become president of the company. Buchanan would in time dominate the Bodcaw company, including its railroad operations.[4]

William Buchanan was a Tennessean who moved to the Texarkana, Arkansas–Texas, area in 1873, shortly after the town had been established as the junction point of the T&P and Cairo and Fulton railroads. In the young community Buchanan set up a diminutive (and portable) sawmill to meet the needs of home and building construction. Later, he became a partner of Joseph Ferguson and set up a more permanent mill a few miles south of Texarkana, feeding to the mill logs from a large acreage owned by Ferguson. Buchanan married Hannah Ferguson, sister of Joseph, and began to ally his business interests closely with Joseph and his brother William T.

The first locomotive of the Minden Tap, forerunner railroad of the L&A, was named Ross Mehan *and is said to have been purchased from the* Queen and Crescent *system. In this April 1890 photograph, its inside-connected driving-wheel arrangement is evident.*

A younger brother of William Buchanan, James A., moved from Tennessee to join the group. The Ferguson brothers and the Buchanan brothers pursued the lumber business with vigor—and with a great deal of success.[5]

Still another pair of brothers would have an impact on the future of Bodcaw Lumber Company—William C. and Thomas A. Brown. William moved from Tennessee to Arkansas in 1869, and Thomas followed in the mid-1880s. These brothers had earlier acquired expertise in the art of lumbering and for many years would concentrate on the milling operations of Bodcaw.[6]

By late 1894 the Bodcaw ownership had shifted, such that the Buchanans owned 45 percent of the company, the Fergusons 29 percent, and the Browns 20 percent. And by this time a standard-gauge logging line had been built south from Stamps to timberlands owned by Bodcaw, with feeder lines tying into the main line at various intervals. These feeders were lightly built to serve logging camps and were moved about as the timber was cut over.[7]

Whether these logging camps had any social and cultural significance is unclear, but a contemporary description of a typical camp in the region gives some feeling for the loggers and their families. In his 1906 book, *Highways and Byways of the Mississippi Valley*, Clifton Johnson described a camp scene in southern Arkansas:

> Near the end of the track was a choppers' settlement, consisting of a score of structures loosely grouped among the trees. They had floors and sides of boards; but the roofs were of canvass, put up tent fashion. Such construction made it a simple matter to pull them to pieces and move them when the vicinity had been chopped over. The moving of the homes to be nearer the work was necessary every six or seven months. The woodsmen had their

By the early 1900s logging activities in southern Arkansas were booming. Here we see an end-of-the-line logging camp, with loads prepared for movement to the sawmill.

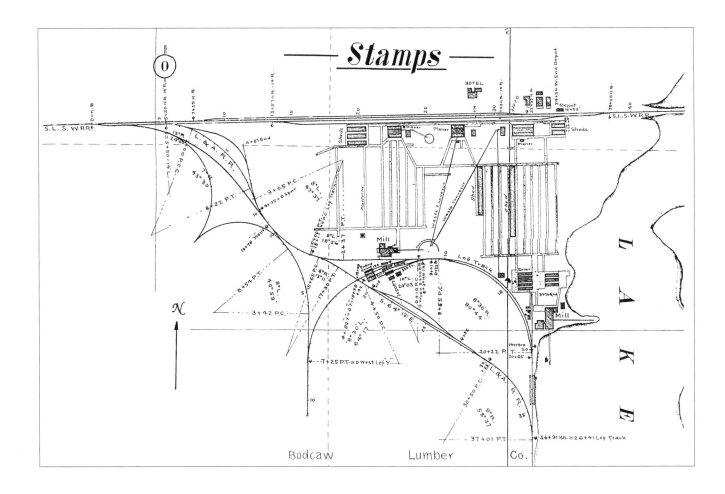

Early trackage layout at Stamps, before the 1902 extension of the line north to Hope. The new alignment for the Hope crossing called for the movement of the main line to the west, with the crossover being just to the east of the zero marker on the Cotton Belt tracks. (Courtesy of Archives and Special Collections, Noel Memorial Library, Louisiana State University–Shreveport)

wives and children with them; and there were bevies of pigs and chickens wandering about, so that the village was quite domestic.[8]

It was inevitable that the logging line would be called upon for transporting passengers and freight, because wagon roads were generally impassable, if they were available at all. Soon the Bodcaw railroad was carrying passengers in cabooses, and a boxcar was purchased secondhand for the hauling of general merchandise. By January 1896 scheduled trains over 27 miles of track were advertised, operating under the name of the Louisiana and Arkansas Railroad. On January 1, 1897, the logging line was set apart as a separate department of Bodcaw, and the first records filed with the ICC were dated June 30, 1897. These records showed that the company owned 5 locomotives, 2 cabooses, 1 boxcar, and 150 logging cars. Details on the locomo-

tives are missing, but two of them were of the 4-4-0 type and were used exclusively for main-line operations (and were equipped with air brakes), and the others were assigned to logging-camp service. William Buchanan was president of the L&A, and his brother James A. served as secretary-treasurer.[9]

The village of Stamps, which had been incorporated in 1892, was a typical mill town of the region and was central to the Bodcaw operations. Mill hands, railroad workers, and loggers received special punch cards as part of their wages, redeemable for goods and services at the town's primary merchandising establishment, the Bodcaw Store. One of the railroad-construction hands, Charles Roach, had this amusing description of the system:

[T]his small piece of cardboard was our key to that wonderful store at Stamps. . . . [W]hen you finished your selections, [the clerk] would punch out the figures on the card and so there was no bookkeeping necessary. The system was known as the "punchout". Many mill employees in town never had a payday because they used up all they earned in buying things to eat and wear at the commissary. Buchanan, the wealthy man back of the trading, doubled his money on everything he sold.[10]

By 1898 scheduled service of the logging road covered 46.5 miles, and Buchanan had decided to incorporate the railroad as a common carrier in interstate service; this would give certain advantages in division of freight rates on outbound lumber shipments and would afford Buchanan certain opportunities for expanding his railroad business. It was clear by this time that Buchanan's railroad ambitions lay far beyond the hauling of logs to sawmills. At the same time, his mill capacity had been increased to 350,000 board feet per day, making it the largest mill in the Yellow Pine Belt and one of the largest in the entire South. When running at capacity, 20 carloads of lumber were shipped out each day. Such a mill had an enormous appetite for logs, and as the Arkansas timber was cut out it was necessary for Buchanan to look southward toward the thick forests of Louisiana, where he had agents in the field procuring choice timberlands. Thus, the initial justification of a main-line common carrier could be the essential business of transporting pine logs to the sawmill at Stamps.[11]

On March 18, 1898, Buchanan incorporated the L&A under the general laws of Arkansas. Previously, on October 23, 1897, a Louisiana charter had been granted to the Arkansas, Louisiana and Southern Railway for the purpose of building northward from Minden, Louisiana; although the principals of the latter line were said to be those of the Minden Tap, it was apparent that the AL&S was locating its line to connect directly with the L&A. Thus, in a coordinated fashion, the L&A built southward and the AL&S northward in 1898. The Minden Tap was sold to the AL&S on July 9, and the last spike connecting the lines was driven near Cotton Valley, Louisiana, on September 29. On Octo-

ber 1, through service was established between Stamps and Sibley, a distance of 60.4 miles. In addition, scheduled service was provided on a 20-mile branch line running eastward from Taylor, Arkansas, to a logging camp called Fomby.[12]

The charter of the L&A was amended December 6, 1898, to permit extension of the line southward from Sibley to Winnfield and Alexandria, Louisiana, and to Natchez, Mississippi. The well-known civil engineer Gus Knobel and his son began their survey south of Sibley on January 1, 1899, projecting an 18-mile extension of the line into virgin short- and longleaf pine forests. On March 28, 1899, contracts were let for the grading of this extension. By September 15 tracks were down on the 18 miles, and grading was active on another 20 miles. A year and a half later, on September 25, 1900, 91.8 miles of main line were in operation, extending from Stamps to Ashland, Louisiana, and the Fomby branch was still active. (On July 14, 1900, the AL&S had been acquired formally by the L&A.) It was clearly evident that William Buchanan was serious about the railroad business—and about competing with others (such as William Edenborn) for revenues from the Red River valley. In January 1900 the *Shreveport Times* had this to say about him:

> He is a brainy, broad-gauge, practical man, with liberal views and systematic business methods, coupled with unbounded philanthropy. He is a man who "earns his cake before he eats it." He makes his money first, and then spends it building his railway. He does not owe a dollar on his road and it is not bonded for a dollar.[13]

Principals of the L&A at this time were: president, William Buchanan; first vice president, F. H. Drake of Minden, who had been president of both the Minden Tap and the AL&S line; secretary, James A. Buchanan, brother of the president. Others on the directorate included Marshall Northcutt, a longtime friend and business associate of William Buchanan, and Robert Buchanan, another brother of the president. One might note in

Map of the L&A based on completion of the main line to Winnfield in mid-1902 and published in the December 1902 Official Guide. *The extensions indicated were eventually built. The Fomby branch is evident.*

passing that the assistant freight agent at Minden was B. S. Atkinson, who would remain with the railroad until September 1939, rising to the post of executive vice president of the full-fledged L&A system.[14]

The hamlet of Ashland, deep in a thick forest of longleaf pine, was chosen as an interim terminus, with temporary engine-servicing facilities and a turntable being installed. Southward construction did not resume immediately because of Buchanan's strong belief in "pay as you go." Revenue from timber and lumber movements enabled resumption of construction in late 1901; by March 1902, 15.4 miles were completed to Goldonna, and the remaining 18.1 miles were being graded to Winnfield, the seat of Winn Parish. The en-

tire line from Stamps to Winnfield was opened on June 1, 1902. Notably, the entire construction effort in 1902 had been accomplished without bonded indebtedness.[15]

Building a railroad without going into debt was an unusual feat, but William Edenborn was using the same approach, and at about the same time, in building a road roughly parallel with the L&A, some 20 miles or so to the south. Edenborn was not in the milling business, but his agents competed with those of Bodcaw for the purchase of timber rights in the forests just to the north of the Red River. Edenborn's line, the Shreveport and Red River Valley Railway, was being constructed southeastward from Shreveport, Louisiana, and from time to time Edenborn had stated that he "was headed toward Natchez." However, by mid-1902 it was clear that Edenborn instead was going to build his line to New Orleans. The rivalry between Buchanan and Edenborn would continue for several years, however.[16]

On June 10, 1902, the Louisiana and Arkansas Rail*way* Company was incorporated in Arkansas, to extend the charter of the Rail*road* Company, and on August 18, 1902, all property and assets of the latter company were taken over. The articles of incorporation showed that William Buchanan owned 2,489 of the 2,500 outstanding shares of capital stock. (As late as June 1900 he owned only about 60 percent of the shares.) Buchanan published the first annual report of the new company on November 10, covering the fiscal year ending June 30, 1902. The report was

impressive in its statistics and optimistic in its promise. A grading contract had been let in August 1902 for a 38-mile extension east from Winnfield to Jena, a town in the heart of extensive pine timberlands, and grading was in progress for a 23-mile addition northward from Stamps to Hope, Arkansas, on the main line of the St. Louis and Iron Mountain. The Hope connection would give Buchanan an alternative to the Cotton Belt for shipments to the north. Work on this extension went smoothly, as Charles Roach recounted:

In less than three weeks the trackwork had progressed far enough for Cap'n. Jack [Wardell] to bring the bunk and kitchen cars up to a spur he had built for that purpose. So one night during the evening meal an engine pulled the entire outfit along the newly laid

Ten-wheeler 174 was out-shopped by Baldwin Locomotive Works in December 1903 and in this view is thought to be at its birthplace, the Baldwin Eddystone facility near Philadelphia. The locomotive in the background appears to be sister 175. (Courtesy of Goodyear Collection, De-Golyer Library, Southern Methodist University)

rail. . . . Once the camp cars were set and the track end ready for the next day's progress . . . we signaled to the hogger [engineer] to hit the line for town. Since our woodburner had to be refueled up and watered, it was necessary to tie up in Stamps. That way we'd switch out the steel and other material for the next day. . . .

Often I'd stand on the head flat of rails watching Mike [Griffin] go the rounds with Wardell, directing the 40 Negroes in what to do and how fast to do it. Every time a rail was placed in the track, a big ginger-colored gang boss would sing out, "spike 'er down, de boss man say spike 'er down!" The hammers would resound in unison. It was music to the ears of any man who loved railroading. I enjoyed the thrill as did everyone else.[17]

Jack Wardell was in charge of construction, and Mike Griffin was conductor on the work train.

The Hope extension also involved re-arrangement of the Stamps trackage and construction of a new joint depot with the Cotton Belt. Furthermore, surveyors were in the field to locate a line southward from Packton (on the Jena extension) to Alexandria. The entire main line now had sixty-pound rail, the lighter forty-pound rail originally laid in Arkansas having been replaced. Importantly, eight new ten-wheel locomotives (which would become numbers 170–177) had been ordered from Baldwin Locomotive Works for delivery in August 1903.[18]

The extensions to Jena, with the ultimate objective of Natchez, and to Alexandria were in part motivated by the Edenborn competition. The Shreveport and Red River Valley line reached Alexandria in October 1902, crossing the river on an impressive steel-truss bridge. As noted in chapter 2, as an interim measure Edenborn established a traffic agreement with the Southern Pacific, which had a line in place between Alexandria and New Orleans. Buchanan had in mind an Alexandria connection with the T&P, with its shorter Alexandria–New Orleans line, and this was part of his justification for the Alexandria extension.[19]

The railroad was certainly busy in 1905. A former station agent of the L&A, A. H. Davis, reminisced about a train ride out of Stamps that year:

The chief clerk gave me a message to ride a long freight extra south with one hundred and

The Stamps, Arkansas, Union Station was about two years old when this photograph was taken in 1904. The operating-headquarters building of the L&A is at the left. The passenger train is just beyond the Cotton Belt crossing and is northbound on the L&A. The car at the rear of the train appears to be William Buchanan's private car Bodcaw.

eighteen empty box cars for distribution to the mills between Stamps and Sibley, and a bunch for that little railroad out of Sibley. . . . Down the line at some place, where I never saw such a lot of logs or a sight like it, several locomotives were hauling them out in long train loads and others going in with the empties [log cars].

The "little railroad out of Sibley" was the Sibley, Lake Bistineau and Southern Railway, which extended about 30 miles south of Sibley into timber properties of the R. A. Long family of Kansas City. Its mill, at the town of Yellow Pine, five miles south of the junction with the L&A and VS&P lines, is a perfect example of the tap-line case studied by the ICC. By hauling lumber for only five miles on its own tracks, the Long-Bell Lumber Company enjoyed a favorable division of the total freight charges for lumber shipments. Northbound cars of lumber were handled by the L&A.[20]

The second annual report of the L&A, for the year ending June 30, 1903, showed tremendous progress. The Hope extension had been placed in service on June 1, 1903; this extension connected with the Iron Mountain main line between Little Rock and Texarkana. Perhaps a more important aspect of the Hope interchange was the connection with the recently completed Arkansas and Choctaw line (Frisco system), which could exchange freight to and from Oklahoma. When the present relaying of rails was complete, seventy-five-pound rail would be spiked down from Hope to Sibley. For the first two years reported, gross receipts of the railroad were $1,011,065, and the surplus came to a remarkable $258,599! And this was after full interest payments, Buchanan having gone through the formality of issuing $2,449,000 in first-mortgage bonds ($16,600 per mile of road) and $2,625,000 in capital stock. Actually, most of these securities were held in his

The log pond of the Minden Lumber Company, a Buchanan property, in the early 1900s. Logs were rolled off the train and down the skid deck to the water. In due course they were conveyed up the inclined jack ladder, shown at the right, to the log deck and fed to the band saws.

Lumber yards of the Bodcaw mill at Stamps in 1904. The view is toward the west, and the mill pond can be seen in the distance.

or his relatives' names, except for the few qualifying shares of his "outside" directors. In transition periods some shares were held by Stamps Construction Company, his firm for building the railroad. William Buchanan was building a first-class railroad and was enjoying substantial profits in the undertaking.[21]

The Jena extension was completed at the end of 1903, except for a 180-foot steel-truss bridge across the Little River near Georgetown. (This was the first bridge of any consequence to be needed by the L&A.) High water during the spring and summer of 1904 delayed completion of the bridge, and through service from Packton to Jena could not be provided until February 1905. The terminal point, Jena, was an old settlement that had become little more than a country post office in the midst of a dense pine forest; but Buchanan now owned most of the forest and proceeded to build up Jena to the point that it was incorporated in 1908. Estimates of lumber yield from the Jena area ran as high as 250 to 300 million board feet per year, for at least twenty-five years. To exploit this lumber potential, Buchanan located three mills in the vicinity, one of which, at Trout (three miles west of Jena), survived until the 1940s.[22]

The L&A issued an attractive brochure in 1904, designed to tell the world about the

railroad and its geographic region. It claimed that the mill at Stamps was the largest in the region, shipping some 82 million board feet of lumber in 1903. The brochure described a seemingly inexhaustible supply of trees for lumbering, yet serious attention was being given to the reuse of cutover land. The railroad boasted that it was being constructed to rigidly high standards, with an eye toward freight-traffic interchanges at several points. This sanguine attitude of management appears to have been justified; on June 8, 1904, the Louisiana Railroad Commission made an inspection of the property and reported:

> The roadbed and track of this road are splendidly constructed, ballasted with gravel and laid with heavy rails on cypress ties, and are unusually smooth for a new road. The depots are all frame structures, but are constructed along modern plans, and in each there are water coolers, and ample provisions for their proper heating. The closets are located at a convenient distance from each depot.[23]

Construction of the Alexandria extension began in early 1905, departing from the Winnfield–Jena line at a station named Packton. On July 1, 1906, 30.46 miles of railroad were placed in operation between Packton and a connection with the Iron Mountain at Tioga, Louisiana, 8.2 miles north of the joint Iron Mountain–T&P depot at Alexandria. Trackage rights were secured from the Iron Mountain and T&P, which included a bridge over the Red River and use of the joint passenger station in Alexandria. Separate freight facilities and yard trackage were developed by the L&A.[24]

The survey of the L&A route into the Alexandria area called for a direct line from Tioga to Alexandria through Pineville, utilizing the Edenborn bridge (of the Louisiana Railway and Navigation Company, the new name of the Shreveport and Red River Valley) to cross the Red River. William Edenborn refused to grant such rights to the L&A, keeping alive the old rivalry between Buchanan and himself; hence the arrangement with the Iron Mountain and the T&P.

At about this time, the L&A entered into a trackage-rights agreement with the Rock Island, Arkansas and Louisiana (by this time part of the Rock Island system, earlier the Arkansas Southern) for use of the L&A between Packton and Tioga. The RIA&L had progressed southward from Arkansas through Winnfield and was paralleling the L&A as it headed toward Alexandria. Prudence showed that there was unnecessary drainage of resources, and the trackage-rights agreement resulted. With this arrangement in the offing, Buchanan decided to go ahead with the original plan of building directly to the Edenborn bridge, completing a 5.02-mile segment in February 1908 to a connection with the LR&N at Pineville Junction. Edenborn was willing to permit Rock Island trains to cross his bridge, and thus for many years only the Rock Island used this short stretch of L&A rails.[25]

Attention next turned to gaining entry to Shreveport, by far the most important com-mercial city in northern Louisiana. A logging road operating 8 miles west of Minden had been built in 1907 and 1908 by F. H. Drake and associates; it was called the Minden East and West Railway Company and had a Louisiana charter dated March 7, 1906. (Clearing had started in August 1905, using a survey aimed at connecting Minden and Shreveport by a direct route.) Buchanan acquired this property through his Stamps Construction Company, the date of sale being March 10, 1909. Rehabilitation and extension of the property began immediately, and operations into Shreveport began on January 1, 1910. The length of the Minden–Shreveport line was 29.16 miles, which included 2.01 miles of rights over the tracks and Red River bridge of the Cotton Belt at Shreveport. The bridge had been completed in March 1907 and was also used by the LR&N.[26]

Buchanan decided to build a commodious and first-class passenger terminal in Shreve-port, and he arranged to have the Cotton Belt

A southbound L&A freight train in 1904. The load of merchandise indicates that the scene is between Stamps and Minden. Ten-wheeler locomotive 172 had been delivered from Baldwin in late 1903.

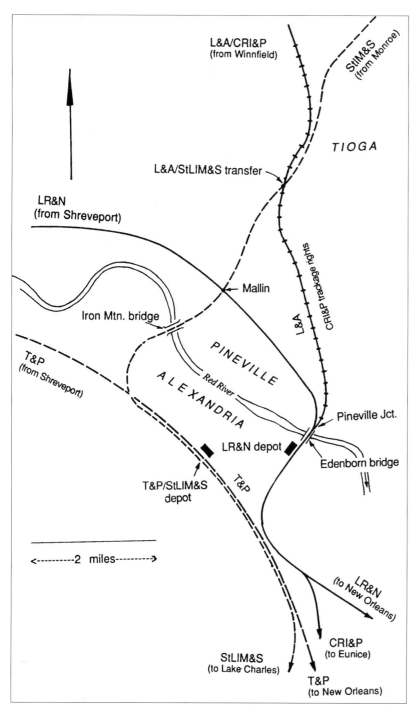

Trackage in and around Alexandria, Louisiana, in the early 1900s. The L&A used
the Iron Mountain–T&P passenger depot. For many years, the Rock Island alone
used the L&A tracks from Tioga to Pineville Junction. After the L&A and the
LR&N were consolidated, the Edenborn bridge and the LR&N depot were used by
all L&A trains.

as an occupant; this terminal, called the Central Station, opened for business on March 1, 1911. Although it might have been convenient for Edenborn's LR&N to use the terminal also, it is likely that the continuing rivalry between Buchanan and Edenborn precluded such an arrangement. Passenger service on the L&A now included two through trains to Alexandria, one from Hope and the other from Shreveport, in competition with the shorter routes of the T&P and the LR&N. By this time it was clear to the trunkline carriers that the L&A was no longer a simple log-hauling road but a serious contender for business of all types. Its location, however, did not offer direct competition with the large carriers; rather, it was a feeder that they respected.[27]

The final construction project of the L&A was the extension eastward from Jena toward Natchez, Mississippi. This work started in early 1911 and had as its destination a connection with the Natchez and Western (formerly Natchez, Red River and Texas, by now a part of the Iron Mountain system) on the east bank of the Black River. Two major stream crossings were involved: a three-span truss bridge (with vertical lift span) across the Little River, and a five-span truss bridge (also with vertical lift span) across the Black River. Construction of these bridges was expensive and time consuming, and it held up operation of through service until September 1913. The completed line connected with the Natchez and Western at a point named Wildsville Junction, 1.6 miles east of the river and 2.0 miles east of the end of the Natchez and Western in the town of Black River. The extension to Wildsville Junction added 24 miles to the L&A system, bringing the total mileage owned to 273.36. Except for 15.5 miles of sixty-pound rail, all of this mileage was now laid with seventy-five-pound steel rail, something worth boasting about in the 1914 annual report.[28]

The 1914 annual report also stated that total mileage operated was 298.5 (including trackage rights), that capital stock issued was $5 million, and that bonded indebtedness was $5.4 million. Bond interest had been met

Central Station at Shreveport, shortly before its 1911 opening. With this impressive structure William Buchanan made a statement to the community that his railroad was a significant force in the transportation industry of the south. He secured the Cotton Belt as a tenant. The view is from Marshall Street, where street cars provided a convenient means for passengers to travel to the downtown business district. Passenger service at this station ended in 1940, when the KCS/L&A operations were consolidated at the Union Station.

The lift bridge over the Black River at Jonesville, Louisiana, on the Packton–Vidalia line, as it looked in 1948. This was a major structure for the L&A, with a total length of 840 feet in the five spans. The view is toward the east. Completed in September 1913, the bridge permitted through freight service between Shreveport and Natchez, Mississippi, and eventually between Dallas and Hattiesburg, Mississippi, in conjunction with the Mississippi Central. (Photograph by C. W. Witbeck)

William Buchanan in his later years.

regularly, and dividends had been paid on the stock for a number of years. Operating ratios (operating cost divided by revenue) were in the range of 65 to 70 percent. Unlike the rival LR&N, there had not been a deficit year since the start of the business.

For the next ten years or so the L&A functioned efficiently, if somewhat undramatically, as a tightly controlled business of the Buchanan family. There were no deficit years, although the exigencies of World War I caused a car shortage on the L&A in 1917 that nearly caused a dip into red ink. When the ICC evaluated the property on June 30, 1917, the L&A owned 32 steam locomotives, 1,181 freight cars, 28 passenger cars, and 58 units of service equipment. Final value for rate-making purposes was $7,748,765, based on property owned. On December 28, 1917, the L&A was among those lines taken over by the U.S. Railroad Administration, and was assigned to the Southwest Region, of which B. F. Bush (from the Missouri Pacific) was director. The railroad was operated by the USRA until it was returned to the owners on March 1, 1920. During this period of government control, wages were increased greatly, and on a strict operating basis the road showed deficits in 1918 and 1919, the only years in its history it would show a loss. However, a later settlement with the government would in effect cancel those losses, and the record of running in the black was preserved.[29]

On March 5, 1921, connections at Natchez were made with the Mississippi Central Railroad, and in August 1921 through freight service was established between Shreveport and Mobile, Alabama, using the Mississippi Central together with Gulf, Mobile and Northern trackage east of Hattiesburg. This service became known as the "Natchez Route" and continued until January 1, 1925, when the Hattiesburg–Beaumont branch of the GM&N was sold to the Hattiesburg and Bonhommie Railroad. After that, cars were interchanged at Hattiesburg, but solicitations for freight movement via the Natchez Route continued until 1967 (see chapter 8).[30]

The principal shops of the L&A were located initially at Stamps. In 1923 and 1924 they were relocated to Minden, with the addition of a hundred-foot turntable, a six-stall roundhouse, and a large, brick backshop building. Additional shops would be completed at Shreveport in 1926.[31]

William Buchanan died at his Texarkana home on October 26, 1923, after a lingering illness. He had shown astute leadership in his development of lumbering and railroad businesses. His fondness for the railroad is quite clear and is related many times by his biographer, Archer Mayor. He chose never to collect any salary from the railroad or the construction company. He owned his personal private car (the *Bodcaw*) and paid for the taxes and maintenance it required. B. S. Atkinson, a vice president of the L&A, had these words about the builder of the railroad:

> Buchanan had a genius for organization, and a reputation through long years of his business life for fair dealing. . . . [H]e knew personally at least three-fourths of his employees, and to a wonderful degree was able to secure from all his employees their active support and cooperation. He also knew intimately hundreds of people living along the line and enjoyed the good will of each and every one of them. . . . [I]n the last years of his life, he loved this property like it was dearer than anything he ever had.[32]

William Buchanan was succeeded in the presidency by his son, W. J. Buchanan. It might have seemed logical for the brother, James A., to take over this position, particularly because he had maintained a strong interest in the railroad since its inception. But James had little interest in management and avoided as much business responsibility as possible. So the task fell to the son, who accepted the responsibility but who inherited little of the father's interest in railroading. Supervision of the operations was delegated, and the property was regarded only as an asset that could bring money into the family when it was sold. Too, the lumber business had passed

its prime in Louisiana, and it was inevitable that the Buchanan family would want to dispose of the railroad that seemed so dependent on hauling logs as well as finished lumber.[33]

The general situation was well summarized by Archer Mayor in his book on the Buchanans:

> [William Buchanan] represented with his life span, by simple chance of birth, the growth and evolution of an era. In the 1870s, as he entered the lumber business, the South was about to steal from the Great Lakes region the title of largest lumber producer. As the railroads and Northern capital discovered the South, Buchanan was there, building his own road and benefiting from the sudden flow of cash. In 1909 Southern lumber production reached a peak of almost 20 billion board feet; in 1913 Louisiana produced the record high of any one state with 4 billion board feet; and William Buchanan's mills turned out their top number of just under 335 million board feet in 1915.[34]

In 1926, not too many months after William Buchanan's death, a syndicate headed by Harvey Couch began to discuss with the heirs the possible purchase of the railroad. The property had been maintained in good condition, and during the 1920s heavier motive power had been purchased in the form of five mikado-type (2-8-2) locomotives. Also, the railroad would suffer little damage in the spring flood of 1927, the only underwater trackage being between Jonesville and Vidalia; the cost of rehabilitation for the L&A was less than $10,000 (compared with $125,000 for the LR&N). The Couch syndicate was also interested in the Louisiana Railway and Navigation Company. Without question, the Buchanan heirs would be interested in getting rid of the railroad. It was while these discussions were in progress that $2.595 million in twenty-five-year L&A bonds were scheduled to mature on September 1, 1927. Because of possible corporate changes, new bonds were not issued (although in 1927 the bond market was fairly

In the 1920s the L&A invested in heavier freight power, purchasing six 2-8-2 oil-burning engines, numbers 551–556, from Baldwin Locomotive Works. This builder's photograph of number 553 bears the date January 1925. (Photograph courtesy of Goodyear Collection, DeGolyer Library, Southern Methodist University)

good); instead, $2.6 million was borrowed from banks on a short-term basis, to pay off the bondholders. The resulting notes would become a problem in future months, as discussed in chapter 6.[35]

At this point in the overall history of the L&A system, it is quite clear that the "early L&A" had been well conceived and operated. It served no large cities, other than Shreveport, and had little through, or "bridge," traffic. It could be considered a "country railroad." Clearly it was instrumental in the development of the region it served, and its profitability remained as a tribute to the foresight and business acumen of its builder, William Buchanan. But it was also clear that the forest-products business, upon which the railroad had thrived for so many years, was changing as the virgin forests were becoming depleted and that the railroad would have to develop new lines of business. The sale of the road was effected, and it was now the assignment of Harvey Couch and his colleagues to carry on the tradition of profitability.

The Couch syndicate of investors took control of the L&A as well as the LR&N (including its Texas subsidiary) in 1928, at a time when the mood in the United States was upbeat and almost any investment was thought to be prudent. The stock market was climbing, and the country was bullish in general. The syndicate obtained a profitable shortline (the L&A) and a worn-out "streak-o-rust" (the LR&N) that had a favorable geographic location. Despite the prevalence of the "plunger" type of investors, who often built houses on sand, this group appeared to have its base on solid rock. The two railroads were in a growing, but still largely rural, region. In the early 1920s the L&A had been favored by petroleum discoveries in Claiborne and Webster Parishes of Louisiana; and whereas in the previous decade logs and lumber accounted for as much as 80 percent of its tonnage, by the late 1920s petroleum and its refined products accounted for 60–70 percent of its tonnage, with forest products dropping to 20 percent or less. Also, the Natchez Route arrangement with the Mississippi Central was providing bridge traffic of consequence.[1]

The LR&N had always enjoyed a good business from the sugar mills and petroleum refineries on the south end, and it handled tank car tonnage to and from refineries in the Shreveport area. For the LR&N, forest-products business had never equaled that of the L&A. But the syndicate saw an opportunity to handle merchandise traffic moving to and from the wharves in New Orleans. The Texas line had never done much more than handle agricultural products derivative of its region, and Edenborn seems not to have sought bridge traffic to and from Dallas, in connection with the Queen and Crescent system east of Shreveport.[2]

So the properties appeared to have possi-bilities, at least from the perspective of 1928. It would be interesting to see how the syndicate might go about increasing the traffic, and profitability, of all of its new properties. Just who were the members of the syndicate?

The leader of the group, Harvey Crowley Couch, was a South Arkansas farmboy who emulated the classical Horatio Alger character in rising far beyond his origins and succeeding fabulously in the world of business. Born in Calhoun, Columbia County, Arkansas, on August 21, 1877, he recognized an early infatuation with trains, building his own "play line" in the yard of the family house—and vowing that someday he would have his own real railroad! At Columbia Academy, a preparatory school near Calhoun, he came under the influence of the headmaster, Pat Neff, who later became governor of Texas and eventually president of Baylor University. Neff recognized young Couch's potential, encouraged him at the time, and became a confidant later in life.[3]

In 1898 Couch took and passed civil-service examinations to qualify him for the job of railway mail clerk. His first assignment was to operate out of St. Louis, running to Texarkana on the Iron Mountain line. A year later he managed a transfer to Memphis, where his run on the Cotton Belt was between Memphis and Texarkana. This new run took him through McNeil, Arkansas, only a few miles from Magnolia, where his parents had moved from Calhoun. Before the end of 1899, he managed still another move, to a mail car operating between McNeil and Bienville, Louisiana, on the new Louisiana and North West Railroad. This route included Magnolia and the opportunity to spend some time with his parents, with Pat Neff, and with Dr. H. A. Longino, who, like Neff, had taken a paternal interest in him.[4]

6

HARVEY COUCH AND THE NEW L&A

Harvey Couch, the one person responsible for the modernization and growth of the L&A and for its acquisition by the KCS.

While working on the L&NW, Couch had an opportunity to become acquainted with many people in the area and to observe the need for telephone service in such towns as Magnolia, Homer, Gibsland, and Bienville. With the financial aid of Dr. Longino, Couch formed a telephone company that initially would serve customers living along the right-of-way of the L&NW. While launching this business, Couch continued to make his mail runs. As the company prospered, Couch had to turn away from railroading and follow an alternative goal of becoming a successful entrepreneur. His small company was succeeded by the North Louisiana Telephone Company, which he sold to the Bell System in 1911 for about $1.5 million. After paying off his investors, Couch was a millionaire—at the age of thirty-four![5]

Success followed success, as Couch moved from telephones to electric utilities, the latter beginning with a small power company serving Arkadelphia and Malvern, towns in southwestern Arkansas, and leading to the organization of the Arkansas Light and Power Company in 1913. He began to seek financial backing among New York investors, to satisfy his need for capital to support expansions of his business.

A key contact here was Charles Simonton McCain, another Arkansas native (from Pine Bluff) who had risen well in the banking world. Couch and McCain had become friends while the latter was an officer of Bankers Trust Company in Little Rock. The two of them would share commercial interests for some time to come, and when, in 1925, McCain became an officer of the Chase National Bank in New York, he was instrumental in setting up the syndicate for Couch.[6]

Others identified with the investors' group included E. A. Frost, a Shreveport lumberman; Randolph Pack, a principal of Corn Products Company; Randle Moore, a Shreveport businessman; and private investors W. N. Adams and Louis Meyers of Arkadelphia and Little Rock, respectively. At Couch's right hand was a young lawyer, Hamilton Moses, who would serve as his chief counsel and, later, would become chief executive officer of Arkansas Power and Light.[7]

Harvey Couch and his company prospered as Arkansas began to appreciate the value of statewide electrical services. Small utility companies were bought up, generating facilities were built, and transmission lines were strung, the only problem being securing the needed capital to carry out these expansions. Couch solved this problem in 1926 by selling Arkansas Light and Power to Electric Bond and Share Company, a large Eastern conglomerate of utility companies. This maneuver gave him better availability of capital while retaining his independence of management. A new company, Arkansas Light and Power, was chartered, to acquire all assets of the old company. Couch could now go ahead with plans to extend services into Mississippi. With funding problems off his mind, he could also turn some of his attention to his earlier love, railroading. He became interested in the L&A, which, after the death of William Buchanan, was for sale. After preliminary negotiations met with success (see chapter 5), the syndicate went into business.[8]

To acquire the L&A as well as the LR&N, a sum of $10 million had to be raised. The following contributors made pledges that reached this goal: Dillon, Read and Company, $3 million; Randolph Pack, $750,000; Harvey Couch, $3.5 million; Rogers Caldwell, $850,000; Charles McCain, $650,000; Coverdale and Colpitts, $250,000; and J. A. Moffett, $1 million. McCain and Pack have been mentioned. Dillon, Read was—and still is—an investment-banking house to which McCain had close ties. (In fact, he would become president of the firm in 1929.) Caldwell and Moffett were also investment bankers. Coverdale and Colpitts was a consulting firm specializing in railroad properties. By and large, the individuals and companies were among those who had supported Couch in his needs for expanding Arkansas Power and Light. The magnitude of Couch's own investment is noteworthy.[9]

By 1927 it was clear that the Edenborn line was to be part of the Couch scheme, and active negotiations with Sarah Edenborn had been under way for several months. Couch decided to fold the Edenborn and L&A acquisitions into one purchase package. The L&A would be procured with an exchange of stock plus assumption of debt. As noted earlier, the LR&N would come at a cash settlement with Sarah Edenborn of $7.5 million (for the $8 million in 5 percent first-mortgage bonds), due May 1, 1928, and $2.5 million on May 1, 1929, to retire a short-term note. As far as the L&A debt was concerned, of the $7 million worth of 5 percent bonds sold in 1902, $5.196 million were still outstanding, with $2.595 million maturing on September 1, 1927; this was handled by a short-term loan from the National Park Bank in New York. (The note would be renewed for several successive years, as approved by the ICC.)[10]

The year 1928 was a pivotal one for the Couch railroad system. The May 1 agreement with Sarah Edenborn has been mentioned. The "new" L&A was chartered on July 1 as a Delaware corporation. The new and old companies reached their agreement on July 11. Application to the ICC for approval of the total plan was filed on August 4, and hearings on the application were held in Washington on October 15 and 16. Importantly, the Couch

interests began to control operations in January 1928, even though the formal change of management did not take place until final ICC approval on February 23, 1929.[11]

What did the Couch group acquire with all these negotiations? The "old L&A" was operating in the black with a well-maintained set of properties. As noted, there had been a shift away from total dependence on hauling forest products. Motive power was reasonably modern, the latest acquisitions having been the six mikado-type freight locomotives bought in 1923–1927. These engines, in the 550 class, could each haul 2,300 tons (about sixty cars) between Hope and Alexandria and twice that much in the flatlands below Alexandria. Station buildings were painted, and three of them (at Hope, Minden, and Shreveport) were of brick construction. The shops at Minden were modern and represented an investment of $1.5 million in 1923–1924. Passenger service was somewhat colorless but provided the local service needed along the routes. Total operating mileage was 842.96.[12]

The LR&N was another matter. All of its properties had been allowed to deteriorate after Edenborn's death, and a great deal of investment would be needed just to bring them up to the standards of the L&A. Rails were light, were tied together by untreated cross ties, and were supported by dirt ballast well infested with weeds. The most modern motive power was a set of decapod (2-10-0) freight locomotives that had been purchased from the government just after World War I (these so-called Russian decapods had been built for shipment to Russia but were found not to be needed). There were brick depots at Baton Rouge and New Orleans, and a single local passenger train took more than twelve hours to travel between Shreveport and New Orleans. At least the facilities in the vicinity of Simmesport and Angola were recently constructed and thus had not yet deteriorated. To conserve cash, the syndicate opted to lease the LR&N, at least initially, for a period of 999 years; in 1934 the LR&N would be dissolved and the property taken over by the L&A.[13]

The real problem was the Texas line. It had become an unloved stepchild that enjoyed

This map of the L&A, taken from a 1929 public time-table, shows the system as Couch put it together. The Farmersville–McKinney and Aloha–Winnfield branches were still in operation, but the Farmersville–Dallas arrangement with the Santa Fe was yet to come.

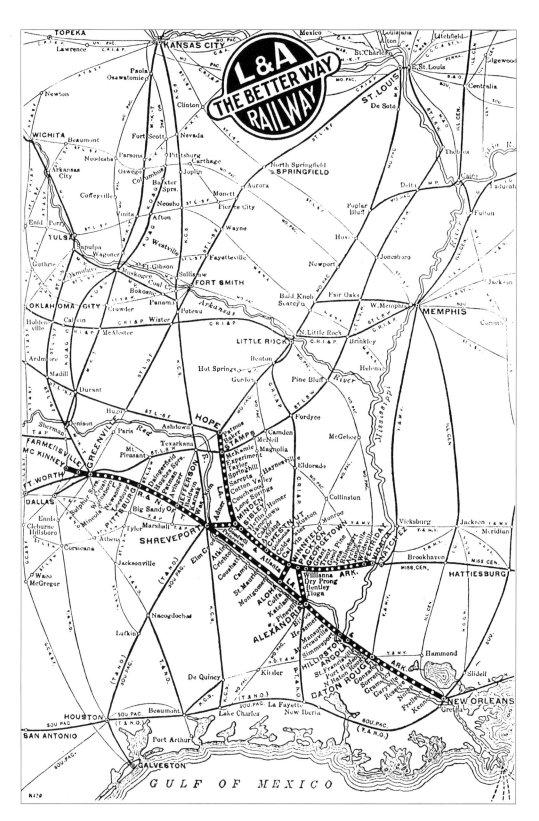

little local business and essentially no overhead traffic. Rails were light and line bent, motive power was castoffs from the Katy that would have been too light for the heavy grades around Daingerfield had the trains served enough customers to be of reasonable length. The only brick depot was one shared with the Katy at Greenville; shops at Hughes Springs and Greenville were considered completely inadequate. The term "streak of rust" must have been coined by an observer of its weed-overgrown tracks. The line had been running an annual deficit despite a relatively low load of fixed charges. The Couch group would rather not have acquired the LR&N of Texas—but Sarah Edenborn insisted that it be part of the package. At least its indebtedness was fairly low—$750,000 in first-mortgage bonds.[14]

The Couch group went to work with the financial resources that were available to it. The support of all the employees was rallied around an in-company organization, the L&A Cooperative Club, a booster-type activity formed early in 1928. This was not a new idea; other railroads such as the Baltimore and Ohio had such organizations, and Couch may well have studied the salutary effects on morale and business that employee-managed clubs could generate. In November of that year the club published the first issue of *Co-Operative News*. A new corporate logo was designed, along with a new slogan, "L&A—The Better Way." The Texarkana headquarters offices, comprised mostly of accounting functions, were closed and the people relocated to Shreveport (in a three-story brick office building at 110 Lake Street, erected in 1914 by the LR&N; executive offices of the L&A were in the Central Station building). Plans were made to shift from the T&P to the Illinois Central (that is, the VS&P) for trackage between Waskom and Shreveport, on more favorable rental terms. The out-of-date shops of the LR&N, located near Cross Bayou, were closed, and some of their machinery was relocated to the Silver Lake shops of the L&A, where a new six-stall roundhouse was constructed.[15]

A move that attracted much attention was the institution of a new passenger train between Shreveport and Hope, named the

Harvey Couch formed employee cooperative clubs at various locations along the line. Publication of the monthly Co-Operative News *began in November 1928 and continued for several years, until it fell victim to the Great Depression. This cover shows mikado-type engine number 556, with a feedwater heater. (Courtesy of Harold K. Vollrath)*

The Shreveporter *ready to depart Central Station for its maiden northbound run, December 30, 1928. Engine 300 has a new coat of olive green paint with gold trim, and its tender is adorned by the herald of Harvey Couch's "New L&A." Behind the engine are baggage/mail car 45, a coach with unidentified number,* Pullman Uraguay, *and café-observation car 609. The train will leave on time at 5:00 P.M., and despite a delay because of ceremonies at Minden will arrive on schedule at Hope, where the sleeper will be turned over to the Missouri Pacific for overnight transit to St. Louis.*

Shreveporter. It would depart Shreveport in the late afternoon, run on a faster schedule than its predecessor local trains, and connect at Hope with Missouri Pacific's *Texan* for Little Rock and St. Louis. An overnight sleeper would be carried between Shreveport and St. Louis, and a café-parlor car (with an observation platform) would provide food and comfort for passengers between Shreveport and Hope. The only stops would be made at Minden, Cotton Valley, and Stamps. Couch hoped that this train would gain some nonregional recognition for the L&A and would be a cause for celebration by the employees.[16]

For the inaugural run on December 30, 1928, engine number 300, a 4-4-0 of 1911 vintage, was cleaned and lacquered in olive green with gold trim; a café-parlor car was purchased from the Missouri Pacific, and other rolling stock was likewise renovated to make up a slick-and-shiny train for publicity as well as marketing purposes. The return trip from Hope would be in the morning, with the sleeper delivered to the L&A by the flagship train of the Missouri Pacific, the *Sunshine Special.* At Hope, arrangements were made

for joint use of the Missouri Pacific passenger station. The run time for the *Shreveporter* was about three hours, which enabled the railroad to get by with only one set of equipment. Each run would comprise, in order, a baggage-mail car, a divided coach, a sleeping car, and the café-parlor car. Adorning the observation platform at the rear was a lighted red-and-white sign with the train name and railroad insignia.[17]

The December 30 inaugural came off on schedule, even though the first train left Hope thirty minutes late because of the delayed arrival of the Missouri Pacific connection. One reporter commented,

It arrived at Minden shining like a new dollar and was greeted by a large number of officials, employes and citizens of the town. Copies of the "Co-Operative News" were distributed through the train for the passengers and we had just enough time to walk through the train and get off as it started moving. Everyone on the line seemed to be "listening in" and checking the progress of this new darling of ours, and when OS-ed by Shreveport— "No. 1 arrived 9:55 A.M." [on schedule].[18]

For the return trip, the train left Shreveport on time at 5:00 P.M., after brief ceremonies at Central Station, and was met "by practically the entire population" of Minden, headed by the Lions Club and the Lions Boys' Band. There were photographers, a band concert, and official greetings. Thus, the new flagship train of the L&A had been launched, and within a few months a second sleeper, Shreveport–Little Rock, would be added. Also, later in 1929 another passenger engine would be added to the roster. This new addition was number 309, a trim Pacific-type (4-6-2) locomotive built in 1913 and purchased from the Florida East Coast Railroad; after an overhaul at Minden, a metal plate bearing the train name was installed on the smokebox cover, and for a number of years this locomotive would be as-

signed exclusively to *Shreveporter* service.[19]

Other moves were made to strengthen the passenger business. Two motor cars were ordered from J. G. Brill Company in Philadelphia, numbers 125 and 126, for use in local service between Shreveport and Hope and for use either on the Texas line or on the river line between Shreveport and Alexandria. A city ticket office was opened in the Washington-Youree Hotel in Shreveport. Offline agents were schooled in soliciting passenger business. And the traffic people kept a sharp lookout for excursion opportunities. One interesting excursion took place on June 18, 1930, when Governor Huey Long, in his usual ruthless fashion, commandeered state workers to converge on Baton Rouge and take his side against a large group of dissidents. On that day two special trains, each

Brief ceremonies were held before the first departure of the Shreveporter *from Central Station. The identity of the individuals is not known. The café-parlor car still has its Missouri Pacific markings, but the red-and-white drumhead sign with the name of the train is distinctively L&A. (Photograph by Bill Grabill, courtesy of Archives and Special Collections, Noel Memorial Library, Louisiana State University—Shreveport)*

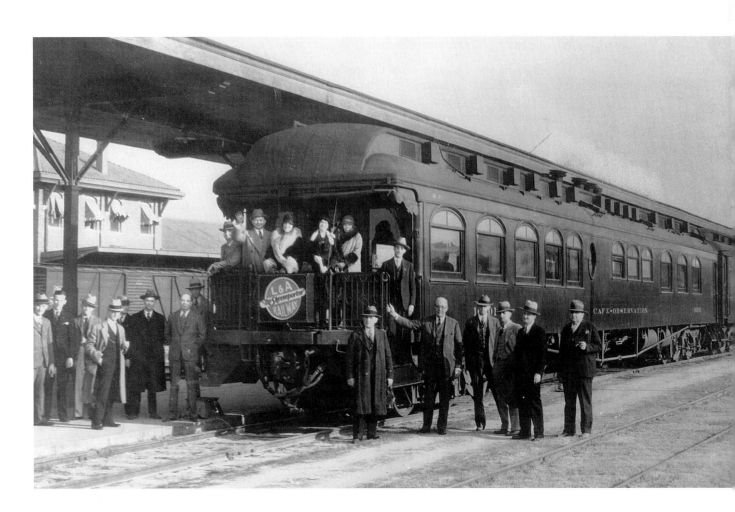

The venerable American-type engine number 51 arriving at Central Station, Shreveport, in the early 1930s, with the local passenger train from Minden. A motor-car replacement for this steam train was not entirely successful. This was the third locomotive owned by the Shreveport and Red River Valley and was not scrapped until 1936. (Photograph by C. W. Witbeck)

containing fifteen "steel-vestibuled cars," made the trip from New Orleans to Baton Rouge and back with 2,400 people aboard! Engines 94 and 97 pulled the trains with little effort, for the route had practically no grades. The scene at Baton Rouge must have been spectacular, and the opposing forces did actual battle, with many being injured in the process. But the governor prevailed.[20]

As far as freight business was concerned, the first task of the Couch management was to build up traffic to and from New Orleans; this meant devoting attention to the run-down segment of the LR&N south of Alexandria. This would enable use of the better-maintained (but more circuitous) "high line" of the L&A between Shreveport and Alexandria and would buy some time for the needed rehabilitation of the "short line" through Coushatta. The work list for the LR&N effort was considerable and included the following:

- Replacing the old seventy-pound rail with heavier section
- Adding gravel ballast and creosoted crossties
- Widening banks to provide a twenty-two-foot crown

- Replacing wood box culverts with concrete boxes
- Extending passing tracks to handle 110-car trains
- Rebuilding the number 2 warehouse in New Orleans[21]

This was an ambitious program, and unfortunately the stock-market crash in October 1929, plus the ensuing depression, prevented much of it from being completed quickly.

There was indeed much to do, and Harvey Couch called on the help of his brother, Charles Peter Couch, thirteen years his junior, who had worked closely with him in building the electric power system. Pete had become known more as a "do-er" than a thinker or planner—one who could go out and get an assigned job done. At the time, Pete was in Dallas, heading up the Southern Ice and Utilities Company, a Couch interest organized in 1927, and though his office remained in Dallas, Pete became a vice president of the L&A. An early matter for his attention was the branch line of the LR&N between Aloha and Winnfield. Because the line had little traffic and the L&A served

Winnfield, the branch was superfluous. Petition for abandonment was made to the ICC, and approval came on April 2, 1930.[22]

By early 1930 there were reports of progress all along the line. Bank widening and track raising in the Mansura area was well under way. New ferry cradles were being installed at both Filston and Angola. Discussions were under way with the Cotton Belt for trackage rights from Greenville to Dallas, to give the Texas line a better overhead freight potential. An agricultural agent, William McComb of Little Rock, Arkansas, was hired to work with farmers in the region to increase agricultural-products revenue for the railroad. By mid-1932 he and his successor, L. E. Robinson, had published five farmers' bulletins, on topics such as crops, diseases, and insects and their control. On the down side, the large Bodcaw mill at Stamps was facing a shutdown because of depleted timber resources, and this held also for the large mills at Trout and Good Pine.[23]

But other freight business opportunities were cropping up. Governor Long embarked on a massive road-building program for the state, and to serve needs for crushed stone, a new quarry was opened near Winnfield, and the L&A obtained a near "exclusive" on this business. The U.S. government decided to install a huge military airfield just south of Bossier City, and in early 1931 surveys of three miles of spurs were being made so that the L&A could serve the construction needs of what would become Barksdale Field. The arrangement for Dallas service was approved

The dining section of the café-parlor car during the inaugural run of the Shreveporter. *The car was purchased secondhand from the Missouri Pacific. (Photograph by Bill Grabill, courtesy of Archives and Special Collections, Noel Memorial Library, Louisiana State University—Shreveport)*

Number 104, a Russian decapod locomotive bought new from the U.S. government by William Edenborn in 1921, leading daily mixed train No. 38 toward Texas on a bright morning in 1931. The scene is along the right-of-way of the Illinois Central west of Shreveport, where the L&A had trackage rights. (Photograph by C. W. Witbeck)

Bringing up the rear of the westbound mixed train to Texas are two passenger cars (coach, baggage-mail) and a caboose. Here, the tail end of the train is at Central Station in Shreveport, for serving passengers and loading mail and express; it will be placed at the rear of the train by a switch engine. Mixed train service on the Texas line ended in 1938. (Photograph courtesy of Lloyd Neal)

by the ICC on June 11, 1930, ostensibly for trackage rights over the Cotton Belt between Greenville and Dallas; however, the L&A trains were handled by Cotton Belt locomotives and crews, and the advantage to the L&A was not nearly as great as anticipated.[24]

The Texas line was brought closer to the corporate fold when, on April 14, 1930, the Louisiana, Arkansas and Texas Railway Company was chartered under Texas laws for the purpose of taking over the properties of the Louisiana Railway and Navigation Company of Texas. There was little more than a name change connected with this move, and it seems to have been made primarily for an improved identity with the L&A system. Connected with the change was the incorporation, on April 7, 1930, of the Louisiana, Arkansas and Texas Transportation Company, a Delaware corporation. The purpose of this company was to augment rail operations with truck handling of freight and express, mostly along the railroad in Louisiana. Such operations were becoming popular among the regional railroads. But for such operations in Texas, it would be necessary to incorporate a separate company, Landa Motor Lines, in 1937.

The LA&T Transportation Company commenced operations on September 20, 1930.[25] Pete Couch was president of the LA&T; by this time he had also become executive vice president of the L&A and had relocated his office to Shreveport. On May 17, 1930, the LA&T trains began to use the VS&P tracks between Waskom and Shreveport, rather than those of the T&P. The Texas line continued to run a deficit and would need a great deal more attention before it could become profitable.[26]

As 1930 ended, the Great Depression had sunk its claws deep into the fabric of American life, but the worst was yet to come. For the L&A, the results were not nearly as discouraging as they were for most railroads in the country. A summary of the years 1928, 1929, and 1930 shows some interesting trends (see Table 6).[27]

Despite the burden of the LR&N, a chronic money loser, the results were not at all bad—and fixed charges were fully accounted

TABLE 6

Louisiana & Arkansas Financial Results

Early Years of the Great Depression

	1928[a]	1929	1930
Operating revenues	$7,284,500	$7,866,700	$6,980,600
Gross income	$1,110,300	$1,632,000	$1,379,800
Net income	$394,600	$826,600	$570,300
Operating ratio	**70.5**	**67.6**	**67.7**

[a] Combined L&A and LR&N.

Source: Company annual reports.

for in figuring net income. Still, the depression seemed to have no end, and on September 15, 1930, the L&A management notified the shop workers that a wage reduction would be forthcoming. (Such reductions were occurring in many areas of business during those early days of the depression.) On October 15 the reduction was identified as five cents per hour. As expected, the Federated Shop Crafts union took up the cause. Negotiations with management consumed several weeks, with the L&A being steadfast against arbitration. Finally, on February 9, 1931, the planned reduction went into effect after Pete Couch had made his final statement: "I have given the [union] request careful and serious consideration, and am compelled to decline to arbitrate this company's proposal."[28]

The year 1931 saw the development of new business that made all but the shop men happy. The Winnfield quarry opened in April, and by June the three tracks at Barksdale Field were busy with incoming construction materials. The morale of the workforce was generally good, and to indicate that all was not glum and serious that year, members of the Shreveport chapter of the Co-Op Club decided to have a Labor Day outing to New Orleans. A special train, consisting of two full Pullmans, two business cars, and head-end equipment, left Shreveport on Friday, September 5, at 7:30 P.M. Pete Couch was aboard, and he permitted free movement into business car 99 and into his private car, the *Magnolia*. At 11:00 P.M. he hosted a watermelon party in the baggage car, and when the Mississippi was crossed many partygoers paraded around the decks of the *William Edenborn* in their pajamas. At New Orleans there was, of course, the French Quarter, and there were also Sunday and Monday baseball games between the Shreveport and New Orleans L&A baseball teams. When the party finally returned to Shreveport on Tuesday morning it is unlikely that they accomplished much for the L&A that day.[29]

The 1931 year-end financial results were most encouraging. The operating ratio dropped to 61.77 percent, and the net income increased almost 13 percent to $729,000. The various moves by the L&A management seemed to be paying off. Upgrading of the property continued, and by the end of the year the Alexandria–New Orleans segment was in admirable shape even though it still lacked new and heavier rail. However, very little attention had been given to the river line between Shreveport and Alexandria, and one could hardly find the rails there because of the verdant vegetation surrounding them. This improvement was on the list but would require a large capital investment.[30]

One historian has called the year 1932 "the darkest, dreariest, most disastrous year of the great depression." Unemployment in the United States was up to 13 million, and the

Charles P. ("Pete") Couch was trusted by his older brother, Harvey, to handle all operating aspects of the Couch railroad empire. He was president of the L&A from 1932 to 1944 and also held the highest offices in the KCS. Often controversial as a railroad man, he was ousted from the system after Harvey's death by a group of Kansas City investors that took control of the properties.

Gross National Product was down to $58.5 billion from $104 billion in 1929. Between 1929 and 1932 the total operating revenues of Class I railroads (which included the L&A) fell almost by half. Nationwide, all railroad-union employees took a 10 percent cut in pay on February 1, and for the L&A this was extended to all personnel.[31]

During these days every fourth family in the country was on relief. Business needed help in financing repairs and improvements in its physical plant, and to this end President Herbert Hoover set up the Reconstruction Finance Corporation (RFC) to enable the government to guarantee loans to industrial organizations. The RFC Act was signed into law on January 22, 1932, by the president. The *Arkansas Gazette* of January 26 advised that Harvey Couch had been nominated as one of the eight

directors of the RFC. Couch and Hoover had become close friends after working together on the relief of victims of the Mississippi River flood in the spring of 1927. Congress promptly approved the nomination.[32]

Couch was appointed officially on February 2, 1932. This meant turning over the management of the power companies and the railroad to others. Pete Couch had been running the L&A as executive vice president, and by midyear he would be elected president. Harvey had confidence in Pete, and by this time Pete had learned a great deal about the railroad business. (Also, Harvey would remain as chairman of the Board of Directors of the L&A.) Before taking office, Pete led another excursion of employees from Shreveport to New Orleans, this time a "Mardi Gras Special." The train left Shreveport with engine number 240, a ten-wheeler (4-6-0) of 1907 vintage that had been acquired from the Katy when the Texas line was purchased by Edenborn. The train carried a day coach, three full Pullmans, and the *Magnolia*, and an additional sleeper was added at Alexandria. Again, the partying began when the train pulled out of Central Station, and the group merged easily with the frolicking crowds in the Crescent City. As in the previous excursion, the train did not dare to use the river line, with its decrepit track, but instead went around by Minden and Winnfield.[33]

By 1932 the Alexandria–New Orleans segment was sufficiently upgraded to allow tonnage freight to move without derailment, permitting more of the coveted New Orleans export business to be gained. It also permitted the addition of a second "name train" to the passenger timetable, this one between Shreveport and New Orleans, with service to Minden, Winnfield, Alexandria, and Baton Rouge. Named the *Hustler,* it was scheduled overnight and included a sleeper between Alexandria and New Orleans (with buffet service) as well as the Shreveport–New Orleans sleeper. This train took its maiden run on Saturday, July 2, 1932, with minimal fanfare. Through the years it competed very successfully with the T&P for the overnight business between Shreveport, Alexandria, and New

The Hustler *approaching Bossier City after its overnight run from New Orleans via Minden, in the late 1930s. Providing the tractive effort is ten-wheeler locomotive number 394, acquired new from Baldwin by the LR&N in 1913 and first numbered 94. The divided coach is sandwiched between the baggage-mail car and the Pullman. (Courtesy of Lloyd Neal)*

Orleans. And it was said to be the only train in the country on which Pullman porters served morning coffee to patrons in their berths.[34]

In the early 1930s there were several developments that would have a lasting influence on L&A operations and economics. As early as 1929 plans had been initiated for a floodway, the Bonnet Carre, that could divert excess Mississippi River water to Lake Pontchartrain and so protect the city of New Orleans. The sad experiences during the Spring 1927 flood heightened interest in this project. The L&A would have to build a long trestle across the waterway, about 25 miles northwest of New Orleans at a narrow neck of land between the river and the lake. The railroad grade would be raised, a strong trestle constructed, and heavier rail provided—all at U.S. government expense! Construction on this project would begin in 1934.[35]

A new railroad-highway bridge across the river at New Orleans was also in the planning stage. It would not involve the L&A directly, but it would create a competitive disadvantage for the railroad, because Southern Pacific and T&P trains would no longer have to use time-consuming ferries at New Orleans. This bridge, named for Huey Long, would be completed in 1935. Another planned bridge would involve the L&A directly: a crossing of

"*The Shreveporter*"

OVERNIGHT SERVICE
Between
SHREVEPORT AND NORTH LOUISIANA
and
ST. LOUIS AND MEMPHIS
VIA L & A—MoPac

Direct connections at St. Louis with fast trains to and from all points North and East.

CONDENSED SCHEDULES

No. 1	DAILY	No. 2
6:30 P. M.	lve St. Louis, Mo..... (Mo. Pac.) arr	8:30 A. M.
10:45 P. M.	lve Memphis, Tenn. (Mo. Pac.) arr	7:10 A. M.
3:10 A. M.	lve Little Rock, Ark. (Mo. Pac.) arr	11:50 P. M.
5:45 A. M.	lve..............Hope, Ark...........arr	9:10 P. M.
6:23 A. M.	lve............Stamps, Ark..........arr	8:27 P. M.
7:24 A. M.	lve....Cotton Valley, La......arr	7:25 P. M.
7:52 A. M.	arr........Minden, La............lve	6:56 P. M.
8:45 A. M.	arr........Shreveport, La.......lve	6:05 P. M.

No. 1—12 Section Drawing-room sleeper, St. Louis to Shreveport, (to Hope on Missouri Pacific No. 1). 12 Section Drawing-room compartment Sleeper Memphis to Shreveport, (to Hope on Missouri Pacific No. 201-1). Observation, Cafe, Parlor Car and all steel coaches Hope to Shreveport. Oil-burning locomotives.

No. 2—12 Section Drawing-room Sleeper, Shreveport to St. Louis (from Hope on Missouri Pacific No. 2). 12 Section Drawing-room compartment Sleeper Shreveport to Memphis (from Hope on Missouri Pacific No. 2-202). Observation, Cafe, Parlor Car and All-steel coaches Shreveport to Hope. Oil-burning locomotives.

Try the Club breakfasts and dinners served on the Shreveporter—you will find them superior in every respect and also moderately priced.

"*The Hustler*"

OVERNIGHT SERVICE
Between
NEW ORLEANS AND BATON ROUGE
and
ALEXANDRIA, SHREVEPORT AND
OTHER NORTH LOUISIANA POINTS

CONDENSED SCHEDULES

No. 204-3	DAILY	No. 4-203
9:00 P. M.	lve.........Shreveport, La..........arr	7:58 A. M.
9:55 P. M.	lve.............Minden, La..........arr	6:58 A. M.
11:41 P. M.	lve........Winnfield, La........arr	5:14 A. M.
1:05 A. M.	lve.........Alexandria, La.......arr	3:45 A. M.
1:49 A. M.	lve...........Mansura, La........arr	3:00 A. M.
5:05 A. M.	arr.......Baton Rouge, La......lve	11:35 P. M.
7:30 A. M.	arr ....New Orleans, La........lve	9:15 P. M.

No. 204-3—8-Section Buffet Lounge Sun-room Sleeper, Shreveport to New Orleans. 12-Section Drawing-room Sleeper, Shreveport to Baton Rouge (may be occupied until 7:30 A. M.). All-steel coaches Shreveport to New Orleans. Oil-burning locomotives.

No. 4-203—8-Section Buffet Lounge Sun-room Sleeper, New Orleans to Shreveport. 12-Section Drawing-room Sleeper, Baton Rouge to Shreveport (open for occupancy at 9:30 P. M.). All-steel coaches New Orleans to Shreveport. Oil-burning locomotives.

Late Supper and Breakfast served on Buffet Cars.

Valet Service --- Bath --- Home Comforts

A simple folder served as the L&A passenger timetable for May 13, 1934. The second named train, the Hustler, *was placed in overnight Shreveport–New Orleans service on July 2, 1932.*

the Mississippi just above Baton Rouge at a point above which the channel was not dredged to accommodate ocean-going vessels. It too would be a combination highway and railroad bridge.[36]

The idea of eliminating the ferry crossing was good news to the L&A management. It so happened that a lightly used branch line of the T&P ran along the west bank of the river from Lobdell, opposite Baton Rouge, to Ferriday, opposite Natchez, and this line could be used by the L&A from Lobdell to the L&A crossing near Torras (between Simmesport and Filston), a distance of some 48 miles. The bridge would be constructed with state funds, and the bonds would be retired through highway and railroad toll charges. The trackage agreement with the T&P was executed on April 10, 1934, and approval by the ICC came on November 12, 1936.[37]

This arrangement was certainly attractive to the L&A, but an even more attractive deal developed while negotiations with the T&P were in progress. The Missouri Pacific (Gulf Coast Lines) had its Houston–New Orleans line interrupted by a ferry crossing of the Mis-

sissippi at Baton Rouge. In its desire to end the ferry operation, the Missouri Pacific proposed to use the bridge, as well as L&A freight and passenger facilities in Baton Rouge, and would purchase a half-interest in the L&A line into New Orleans (replacing trackage rights over the Y&MV). Thus, the L&A would have the same tenant that had irritated Edenborn many years earlier. But now the idea was good news to the L&A, and hearings by the ICC were held in Baton Rouge between January 27 and February 3, 1931. Harvey Couch spoke in favor of the proposal, but, as might be expected, the Illinois Central, which controlled the Y&MV, violently opposed it. Ultimately, the ICC disapproved the plan. The Missouri Pacific would not use the bridge until after World War II. It is interesting that the Baton Rouge bridge idea existed as early as 1930, ten years before the bridge would go into operation.[38]

The mid-1930s showed a deepening of the depression locally as well as nationally. One diversion brightened life in Shreveport: on February 2, 1933, Barksdale Field was dedicated, and L&A shuttle trains operated all day to carry a good part of the 50,000 attendees between Central Station and the end of a spur line at the field.[39] But things were not going well for the railroads in the region, and most of them sank into receivership—Missouri Pacific, Rock Island, Cotton Belt, Frisco. The Kansas City Southern, a future partner of the L&A, was barely spared this fate. But the L&A stayed in the black, although the year 1932 was a close one, with a meager $27,500 net profit after full payment of fixed charges. Profits were better in 1933 and 1934, with net revenues of $151,200 and $291,800, respectively. Wages had been kept under control, with earlier pay cuts continuing in force. The Bonnet Carre trestle was completed late in 1934 and placed in service in the spring of 1935. It was an impressive structure, measuring 9,687 feet in length and comprising 484 I-beam steel spans supported by seven-pile creosoted wooden bents. At each end there was a 0.5 percent grade to move the level up to some twenty feet above the existing embankment of the railroad. The L&A was reimbursed $1.075 million by the U.S. government for the cost of construction. Also during the year, about 10 miles of eighty-five-pound rail were installed south of Alexandria.[40]

Every available passenger car was pressed into use for excursion trains that shuttled back and forth between Central Station and Barksdale Field when the latter was dedicated on February 2, 1933. Some 50,000 people attended the ceremonies, and the L&A donated its services for the occasion. Here, ten-wheeler locomotive number 505 leads a special train past the L&A shops and roundhouse in Shreveport; it will cross the Red River bridge, head south toward Alexandria, and then take the spur line into the field. (Photograph by C. W. Witbeck)

A mid-thirties project of the U.S. government was the Bonnet Carre spillway to carry floodwaters from the Mississippi River to Lake Pontchartrain. This required a 9,687-foot trestle, shown here in a photograph taken in February 1935 from the rear of an L&A train northbound on the old line. (John W. Barriger photograph)

The L&A management was justifiably proud of the new 561-class mikado-type freight engines. All five of them were on display at Central Station, Shreveport, in August 1936, shortly after they arrived from the Lima Locomotive Works. The view beyond the platform umbrella shed includes the second floor of the L&A freight station. (L&A photograph, courtesy of Louis Saillard)

TABLE 7

Location of L&A Engines

8:00 A.M. on March 28, 1936

Number	Type	Service	Comments
79	0-6-0	In the yard	In Shreveport
90	2-8-0	In the yard	In Shreveport
91	2-8-0	In the yard	In New Orleans
95	4-6-0	Train number 68	Arrived in Hope on March 27
96	4-6-0	Train number 68	Departing from Hope on March 28
97	4-6-0	Dodger	In Jena
98	2-8-0	In the yard	In Alexandria
99	2-8-0	In the yard	In Shreveport
100	2-10-0	Being repaired	In the New Orleans shop
101	2-10-0	Train number 16	Arrived in Angola on March 27 (northbound)
102	2-10-0	Train number 39	Arrived in New Orleans on March 27 (southbound)
103	2-10-0	Train number 51	On the Texas line
104	2-10-0	Train number 39	On the Texas line
105	2-10-0	Train number 38	On the Texas line
106	2-10-0	Train number 52	On the Texas line
170	4-6-0	On hand	In Minden
172	4-6-0	Being repaired	In the Minden shop
173	4-6-0	On hand	In Minden
174	4-6-0	On hand	In Minden
177	4-6-0	Extra North	On the Texas line
203	4-6-0	In the yard	In Baton Rouge
204	4-6-0	Being repaired	In the New Orleans shop
205	4-6-0	In the yard	In New Orleans
207	4-6-0	In the yard	In Baton Rouge
243	2-8-0	In the yard	In Minden
301	4-4-0	On hand	In Minden
302	4-4-0	On hand	In Shreveport
309	4-6-2	Train numbers 1 and 2	*Shreveporter*, Hope–Shreveport
392	4-6-0	Train numbers 3 and 4	*Hustler*, Shreveport–New Orleans
393	4-6-0	Being repaired	In Minden
394	4-6-0	Train numbers 3 and 4	*Hustler*, New Orleans–Shreveport
425	2-8-0	Extra	New Orleans–Reserve turn
500	4-6-0	In the yard	In Angola
501	4-6-0	Train number 39	Shreveport–Filston via Coushatta
502	4-6-0	Work	Out of Minden
503	4-6-0	Break-in	In Minden (after repairs)
504	4-6-0	Train numbers 68 and 69	On the Hope–Texas line
505	4-6-0	Train number 51	In Vidalia (from Packton)
506	4-6-0	On hand	In Shreveport
507	4-6-0	Train number 38	South end, New Orleans–Angola
508	4-6-0	Train number 15	South end, Angola–New Orleans
509	4-6-0	Train number 52	Departed Vidalia for Packton
510	4-6-0	Train number 39	In Filston (en route to New Orleans)
511	4-6-0	Train number 38	Alexandria–Shreveport via Coushatta
544	2-8-2	Train numbers 51 and 52	Minden–Winnfield
551	2-8-2	Being repaired	In the Minden shop
552	2-8-2	Train number 216	In Hope
553	2-8-2	In the yard	In Shreveport
554	2-8-2	Train number 215	In Shreveport
555	2-8-2	Train number 16-115	Minden–Shreveport
556	2-8-2	Train number 116-15	Shreveport–Minden

Source: Company records.

By 1935 business was good enough that problems with insufficient motive power began to develop. On a typical day in 1936, as shown in Table 7, the available locomotive fleet was widely dispersed, and serious consideration began to be given to the purchase of new motive power. At the time diesel power was not thought to be fully developed, so plans were finalized to buy six new, heavy mikado-type (2-8-2) steam engines from the Lima Locomotive Works. These engines were delivered in August 1936 and were indeed impressive for a relatively small road like the L&A. They were given the classification M-22, but were more familiarly known as the "560 class"; they were rated to pull at least 2,900 tons of freight over the heaviest grades on which their axle loading could be accommodated. Their Cooper's E-48 bridge rating meant that they could not be used on the Texas line or on the Vidalia branch. Bridges south of Angola could bear their weight, but with grades so mild such power was not really needed for hauling tonnage into New Orleans. (In that territory they were rated at 5,500 tons, or some 100 loaded freight cars.)[41]

Trouble was brewing in 1936, however. The "big four" brotherhoods—engineers, firemen, conductors, and trainmen—wanted to share in some of the profits that were accruing to the railroad. This was particularly true among workers on the Texas line, where sharp wage reductions were proposed because of deficit operations. Mediation did not result in restoration of the wage cuts made in 1931 and 1932. For this reason, labor relations on the L&A were a bit strained. When the railroad insisted on going through with the wage cuts the brotherhoods went out on strike, on September 19, 1936, primarily in sympathy for the Texas line workers. The railroad was shut down completely on that day, but was soon up and running with strikebreakers brought in by Pete Couch. As before, Couch chose not to deal with mediators, declaring in a September 24 telegram to George Cook, secretary of the National Mediation Board, that the railroad would take care of its own

problems. Couch vowed that he would only meet with representatives of each brotherhood separately, not as a group.[42]

The strike lasted for about two months and was both bitter and expensive. Minden was especially hard hit; the L&A was the biggest industry in town, and the classical case of outside management versus hometown workers prevailed. And as had happened in other locations at other times, local residents supported the strikers. Merchants posted notices that they would not ship on the railroad. The women of the community rallied to the cause in a very active way. In one case they assaulted an operating crew member; in another they joined with the men in besieging a special train near Winnfield. The train carried a football crowd; passengers lay in the aisles of the coaches, to avoid gunshots, but seemed to make a party of the affair, passing drinks among each other while under siege! At Jonesville women locked a conductor in his caboose.[43]

At times crews were chased into the surrounding woods. A guard on a passenger train was shot and killed from ambush, and the engineer and fireman were wounded. Three men were killed in a head-on collision of freight trains near Georgetown on the Packton–Vidalia line; unofficially, blame was placed on the railroad for allowing untrained strikebreakers to handle the trains. Except in New Orleans, local law-enforcement officers gave little cooperation to the railroad. An old-timer of the L&A observed that "Pete Couch was born 500 years too late—he would like to be a feudal lord but is out of step with the times." In all, some six deaths were directly attributable to the strike.[44]

In due course the strike ended, on November 20, when the railroad acceded to most of the unions' demands. Even though the strike had been costly, the operating ratio remained low and the profits were not heavily depressed: $428,900 in 1935 and $334,400 in 1936. Improvements continued, with 64 miles of ninety-pound rail being laid on the south end. It was now time to do something about the "short line" or "river line" between

Shreveport and Alexandria. To this end application was made to the Reconstruction Finance Corporation (RFC) for a loan of $350,000 for the purpose of upgrading the line. By this time, incidentally, Harvey Couch had resigned from the RFC directorate (he did so on August 29, 1934) and, with his associates, had begun to buy heavily the common stock of the KCS. One notable purchase was a block of 35,000 shares handled through Paine Webber and Company, a New York brokerage firm. To avoid possible conflict of interest, Couch did not continue as an L&A official but retained the presidency of Arkansas Power and Light, operating out of his Pine Bluff office.[45]

The RFC loan was approved, and by the end of 1937 a stretch of 60 miles of the short line had been rebuilt with ninety-pound steel, new crossties, and heavy ballast. Another 1937 event of note was the start of construction of a very large paper mill near Springhill, north of Minden on the line to Hope. The Southern Kraft Division of International Paper Company had chosen the site with the assistance of Harvey Couch, and the mill would require large quantities of pulpwood to be shipped in from the surrounding territory. The L&A was the only road to serve the mill, and management busied itself considering the needs for additional rolling stock to handle the insatiable appetite of the pulping operations.[46]

Harvey Couch may have been interested in the KCS, but his paternal interest in the L&A continued. He often hosted groups of L&A management people at his retreat, Couchwood, on Lake Catherine near Hot Springs. He was ever cognizant of the morale-boosting benefits of such affairs.

During this time the Rock Island railroad was developing a plan of reorganization to emerge from bankruptcy, and one part of its system that might be on the market was a line called the Rock Island, Arkansas and Louisiana. Although an operating unit of the Rock Island system, the RIA&L bonds were held privately, and the bondholders were interested in selling the property. This line ran south from Little Rock through El Dorado, Arkansas, and Winnfield, Louisiana, to Eunice, Louisiana, where it connected with the Southern Pacific. Operations south of Winnfield to Alexandria were handled by trackage rights over the L&A. A branch line in Arkansas served the lumber-mill town of Crossett. In the early 1920s the RIA&L had handled large quantities of petroleum in the vicinity of El Dorado, and it continued to profit from the handling of forest products. Harvey Couch believed that it could be integrated nicely with

Heavy mikado locomotive number 561 shows off its trim lines as it rounds a curve near Silver Lake Junction, Shreveport, in late 1936. (Courtesy of Goodyear Collection, DeGolyer Library, Southern Methodist University)

the L&A and thus sought to purchase it from the Rock Island receivers. Application for ICC approval was made in February 1937. For its protection, the Louisiana and North West requested that it be acquired by the L&A as part of the total package.[47]

In a separate action, the L&A sought approval to acquire the Texas line. An old Texas law requiring that all railroads operating in Texas be headquartered there stood in the way, but there were certain advantages, legal and economic, in merging the LA&T into the L&A. By this time things were looking better for the Texas operation; on October 17, 1937, trackage rights into Dallas were shifted from the Katy (Greenville–Dallas) to the Santa Fe (Farmersville–Dallas) with much better operating arrangements. LA&T crews and equipment could roll right into the city and also take advantage of Santa Fe freight-yard space at Dallas. However, little money had yet been spent on the Texas properties, and trains had to move rather gingerly over the decrepit roadbed. And motive power was far from adequate: in a September 2, 1936, telegram to Pete Couch, R. R. Farmer complained that engine number 172, pulling a work train and local, had to run for water so often and double even the lightest grades (that is, break into two parts) that it was taking fourteen or fifteen hours a day to cover the 171 miles between Greenville and Shreveport. Farmer pleaded, "Would it be possible [to] let us have an engine that is larger than the 172?" Couch had N. Johnson, superintendent of the L&A, respond on September 4th:

> We are running two 550 class engines to Southern District Tuesday, September 8th. Hope to release the 100 class Thursday 10th, and deliver [to] you. As fast as we can work the 550's to the Southern District and release 100's will deliver until we have delivered three.[48]

The 100 class engines were numbered 100–106 and were the Russian decapods bought by William Edenborn shortly after World War I. They had good tractive effort and a bridge rating of E-37, barely within the E-38 limits of the Texas line. Number 172 was thoroughly antiquated: with three sisters, it had been delivered to the L&A in 1903. Although two of these four were scrapped in 1934 and 1936, number 172 would remain as a yard engine at Greenville until it was sold in 1946. This story shows that Pete Couch was a person of action and also that management interest in the Texas line was increasing.[49]

The mid-1930s continued to be kind to the L&A (see Table 8). With the nation's railroads generally in deplorable financial shape, its condition was almost unbelievable in financial circles. Although President Franklin Roosevelt's New Deal had given the economy a slight boost in 1935 and 1936, a downturn occurred in 1937. Harvey Couch and his associates were looking good indeed with their investment in a regional railroad in the depths of the slow-economy South.[50]

TABLE 8

Financial Results of L&A Operations

Depth of the Great Depression

Year	Gross Revenue	Net income	Operating Ratio
1934	$4,467,600	$291,800	65.8
1935	4,792,100	428,900	65.1
1936	5,537,800	334,400	67.8
1937	5,993,800	409,800	67.2

Source: Company annual reports.

By this time, Harvey Couch had acquired control of enough KCS stock to rate a position on its Board of Directors, and he not only joined the board in February 1937 but also became chairman of the Executive Committee of that body on May 27, 1937. Some interesting power plays were involved. Leonor F. Loree, called a "Patriarch of the Rails," had been chairman of the KCS board (and chairman of its Executive Committee) since 1907. He enjoyed an outstanding reputation as an engineer and railroad-operations man, and he had been president of the

Three KCS directors on March 24, 1937, en route to an inspection of the soon-to-be-acquired L&A properties. Left to right: Charles E. Johnston, KCS president; Kenneth Steere, a financier from New York; and Harvey Couch, KCS chairman. Couch had recently succeeded Steere as chairman of the KCS board. In the background is the joint KCS/Frisco passenger station at Fort Smith, Arkansas. (Photograph courtesy of John W. Barriger III)

Delaware and Hudson for the same period. He knew the railroad business backward and forward and had his supporters on the KCS board. The railroad had done quite well under his domineering leadership, but he was approaching the age of eighty, and the Couch interests felt that it was time for him to go. Under pressure he agreed to resign, effective January 1, 1937. The next year he would retire from the D&H, and he would live only until September, 1940. Loree was replaced in February 1937 by Kenneth Steere, of Paine Webber, the firm that had handled Couch's purchase of KCS stock and which had acquired voting rights of much additional stock. Steere, not at all a railroad man, simply retained his board position. For operations, Couch had Charles E. Johnston, who had been president of the KCS since 1928.[51]

The KCS had originally been built as the Kansas City, Pittsburg and Gulf, and its main line between Kansas City and Port Arthur, Texas, had been completed on September 11, 1897. Its builder was Arthur Stilwell, a flamboyant promoter from Kansas City who followed the dream of a short line from Kansas City to the Gulf. His idea was a good one, of course, but by the time the road had become profitable he had been ousted from it by impatient investors who did not share some of his strange ideas about running (and financing) a railroad. In 1936 the KCS had a gross revenue of $13,831,778, with 879 route-miles operated, and an attractive operating ratio of 63.1 percent. Net income was $580,375, as the road rebounded from deficits in 1932 through 1935. Its profit margin, though not as good as that of the L&A, was much better than that of most other railroads in the region.[52]

Couch and Johnston appear to have differed on a number of issues, and Johnston finally agreed to resign as president of the company, effective January 1, 1939. One point of difference seems to have been a plan of Couch for the KCS to acquire the L&A. In a letter dated February 26, 1938, Johnston expressed what appeared to be logical views on the acquisition:

I have long favored a plan that would extend the Kansas City Southern into New Orleans, and have at various times recommended the acquisition of lines to accomplish this. At one time purchase of the Louisiana Railway & Navigation Company was recommended, and another time the Louisiana & Arkansas was recommended. However, these acquisitions were not made due largely to the high cost and the realization that extension of the Kansas City Southern over its own rails into New Orleans might seriously disturb competitive conditions and a risk of losing more traffic than might be gained.

. . . While I still consider it very desirable that the Kansas City Southern, if practical to do so, should reach the port of New Orleans, this picture has changed in recent years in that the other old and new Gulf ports have grown to be comparatively much more important in the movement of water-rail traffic, and New Orleans, while still perhaps the most important port on the Gulf, does not now dominate the situation as in the past years. . . .

For the Kansas City Southern to reach New Orleans, the old Louisiana Railway & Navigation Company (now a part of the L. & A. system)—on account of distance and low grades—provides the most attractive route. Final decision in the matter, however, should hinge entirely on the cost to acquire this property. Consolidation of the Louisiana & Arkansas and Kansas City Southern would not improve the situation of the Kansas City Southern as it now is with respect to handling of land-water tonnage other than through the port of New Orleans.

A decided danger in the combined picture lies in the future operation of what is known as the Louisiana, Arkansas & Texas, extending from Shreveport to Dallas. It is not an economical line to operate; has no ownership of terminals at Dallas; enters both Dallas and Shreveport over a foreign line; and its grades, curvatures and distances are unfavorable to meet competitive conditions. . . . I question seriously that the Louisiana, Arkansas & Texas should be considered in any plan of consolidation incorporating the Kansas City Southern and the Louisiana & Arkansas.[53]

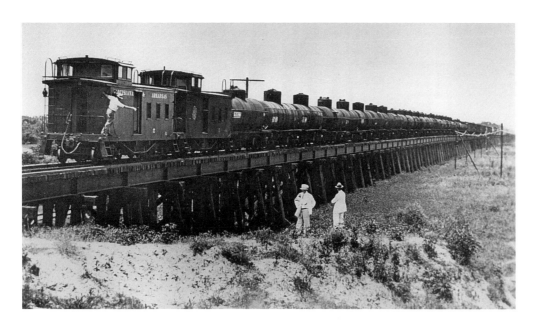

The first train to cross the Bonnet Carre trestle, in 1935. Witnessing the movement from below is E. F. Salisbury (facing the camera), chief engineer of the L&A. The train is northbound, and the old alignment is partly visible through the trestle bents. (Photograph courtesy of Harold K. Vollrath)

Johnston's departure gave Harvey the opportunity to bring his brother into the management of the KCS, and Pete would become president in August 1939. During the interim Harvey would perform as both president and chairman, and other important events would also happen for the KCS and L&A. On November 2, 1938, the KCS applied to the ICC for authority to acquire control, through purchase of capital stock, of the Louisiana and Arkansas Railway Company. And shortly afterward, on November 21, application was made to the same body for authority to issue up to 510,000 shares of common stock and up to 40,000 escrow receipts, pursuant to a plan of unification dated September 12, 1938. In the application it was noted that the KCS and L&A/LA&T operated 878.78 and 846.62 road miles of track, respectively.[54]

Perhaps the biggest news of 1938 was the completion of the huge paper mill near Springhill. On January 4 of that year the Couch brothers escorted 200 L&A traffic representatives to the construction site and to the adjoining new mill community at the station of Cullen. The capital cost of the mill was given as $12 million, and when running at full capacity it would consume the contents of 100 cars of pulpwood each day and would ship out some 50 cars per day of paper and chemical products. The Couch brothers announced to the group that the railroad was spending $800,000 for 550 pulpwood rack cars, to be delivered in time for the midyear startup of the mill. It was indeed a coup by the L&A to become the mill's only railroad connection, and through the years a great deal of attention would be given to it: some fifty railroad employees and two switch engines were assigned to the Cullen location. For many years there would be the familiar sight of pulpwood cars being loaded at remote sidings, to be picked up by L&A locals or by other railroads for transfer to the L&A.[55]

The proposed merger of the KCS and L&A was given due consideration by the ICC. Hearings were held in Washington on January 23 and 24, 1939, and on May 3 the ICC released its order authorizing control of the L&A by the KCS and also the issuance of stock as proposed. Then changes began to take place under the new management. For one thing, Pete Couch was made president of both railroads and was elected to the KCS Board, effective May 23. Another development at this time was ICC approval, on April 20, 1939, of the merger of the Louisiana, Arkansas and Texas (the "Texas line") into

An aerial view of the International Paper Co. mill at Cullen, near Springhill, Louisiana. The mill, built in 1937–38, created a large amount of traffic for the L&A. The view is toward the north, and the L&A tracks and Cullen depot can be seen on the right. A victim of advancing technology and depleting raw material, the mill closed in 1978. (Photograph courtesy of International Paper Company)

the L&A. An epochal event, it countermanded Texas law requiring all railroads in the state to be headquartered in Texas. The attorney general of the state entered into the argument, but the decision of the ICC prevailed. The L&A had to agree not to close the shops in Greenville but was permitted to close the general offices in that city. R. R. Farmer took retirement, and most of the other office employees in Greenville were transferred.[56]

Still another development dealt with motive power: the use of diesel-electric engines

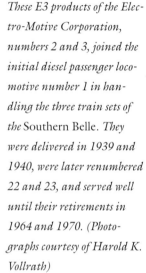

These E3 products of the Electro-Motive Corporation, numbers 2 and 3, joined the initial diesel passenger locomotive number 1 in handling the three train sets of the Southern Belle. *They were delivered in 1939 and 1940, were later renumbered 22 and 23, and served well until their retirements in 1964 and 1970. (Photographs courtesy of Harold K. Vollrath)*

for railroad locomotives was becoming accepted, and the success of the Union Pacific and Burlington lines with streamlined passenger trains was also generally recognized. It is likely that Couch, along with thousands of others, was able to view the new streamliners of these two railroads at the 1934 World's Fair in Chicago. Why not a streamliner for the KCS and L&A? The idea moved forward, and by early 1939 orders were placed with Electro-Motive Corporation for three diesel locomotives and with Pullman-Standard Car

View of the Baton Rouge bridge as it neared completion in spring 1940. This bridge made a tremendous difference in the operating efficiency of the L&A because it permitted retirement of the cumbersome Filston–Angola river transfer. The inauguration of the Southern Belle *awaited the completion of the bridge in September; it would be difficult to imagine such a fast streamliner cooling its heels for an hour during the slow river-transfer operation!*

Manufacturing Company for eleven lightweight passenger cars with a distinctive, streamlined styling, it being reported that Harvey Couch worked closely with the builder at the design stage. Matching sleepers would be constructed by Pullman and operated by that company as part of the KCS trains. This equipment would be emblazoned with a new logo with the inscription "KCS/L&A Lines."[57]

For reasons more financial than openly apparent, the L&A would continue to operate as a separate company even though it was wholly owned by the KCS. Headquarters would be retained in Shreveport. In fact, formal "purchase" of several steam locomotives from the KCS would be made, involving power too light for the KCS but quite suitable for the low grades of the L&A. A major undertaking of the L&A was to complete the rehabilitation

of the river line in order that the streamliners and heavy freight trains could take advantage of its good alignment and shortened distance. Thus, matters were beginning to come together: a larger corporate operating base, a new bridge over the Mississippi, new industries on line, and a symbol passenger train to represent the L&A (and the KCS) to the world as a modern, first-class operation. In addition, the war in Europe was helping to hike revenues and profits for the L&A.[58]

Two of the diesel units were on hand by August 1939 and were placed in Kansas City–Shreveport service. They were given road numbers 1 and 2 and were Electro-Motive E-3 types with 2,000 horsepower each. The third diesel, number 3, with the same specifications, did not arrive until June 1940. The streamliners were to run between Kansas City and New Orleans, and to meet the planned schedules three train sets would be required. Each set would comprise a baggage-mail car, a chair car, a Pullman sleeper, and an observation-parlor-diner car. The three sets would utilize nine company-owned cars; hence the order of eleven cars to provide backup flexibility.[59]

The year 1940 was perhaps the most exciting one in the L&A's history. The economy was booming, although dark clouds of war were on the horizon of the United States. The new paper mill was moving toward full operation. Motive-power needs had been bolstered by the purchase of eight steamers from the KCS, and the relatively new heavy mikados (560 series) were performing well. All freight locomotives carried auxiliary water cars to increase run times: with such help a locomotive could operate from Shreveport to Filston with only one water stop and no need for adding fuel oil. The river line was put into use, which shortened schedules noticeably. Modest repairs were made to the T&P line between Torras and Lobdell, although the old and light rail plus poor ballast remained a problem and provoked severe speed restrictions. The Baton Rouge bridge, somewhat behind construction schedule, would be ready by late summer. As a result of a contest, the name *Southern Belle* was selected for the new streamliner, possibly influenced by a train with the same name that had operated in England for many years.[60]

In 1940 the railroad was also able to unburden itself of the branch line from Farmersville to McKinney, Texas. This was part of the Greenville extension to the west that had been completed during the 1881 takeover of the East Line and Red River by the Katy. Service on the line had dropped to a triweekly freight train that had to move very slowly over the original fifty-two-pound rail and a shaky roadbed that had never known ballast. The primary business of the branch was onion shipments from Princeton and interchange cotton movements. The application for abandonment was made to the ICC in September 1939, and approval by that body was obtained on February 20, 1940. McKinney and Princeton would

be served by Landa Motor Lines. This company was permitted to handle freight between Shreveport and Dallas as well as between Farmersville and McKinney. It did not actively commence operations until March 7, 1941.[61]

Major changes in passenger-train schedules and operations went into effect May 26, 1940. For the first time, L&A trains began to use the Union Station in Shreveport. Also for the first time, fast passenger service began on the river line. Diesel power continued in use north of Shreveport. The *Hustler,* which in 1939 had been combined with the *Shreveporter* between Minden and Shreveport, now became an integral part of through Kansas City–New Orleans service; a "deluxe chair car" went the entire distance, and the sleeper was added at Shreveport. The train was advertised simply as number 1 southbound and number 2 northbound, and its diesel power north of Shreveport was noted. South of Shreveport the river line was used, with steam power, and passenger service on the high line via Minden and Winnfield was provided by bus. Train number 1 was clearly a forerunner of the *Southern Belle,* which still awaited receipt of all passenger cars from Pullman as well as completion of the Baton Rouge bridge.[62]

At last all was in readiness. The bridge was opened to L&A rail traffic prematurely on August 10, because of blockage of the line south of Angola by slides. Dedication ceremonies for the bridge came on September 1. The *Southern Belle* had a ten-day publicity tour of the route followed by a "preview ceremony" in New Orleans on August 24. For this event a special trip of the *Belle* was made, leaving Kansas City on August 23 and along the way picking up beauty queens selected by local groups at Kansas City, Pittsburg, Kansas, Joplin, Missouri, and so on down the line. When the train arrived in New Orleans fourteen comely ladies were aboard, and the reigning queen would be selected from among them by a panel of judges. According to KCS publicity,

At 7 o'clock [in the morning] the train eased into Rampart Station in New Orleans. . . . The

The schedule for the north-bound Shreveporter *was arranged for convenient travel to the north and east through the St. Louis gateway.*

The KCS/L&A spruced up its passenger timetable when joint train service began in 1940. Here a photograph of a real southern belle, Margaret Landry, is superimposed on her namesake train. The schedules inside show double daily passenger service between Shreveport and New Orleans, with bus coverage of the "high line" territory south of Minden. The Shreveporter *was still carried as a named train between Hope and Shreveport, but the equipment (other than the sleeper) returned to Hope as part of a mixed train.*

group went to the Roosevelt Hotel for breakfast and the young ladies toured New Orleans in horse-drawn carriages. They then went to Arnaud's for lunch, after which they hurried to Pontchartrain Beach for the final judging. . . . When the judges called Margaret Landry's name, she broke out in tears.

Margaret Landry had boarded the train at Baton Rouge early that morning, and now she had been selected the ruling queen, "Miss Southern Belle." She participated in publicity activities of the railroad for several years.[63]

For their first official runs, the two *Belles* left Kansas City and New Orleans on September 2. The southbound schedule called for a 10:00 A.M. departure from Kansas City, with a 7:00 A.M. arrival the next day at the Rampart Street station in New Orleans. For the northbound journey there was an 11:00 P.M. departure from New Orleans and a 7:55 P.M. arrival in Kansas City. Between Shreveport and New Orleans an extra sleeper (fugitive from *Hustler* operation) and one or two extra heavyweight head-end cars were added. And a second train was added on the river line, a connection for the *Flying Crow*, which ran between Kansas City and Port Arthur, Texas (as it had for years). This train went south from Shreveport in the afternoon and north from New Orleans in the morning. No through cars between Kansas City and New Orleans were carried, but the transfer at Shreveport was across-the-platform.[64]

The bridge opening cut at least one hour off the running time for passenger trains and permitted the ferry operation to end. For freight trains, however, it introduced some problems. One difficulty was that the seventy-pound rail between Torras and Lobdell was too light for the heavy power of the L&A. The branch line had not been built to high standards and almost literally had been allowed by the T&P to vegetate. Another problem was the 1.25 percent grade on the approach to the bridge from the west: this usually required a helper engine, or doubling the grade. Still, one can understand why the Couch brothers were euphoric and indulgent

with their time when it came to the *Southern Belle*, which was generally acknowledged to be Harvey's brainchild. The *Belle* was indeed an attractive train, with an exterior color scheme of olive green sides with red and yellow trim and aluminum-painted roofs. The interiors were richly decorated, and every effort was made to transport passengers into a new world when they boarded the train. As can be imagined, the display train attracted throngs of people when it toured the line. The railroad was aggressive with publicity; and a song, "Southern Belle," was even written about the train and distributed as sheet music.[65]

TABLE 9

Financial Results of L&A Operations

Outset of World War II

Year	Gross Revenue	Net income	Operating Ratio
1938	$5,815,867	$521,836	65.0
1939	6,769,395	737,630	62.6
1940	7,870,019	789,796	65.2

Source: Company reports.

Indeed, business was almost too good. But the financial results for the last years of the decade provided solid support for the enthusiasm of the L&A group (see Table 9). The influence of the paper mill may be judged from the following data. In 1940, 8,794 carloads of paper and chemical products were shipped from the mill, and 17,500 carloads of pulpwood were received. Of the latter, about one-third were originated online, and the others were received by the L&A from neighboring roads such as the Illinois Central and the T&P. The following year the figures rose by about 50 percent. And if this were not enough, plans were afoot to build a large steel mill near Daingerfield on the Texas line—with the L&A being the only road to serve it![66]

The ICC deliberated the acquisition of the RIA&L for more than three years, which was not unusual in that the reorganization of the entire Rock Island system was under consideration. During this period the ICC approved the affiliation of the L&A and the KCS, which weakened the L&A's argument that it needed an outlet to the north. On October 31, 1940, the ICC decided that the best interests of the public (including the L&A) would be served if the Rock Island were allowed to emerge from bankruptcy intact. By this time, Harvey Couch seemed to have lost interest in acquiring the RIA&L.[67]

But even into a happy life some rain must fall, as the saying goes. Harvey Couch had been troubled by various minor illnesses in 1940, and late in the year he suffered a heart attack while on a business trip to the East. At the end of the year he retired to Couchwood. This rural complex featured a central, large, log cabin–type structure with a number of satellite buildings, and it was Harvey's retreat from the business world as well as a prime location for entertaining business and political guests. Although he was not confined to Couchwood in the latter part of 1940, he seemed to recognize that he was nearing the end. He turned over much of his Arkansas Power and Light affairs to Hamilton Moses and his KCS/L&A affairs to Pete Couch. After the beginning of 1941 he never again left Couchwood, and he died there early in the morning of July 30. The funeral was held at Pine Bluff, where he had maintained his pri-mary residence for many years, on July 31. Of importance to this narrative, one of the diesel locomotives and several cars of the *Southern Belle* were diverted to Pine Bluff to serve as a funeral train, carrying the body from Pine Bluff to Magnolia for burial, using the Cotton Belt to McNeil and the Louisiana and North West the rest of the way. The press covered the funeral proceedings in great detail and remarked on how the *Belle*—or a part of it—could be the only means that Harvey would want to use on his last trip.[68]

Thus, the Harvey Couch era of the L&A ended. There is no question but that he had exerted a profound influence on the railroad, and it seemed that all his ideas were good ones. The continued progress and profitability of his electric-utility business are not chronicled here; nor is the extensive effort that he made in public service and charitable endeavors. Details on his "whole" life may be found in the two biographies that have been published in book form and in the many newspaper articles that underscore what a rich life he had led and how tragic it was that he should die at the age of sixty-three.

Now the leadership of the L&A would rest on the shoulders of brother Pete. Many people were concerned about this. The railroad was about to meet a severe test—that of handling wartime traffic. Was Pete up to it?

The entry of the United States into World War II in December 1941 found the L&A already busy with wartime efforts. Its passenger trains were crowded with people and overloaded with mail and express shipments. Its switch engines were laboring diligently at such places as Cullen, Greenville, Minden, Alexandria, Baton Rouge, New Orleans, and Shreveport. Extra freight trains on the main lines were standard practice. Work on upgrading the Texas line was under way, with ninety-pound rail and fresh ballast being laid west of Waskom, toward Jefferson. The ICC had approved an arrangement that permitted the L&A to rehabilitate completely the T&P line from Torras Junction to Lobdell, and by the end of 1941, 37.5 miles of ninety-pound rail had been installed on this property that did not belong to the L&A.[1]

The Longhorn Ordnance Works, at Karnack, Texas, 37 miles west of Shreveport, was one of the early war-related installations along the L&A. Construction began in late 1941. This plant would produce enormous quantities of tri-nitrotoluene (TNT), the high explosive so vital to the effort of the Allies. Farther to the west on the Texas line, near Daingerfield, plans were going forward for a large steel mill based on East Texas iron ore and Oklahoma coal or Texas lignite. At a new station designated Doyline, 4.4 miles west of Minden on the Shreveport line, the Louisiana Ordnance Plant was also under construction. This installation, an "ammunition plant," would take high explosives and load them into shells of various types. In the Baton Rouge–New Orleans area, government-sponsored chemical plants and oil refineries were being expanded, especially for the production of high-octane fuel and raw materials for synthetic rubber. The L&A was able to take advantage of this surge in business activity, despite being short

of motive power; in this regard regular calls were made to the KCS for assistance.[2]

To be sure, sad events also took place. Foremost was the loss of Harvey Couch and his vision and business acumen. The colorful *William* and *Sarah* steamboats were no longer plying their river course between Filston and Angola, but they remained useful in towing service for Standard Oil at Baton Rouge. The inclines and trackage at Filston and Angola were abandoned and dismantled. It was sad also to note that the last Buchanan sawmill, at Trout (just west of Jena), was beginning to wind down its operations. Now, reforestation of the woodlands was in full sway, much of it directed toward the hungry appetite of paper mills for pulpwood billets. And the chuffing of steam locomotives was heard only occasionally on the former main line of the LR&N from Angola to Baton Rouge; petitions for the abandonment of this section were being made to the ICC.[3]

With the domestic war effort surging forward in 1942, all parts of the system were busy, including the previously neglected Texas line, now finally receiving some top-management attention. No passenger service was provided in Texas, the last mixed train having run on October 19, 1938. Bus transportation appeared to suffice for local needs, and the T&P was certainly capable of handling through passengers between Shreveport and Dallas. On the rest of the system, there was double daily passenger service between Shreveport and New Orleans, the *Southern Belle* being paired with the *Flying Crow*. The *Belle* used diesel-electric locomotives, but all other trains, freight and passenger, remained with steam power. The L&A did manage to obtain priorities to purchase two 1000-HP diesel switch engines from the Electro-Motive Division of General Motors. These NW-2

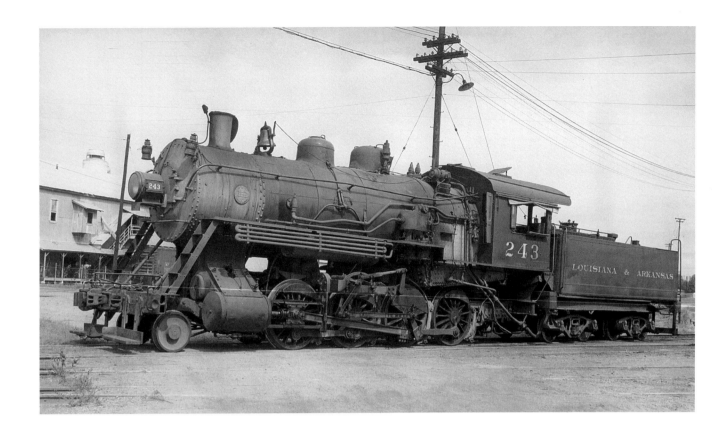

A 1903 product of the Brooks Locomotive Works, consolidation engine number 243 was purchased in 1924 by the LR&N for service on the Texas line. Along with its sister engines, numbers 241 and 242, it came from the Buffalo, Rochester and Pittsburgh and was rated at 1,000 tons on the westbound ruling grade between Hughes Springs and Winnsboro—20 percent less than the tonnage rating of the 100-series decapods that later served the same territory. Here number 243 is somewhere in East Texas in the 1940s, now lettered for the L&A. It was scrapped at Minden in 1950. (Photograph by Robert Foster; courtesy of Lloyd Neal)

types, numbers 1125 and 1126, arrived in January 1942. They were the first diesels to be owned by the L&A, and there would be no further such additions to the roster until diesel F7A number 59A came along in October 1948.[4]

In East Texas, the Longhorn Works started operations in October 1942 and almost immediately began to set production records. The elaborate trackage around this plant was serviced by two center-cab General Electric diesel-electrics of the U.S. Ordnance Department, and each day strings of tank cars were switched through the gates by the L&A local; these cars, containing ammonia, sulfuric acid, nitric acid, and toluene, were exchanged for outgoing boxcars of flake TNT. One could stand at the entrance to the plant and observe through freight trains headed west and gathering momentum for the 0.5 percent grade just beyond the Karnack depot. Many of these freight trains were double-headed, with assorted ancient steam engines that had been rehabilitated at Minden for the wartime needs.[5]

By the end of 1942 most of the little-used St. Francisville–Baton Rouge branch had been retired. The portion between St. Francisville and Paloma was abandoned, and the Paloma–Maryland portion was sold to the

South Shore Railway, a private carrier, to connect with its existing line north from Paloma to Jackson. The Maryland–North Baton Rouge segment was retained by the L&A for industrial switching. This left the orphan line from Angola to St. Francisville up for sale or abandonment; while continuing to operate, mostly for the benefit of the state penal farm at Angola, it exchanged with the Y&MV at St. Francisville.[6]

Miles away, in the executive suite in Kansas City, Pete Couch, chairman of the boards and president of both the KCS and the L&A, now bereft of his brother's protection, was in deep trouble. A Kansas City group led by R. Crosby Kemper, president of the City National Bank and Trust Company, was attempting to wrest control of the KCS from the "New York group" that was basically the Harvey Couch syndicate. Kemper was a member of the KCS Board of Directors and a supporter of Harvey Couch—but not of Pete Couch. The Kansas City group included Grant Stauffer, president of Sinclair Coal Co., one of the largest shippers on the KCS, and James J. Lynn, president of U.S. Epperson Underwriting Co. The Kansas Citians, with allies from the KCS territory, were intent on placing fifty-three-year-old William N. "Bill" Deramus in charge of the railroad system. A railroader since 1903, Deramus hired into the KCS in 1909 as a telegraph operator and had risen to the executive vice presidency on August 1, 1939. His capability was acknowledged by industry peers, and his KCS supporters had little respect for Pete Couch, who certainly did not have the depth of Deramus's experience and, furthermore, had marred his reputation by a propensity for liquor. The locals garnered enough votes to unseat Pete as president and replace him with Deramus. The latter was elected president of the KCS on September 22, 1941, and of the L&A on October 1, after a struggle that received national attention.[7]

Pete Couch had enough votes to remain on the board and was allowed to retain his chairman's position, for he could do little harm in his minority position. During the next three years the Kemper group expanded to include S. E. Gilinsky, an Omaha produce merchant; John D. Ewing, owner of the *Shreveport Times;* Randle T. Moore, a Shreveport lumberman; and Joseph D. Brown, a Fort Smith, Arkansas, attorney. And there were others from the territory served by the

KCS and L&A. Through open-market purchases the Kemper group ran up its holdings of KCS voting stock to 47 percent of the outstanding shares. Furthermore, they reached an understanding with Dutch interests, holding an additional 20 percent of the voting shares, that those shares would remain completely neutral in the event of a proxy fight with the New York group. (The Dutch holdings were based on the financing of the original construction of the KCS.)[8]

The showdown came on April 4, 1944, when Pete Couch was ousted completely from both railroads, and Brown, Ewing, Gilinsky, Lynn, Moore, and Stauffer moved onto the KCS board. Deramus became chairman of the board, and Stauffer chairman of the Executive Committee. Main Street had outmaneuvered Wall Street, but Charles McCain, so influential in helping finance Harvey Couch, was one member of the New York group who would remain on the board for many years.[9]

Pete Couch immediately headed for Shreveport to pursue other interests. He and other members of the Couch family still

The first diesel-electric locomotives purchased by the L&A were 1000 HP switchers, numbers 1125 and 1126, delivered from the Electro-Motive Division of General Motors in January 1942 with the designation NW-2. Here number 1126 is on what appears to be the Shreveport turntable of the KCS. (Photograph courtesy of Goodyear Collection, De-Golyer Library, Southern Methodist University)

A freight train leaving Minden for Winnfield and Vidalia, pulled by Louisiana Midland ten-wheeler locomotive number 503, formerly L&A number 503, on July 17, 1948. This appears to be a Natchez Route train, normally pulled by L&A power between Minden and Vidalia. The Minden turntable is at the far right. (Photograph by C. W. Witbeck; courtesy of H. H. Holloway Jr.)

owned a sizable percentage of the voting shares, however, and for many years some member of the family would remain on the Board of Directors of the KCS/L&A. The first family representative was Johnson O. Couch, son of Harvey and an employee of the KCS. In effect, the move to put Deramus in charge served to integrate further the two lines and to remove much of the identity of the L&A as a separate railroad enterprise.[10]

Returning to the L&A territory, the redundant Angola branch, now reduced to 19.63 miles between Angola and St. Francisville, was finally disposed of in late 1943. The L&A had applied to the ICC for abandonment, but the State of Louisiana protested on the basis that the line was necessary for the penal farm at Angola. The railroad brought in oil for the boilers and carried out farm produce as well as blackstrap molasses from the sugar-refining operations. The L&A offered to truck these materials, operating through its subsidiary, the L&A Transportation Company. The ICC denied abandonment, so the line was sold to the Holloway interests, who would operate the line as the West Feliciana Railroad, a common carrier with intrastate status. By early 1948 this short line would be abandoned, underscoring the contention of the L&A that it could not be profitable.[11]

In late 1945, the Vidalia branch was put on the market, being recognized as a marginal property in the longer-range plans of the KCS management. On August 24, 1945, just after the end of the war in the Pacific, a new railroad was organized, the Louisiana Midland Railway Company. This enterprise was formed to purchase the properties and rights of the L&A line between Packton and Vidalia. The "rights" included the lease of Missouri Pacific tracks from Wildsville Junction (across the Black River from Jonesville) to Concordia Junction (Ferriday) and trackage rights over the Missouri Pacific from that point on to Vidalia. Hamric Holloway of Baton Rouge, the identified purchaser, had prospered in the sand-and-gravel business and now, with the aid of his son Hamric Jr., was ready to satisfy a long-time urge to have his own line-haul railroad. (He had earlier purchased parts of the Angola–Baton Rouge line, operating them as the West Feliciana and South Shore lines, as noted above.) In this sense he was fashioned from the same material as William Buchanan, William Edenborn, and Harvey Couch.[12]

The LM bought the Vidalia branch for $2.5 million; the purchase included three steam locomotives (numbers 101, 102, and 104, all Russian decapods of the 2-10-0 wheel arrangement). On January 1, 1946, operations were taken over by the Midland. As part of the purchase agreement, as observed by the ICC,

The operation was unusual in that the LM [Louisiana Midland] did not run its trains with its own employees. . . . [T]he L&A employees would operate trains for the LM as the LM might direct. These were freight trains Nos. 51 eastbound and 52 westbound, operating seven days a week from Packton to Vidalia and return. The same two brakemen would work the round trip. . . . The turnaround at Vidalia took the crew's mileage beyond 100 miles per day and resulted in the crewmembers collecting pay in addition to the basic pay.[13]

Thus, the Natchez Route was preserved and Mississippi–Texas freight trains continued to roll through such towns as Jonesville, Georgetown, and Ashland. The steam locomotives purchased from the L&A were usu-ally assigned to local service, with the power for through freight trains 51 and 52 being supplied by the L&A. The Midland operations were under the direction of General Manager L. B. Williams, who had been one of Edenborn's key employees; operating headquarters were in the depot building at Jena.[14]

With the winding down of the war in 1945 the L&A—even the former "ugly-duckling" line in Texas—was doing exceedingly well. The Texas line had been rehabilitated (though left with some steep grades and sharp curves), and the rail and bridges were now heavy enough to support 550-class mikado engines. These engines could take strings of freight cars into Dallas, the Santa Fe yards and shops at that location being used by the L&A with the Santa Fe handling the switching. The government-sponsored steel mill at Daingerfield had not yet been placed in operation and was sold to newly organized Lone Star Steel Company; the sale included a 7.6-mile spur line from the L&A at Veals, Texas. This spur was incorporated on August 4, 1948, as the Texas and Northern Railway Company.[15]

The bluff at Natchez, Mississippi, required a switchback to gain elevation, as shown in this June 1948 view. The James Y. Lockwood *transfer steamer, shown at the foot of the incline, was replaced by a diesel-powered tugboat in 1961, and the entire transfer operation was shut down in 1982. (Photograph by C. W. Witbeck)*

Joseph Goulden called the latter half of the 1940s "the best years" for the country: the Great War was over, and the Korean War had not begun. Industry was busy catching up with the needs of war-deprived citizens and returning veterans. The country had an expansive feeling, founded on successes in Europe and the Pacific. On the other hand, the high volumes of rail-freight traffic for military support could not be expected to continue. But these years were indeed good ones for the L&A (see Table 10). The growth in traffic during the war years was significant, and the railroad managed to counter the national trend and maintain traffic at high levels. The L&A territory was rich in petroleum refining and petrochemicals manufacturing, and these industries undertook large capital expansions in the late 1940s. The KCS management became more attentive to the L&A—and could not deny that the smaller road was generating as good a profit as the larger one. In 1946, the first full peacetime year, both roads showed net earnings equal to 12.2 percent of gross operating revenue—a margin that would be the envy of any company in any industry.[16]

Capital projects for the L&A were extensive. A new eight-track yard holding 374 cars was installed at Baton Rouge. Construction went forward on a new shops and yard facility for New Orleans, the location to be at Shrewsbury (in the suburb of Metairie) on the outskirts of the Crescent City. New brick depots were built at Cullen and Springhill, and a new frame one was erected at Cotton Valley. Importantly, the railroad was cooperating with the City of New Orleans in its planning for a new union passenger terminal, to replace the extant five stations spread out around the downtown area.[17]

A strong motivation for the new terminal was the elimination of many grade crossings in New Orleans. By 1945 pressure from the Chamber of Commerce forced the mayor, Robert Maestri, to create a Railroad Terminal Board to launch a definitive cooperative project between the city and the railroads. An earlier study had placed the new terminal near the Rampart Street station of the L&A but would do away with the L&A trackage, warehouses, and shops. The study, by a group of consulting engineers, was thorough and pro-

TABLE 10

Freight-traffic Densities on the L&A

1938 & 1945 [a]

	1938		1945	
	Southbound	*Northbound*	*Southbound*	*Northbound*
Shreveport–Minden	5.9	7.6	15.7	14.9
Minden–Winnfield	5.8	5.1	6.7	9.2
Winnfield–Alexandria	6.8	3.4	9.2	3.7
Mississippi River–New Orleans	9.0	4.0	16.6	7.7
Winnfield–Vidalia	2.6	1.6	—[b]	—[b]
Hope–Minden	3.4	3.6	7.9	9.0
Dallas–Greenville	1.3	1.4	5.0	4.3
Greenville–Shreveport	2.2	3.5	7.7	7.5
Shreveport–Alexandria	3.0	0.9	—[c]	—[c]

[a]   The data represent 100,000 net tons miles per mile.

[b]   In 1945, the Vidalia branch was considered sold to the Louisiana Midland.

[c]   Data are not available.

Source: Company records.

vides insight into the mode of operation of the L&A in the 1943–1944 period (see Appendix A). On April 15, 1947, voters approved a bond issue to cover about half of the total estimated cost of $33 million, with the railroads to pay the other half. This idea was not especially well received by the railroads, because they were progressing quite well with the five-station idea and were not overly concerned about traffic tie-ups caused by their trains. But they provided proper cooperation, and the project went forward. One result of the action was a need by the L&A to move its shops out to the Shrewsbury ("West Yard") location and cure a long-standing problem of widely separated shops and freight-terminal facilities. (Switching operations in New Orleans had always been awkward: see Appendix A.) Thus new developments for the L&A at Shrewsbury included opening a new yard office and other modern facilities in April 1950. But it would be several years before the new union passenger terminal would open.[18]

At about this time the KCS/L&A management demonstrated a concrete interest in providing highest-quality service to its passenger-train patrons. The 1940-vintage streamlined equipment was largely worn out, and on April 3, 1949, new equipment went into service after being exhibited at forty locations along the railroad. The equipment had been on order for several years and included two mail-bag-gage-dormitory cars, six chair cars with "sleepy hollow" seats, eight sleepers with bedrooms and roomettes, two dining cars, and three tavern-lounge-observation cars. With new F7-type diesel electric locomotives to pull the trains, the investment in this equipment was said to be about $24 million.[19]

The *Belle* schedule between Kansas City and New Orleans was speeded up to eighteen hours, which made two train sets workable. Also, the older passenger equipment was rehabilitated for use in secondary trains, and the April 3, 1949, schedule showed three trains each way between Shreveport and New Orleans! This thrice-daily schedule included restoration of passenger trains to the L&A high line, with numbers 5 and 6, the *Flying Crow*, stopping at Minden, Sibley, and Winnfield;

The facade of the Rampart Street Station, New Orleans, in the late 1940s. The neon sign includes an airplane to indicate the business of KCS Skyways, a 1946–1949 cargo-carrying venture that did not pan out. The building was demolished after the New Orleans Union terminal opened. (Photograph courtesy of Charles Winters, Fink Collection, University of Oklahoma)

The quiet platform of the Rampart Street Station in New Orleans on an afternoon in the 1940s. Arrivals and departures were in the morning and evening, at which times the scene was bustling. The stub-end arrangement required arriving trains to head into the station and then back to the Shrewsbury wye for turning. (Photograph courtesy of the New Orleans Times-Picayune*)*

The New Orleans Terminal
Project brought many
changes in the rail lines of
New Orleans. Here, "before"
and "after" maps include the
changes undergone by the
L&A. (Reproduced from
Railway Age, April 26,
1954)

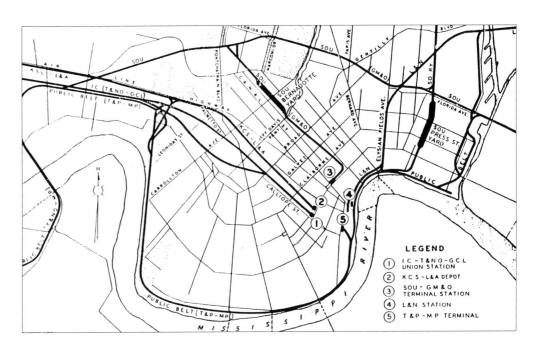

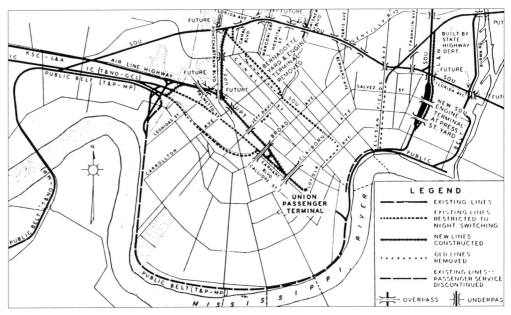

and nine other stations had flag-stop accommodations. This was a day train that carried coaches and a diner-lounge. The third train, numbers 9 and 10, was on the old *Belle* schedule and provided overnight sleeper accommodations between Shreveport and New Orleans. This extensive service between the Louisiana cities seems overly aggressive in view of postwar commercial airline and automobile inroads, and indeed one of the trains (numbers 9 and 10) would have to be re-

moved from the schedules in late 1950.[20]

The new passenger terminal at New Orleans opened on April 14, 1954, and on the day before, the last L&A trains arrived and departed from the Rampart Street station, just two blocks or so from the new terminal. The new facilities were indeed impressive, with twelve stub-end tracks of ten- to twenty-car capacity and six concrete platforms with butterfly sheds. They also boasted a five-track coach-servicing yard, an eight-track hold

New Orleans Union Passenger Terminal

The New Orleans Passenger Terminal opened in April 1954 and was the most visible component of a $56 million project that included the elimination of grade crossings, the closing of five separate passenger stations, and extensive rerouting of rail trackage around the city. But the patrons of the Southern Belle *now had a much more comfortable facility for their Crescent City arrivals and departures.*

yard, a double-track wye for turning trains, and well-equipped buildings for servicing diesel locomotives and passenger cars. The statistics were formidable: more than eighty grade crossings were eliminated, and many others were made much less dangerous; and the total cost had escalated to $56 million, about 44 percent of which was paid by the railroads. The station building itself had a sandstone-and-granite exterior and was fully air conditioned. By the time of the opening, however, passenger-train service was on the decline, and the twenty-three trains arriving and twenty-three departing would have seemed rather ordinary in wartime.[21]

Now the *Southern Belle* and its companion train, the *Flying Crow,* had an attractive and exciting terminus in which to disembark or board passengers. During the May 1 dedication ceremonies, young Corrine Morrison, daughter of Mayor DeLesseps Morrison, broke a bottle of waters gathered from both oceans, the Gulf, the Great Lakes, and the Mississippi River tributary system (all touched by scheduled trains departing from the station). Accompanying the dedication ceremonies was a display of modern passenger-train equipment that included a fourteen-roomette, four-double-bedroom car of the *Belle.*[22]

The passenger-train business makes for interesting reporting, but it was, of course, the freight business that kept the profits rolling in during the 1950s. National inflation was low and business recessions largely absent, partly because of the Korean War. One important line of business was in paper and forest products. Most of the larger sawmills along the L&A had closed, giving way to small specialty mills that processed hardwoods. But the pulp-and-paper business, especially in the Springhill vicinity, was booming. Mention has been made earlier of the International Paper Company mill at Cullen, near Springhill. A report in 1952 showed such statistics as 3,000 or more cars of pulpwood billets received each month, along with 150–200 cars of other commodities. (The Minden north yard was the gathering area for pulpwood cars, and extra freight trains were often used to move the cars to the Cullen area.) During the same month, some 1,500 cars of paper and chemical products left the plant. This activity utilized fifty L&A employees, including four train crews using two switch engines, each on two-shift schedules. In addition to International's needs, these crews served several chemical plants that were fed by products from the paper mill. The legacy of Harvey

View from the five-stall roundhouse at Shreveport, looking east toward Silver Lake Junction and the Red River bridge, on July 18, 1948. The intrusion of diesel power into the domain of steam is evident from the nose of a 2,000-horsepower Fairbanks-Morse unit. Number 51, a heavy 0-8-0 switcher, was acquired from the Florida East Coast in 1930. (Photograph by C. W. Witbeck)

Couch, who had been instrumental in attracting the paper company to L&A trackside, lived on in this profitable undertaking.[23]

The latter half of the 1950s saw a consolidation and general upgrading of the L&A properties, coordinated through the KCS. One notable example was a gross improvement in the Shreveport facilities. Since the acquisition of the L&A by the KCS in 1938, two freight yards had been in use at that city, the old Silver Lake yards of the L&A being connected with the KCS Harriet Street yards by a line that ran past the Union Station and in fact ran down the middle of Lake Street. The L&A yards were not large enough to accommodate the hundred-plus car freight trains that were being dispatched to New Orleans, it being necessary to ferry half the train over to Bossier City and then return for the other half. Moreover, the use of two roundhouses and sets of repair shops was patently inefficient. Accordingly, the railroad set about developing a new, integrated classification yard and shops on 257 acres purchased near the town of Blanchard, just north of Cross Lake and the city limits of Shreveport.[24]

Two other early-1950s projects involved line changes. In Texas, the eastbound hill between Daingerfield and Veals had, at 1.6 percent, represented the limiting grade on the system; a 550-class mikado locomotive could only handle 1,450 tons without help, as could an F7 diesel (1,500-horsepower) unit. During 1952, a new alignment was placed in operation that increased the tonnage ratings for all

locomotives by about 35 percent. In Louisiana, problems had continued with the L&A/T&P trackage between Simmesport and Lettsworth. According to Paul Sippel,

we had to re-lay with new rail and ballast the entire line from Torras Junction to Lobdell because the old [T&P] line would not stand the heavy traffic. We sloped, widened the embankment, and drained the road bed. Even had to purchase for this purpose additional right-of-way, and agreed to maintain fences for the adjoining property owners . . . and still . . . we found the track hard to maintain, especially south of New Roads where it runs along the Mississippi River levee. [We] also had to build about five miles of new track for the approaches and crossing of the Morganza Spillway.[25]

In addition, a tight curve at Torras Junction, where the T&P connection was made, not only slowed the passenger trains but was a cause of numerous derailments. To correct this situation, a new six-mile line was surveyed between Simmesport and Lettsworth that bypassed Torras Junction, shortened the total distance by four miles, and permitted high-speed running by the passenger trains.[26]

This new line in Louisiana was placed in operation in 1953, but not before a terrible wreck, by far the worst in the history of the L&A, occurred 1.67 miles north of Lettsworth. On August 10, 1951, a northbound troop train collided head-on with the southbound *Southern Belle,* killing thirteen people and injuring another eighty-two. The troop train, with diesels 59D and 78C and sixteen cars, was traveling at 40 miles per hour and disregarded a train order to take a siding at Lettsworth. The *Belle,* with diesels 23 and 32A and six cars, was traveling at the speed limit of 55 miles per hour. The accident occurred at 7:02 A.M. on a long curve, where trackside vegetation obscured visibility. The list of dead included seven train-service employees. Paul Sippel, then assistant to the president, joined President Deramus in a chartered flight to the accident scene. In his recollections, Sippel made the following observations:

[We] spent over 24 hours at the wreck, without sleep and . . . without food. I lived on black coffee, which was made on the wrecker, and it made me sick. The weather was hot, and the flames from the coaches must have been 2,000 or more degrees because it [*sic*] melted the aluminum and even the steel of the Pullmans and coaches. After a long, long search, we finally found the last missing man, who was a Marine, in one of the Pullmans, and it was because the sun happened to be shining through a crack or break in the wall. Only his torso remained.[27]

Little of the equipment was salvageable. The accident made national headlines, and it also drew attention to the then-controversial use of radio dispatching, recently initiated by the L&A.

Returning to the new shops and yards for Shreveport, the projected capital investment of $6 million was approved by the Board in 1953, and the project was reported well on its way to completion in April 1955. By this time named Deramus Yard, it had some impressive features: 60 miles of track, trackage to accommodate 4,500 cars, thirty classification tracks, and thirty-seven structures, including a three-story office building, a freight house, and repair shops for locomotives and freight cars. At the time of its opening, about one thousand workers were at the site. Dedication ceremonies were held on March 24, 1956, with speeches by William Deramus and James Gardner, mayor of Shreveport. The KCS started using the facility on April 1; the L&A, on April 22. Concurrently the older shops of the L&A and KCS were shut down, as were the shops at Minden (except for providing light running repairs to equipment). This consolidation led to many efficiencies, and the long trains headed south or north could be made up at Deramus. Yet southbound L&A freight trains still had to find their way down Lake Street, rumbling across the Marshall Street overpass and past the now-neglected Central Station building.[28]

As a part of this Shreveport realignment, a new route was constructed to connect with the Texas line at Karnack. Through the years,

NEW DERAMUS YARD
Shreveport, Louisiana

L&A trains used the VS&P (now Illinois Central) tracks between Shreveport and Waskom, together with company tracks between Waskom and Karnack. The new line measured 16.58 miles, was laid with hundred-pound rail, and ran directly (with only one curve) between Karnack and a point (appropriately named Texas Junction) just north of the new Deramus Yard. The 13.64-mile-long track between Karnack and Waskom was abandoned. No longer did L&A trains have to move through a complicated, two-switch crossing over the T&P at Waskom and pay for use of the Illinois Central tracks. With the yards now north of Shreveport, the direct connection

The new Deramus Yard just north of Shreveport was featured on the cover of the 1955 annual report of the KCS. Dedicated on May 1, 1955, the yard became the railroad's principal shop-and-yard facility. It enabled the closing of the KCS and L&A shops at Shreveport as well as the L&A shops at Minden.

L. & A. NO. 53 ON THE
NEW TEXAS CUTOFF

saved well over an hour of running time for Texas-line freight trains. Operations over the new cutoff began on April 22, 1956, coincident with the use of the new yards.[29]

Another milestone was passed in 1956. The last steam locomotive on the L&A roster, number 253, an eight-wheel switcher, was retired and given to the city of Texarkana, Texas, for display at the Four States Fairground. The railroad had been essentially completely dieselized since 1953: in March of that year a large shipment of diesel locomotives was received from General Motors. It had become quite clear that the colorful steam locomotive, with its many aficionados within the KCS/L&A organization, simply could not compete economically with the diesel locomotive.[30]

And so the 1950s ended with the KCS and

L&A well integrated; new, centralized shop facilities (the KCS shops at Pittsburg, Kansas, were greatly reduced in scope); passenger service intact between Shreveport, Hope, and New Orleans; expanded facilities at Baton Rouge and New Orleans for both passenger and freight movements; and through service between the Southeast and the Dallas gateway. Profits continued to be good, and there seemed to be little cause for complaint.

The 1960s were not long under way when an event occurred that had a far-reaching effect on the L&A, as well as the entire KCS system. On November 2, 1961, William N. Deramus III, the forty-five-year-old son of the KCS chairman, resigned as president of the Missouri–Kansas–Texas railroad to become president of the KCS/L&A, succeeding his father, who remained as chairman of the

Northbound L&A train number 10 eases down the 1.3 percent grade western approach to the Mississippi River bridge at Baton Rouge in 1960. Heading the short train is F-3 engine number 32; a baggage-express car, a chair car, and a snack-observation car follow. At Shreveport the train will connect with number 16 from Port Arthur to form an overnight train to Kansas City. (Photograph by J. Parker Lamb)

(Opposite page) Westbound freight train number 53 on the cutoff between Blanchard, Louisiana (near the new Deramus Yard north of Shreveport), and Karnack, Texas, that was opened in 1955. The new line measured 16.48 miles and shortened the total distance by some 13 miles. It also eliminated the need for trackage rights over the Illinois Central west of Shreveport. In the photograph, which appeared in the 1956 annual report of the KCS/L&A, F-7A locomotive number 76 is in the lead, with three sisters following.

This portrait of William N. Deramus Jr. appeared in the KCS annual report for 1965, issued shortly after his death. Deramus, who served the KCS and L&A lines for more than fifty-six years, was president from September 22, 1941, to November 2, 1961. He was a strong supporter of the Harvey Couch tradition and received much credit for building the L&A into a "big little railroad."

board. Before going to the Katy, the younger Deramus had been president of the Chicago Great Western, where he became well known as a proponent of superlong freight trains, with as many as 275 cars each and powered by up to ten diesel units. (The CGW was controlled by a Kansas City group, several members of which were influential with the KCS; the senior Deramus was a member of the CGW board.) At the Katy, he was parsimonious in spending money for the physical plant, and his successor, C. T. Williams, found a property with many deferred maintenance problems. Deramus's act of secretly moving the Katy accounting office from St. Louis to Texas over a weekend, to the utter surprise and dismay of those who worked in the office, made national news. At any rate, he came to the KCS, to a property that had been well maintained by his father and to a company that had made enviable profits. Almost coincident with his arrival, the Board of Directors approved a plan of diversification that would put other businesses in bed with the railroad—and make use of some of the surplus funds from the railroad. On February 6, 1962, Kansas City Southern Industries, Inc. (KCSI), a Delaware corporation, was chartered; it began formal operations in November of the same year.[31]

With the advent of KCSI the old L&A began to lose its identity in annual reports to stockholders, and with the 1966 report of KCSI it had disappeared completely. (It was still reported separately to the ICC, however.) The ICC granted permission to eliminate the *Shreveporter* on January 24, 1962, the train having been coaches-only since the sleeper was dropped on April 30, 1961. Further analysis of the history and development of the L&A after 1962 requires integration with the KCS, which is outside the scope of this treatise. Accordingly, in chapter 8 the L&A story will be concluded with only a few highlights from the railroad's operations during the next thirty years or so.[32]

SUBMERGED IN THE HOLDING COMPANY

The Final Dissolution

William N. Deramus III inherited a railroad system that was in excellent shape physically and had modern motive power, an ample freight-car fleet, and passenger trains that were at least meeting out-of-pocket costs—yet ominous clouds blocked the sunshine. In an economy move beginning in 1957, maintenance-of-way-force head count was steadily lowered, and by 1962 there were 61 percent fewer employees in this area than there had been in 1957. Mechanization explained some of this reduction, but many needed track-work jobs simply were not being completed, and undetected flaws in the track-work structure were about to become evident. The deleterious effects of deferred maintenance of way can take a few years to become woefully apparent, but trouble surely comes. Wooden cross ties simply do not last forever, rock ballast cannot resist completely the tendencies for fouling by dirt, and rail joints must have attention if they are to remain smooth. It seemed apparent that cash flow from the railroad was being diverted to the needs of other components of Kansas City Southern Industries. The railroad was not getting enough cash to deal with much of the needed maintenance. Still, to outward appearances everything looked solid—and the profits were continuing.[1]

It did not take Deramus long to institute superlength freight trains on the system, following his practice at the CGW. The idea was to place enough power at the head end to conquer the grades of the Ozark and Ouachita Mountains but not to change the power when flatlands were encountered. This obviated the need for helper service in the hills, but it may not have been an optimum arrangement for the use of available locomotives. The idea of long freight trains had the obvious advantage of lower operating wages per car carried, but it had disadvantages in op-

eration and, importantly, it upset customers whose shipments were delayed until sufficient loads had been accumulated to justify the departure of a train. Whereas two or three through freight trains each way had been standard on the L&A main line in Louisiana, one train per day became the norm, with no apparent upper limit on the number of cars per train. If sidings were not long enough, schedules were carefully controlled to ensure meets where there was siding capacity.[2]

An event of some importance to this story came in February 1966, when the Illinois Central applied to the ICC for permission to purchase the Mississippi Central Railroad. The MC was providing an important link in the Natchez Route and was supporting some of the cost of soliciting traffic for the route. The daily freight trains rolled on the LM between Packton and Vidalia, and the L&A enjoyed good divisions of rates for its handling of its cars west of Packton. The Illinois Central had other ideas for the MC, however, and indicated that the Natchez Route would be severed if the purchase went through. Hearings on the purchase were held in Natchez on August 1–3: the LM intervened on the basis that it could not survive if the Natchez Route came to an end and requested that it too be purchased by the IC. After a great deal more investigation, the ICC finally gave the IC permission to purchase the MC, but the LM would have to be included in the package. This qualified permission came on April 7, 1967. On April 28 the IC formally acquired the assets of the MC for $2 million, and on the next day it paid the Midland $475,000 for all of its properties.[3]

The through freight trains between Vidalia and Packton were discontinued immediately. Only local service was provided, much of this in pulling loaded pulpwood cars

William N. Deramus III inherited the KCS/L&A leadership from his father. Trained in the law, he spent his entire career in railroading, serving as president of the Chicago Great Western and Missouri–Kansas–Texas before moving to the KCS/L&A in 1961. Through the years his management style was controversial: railroad people called him "militaristic" and "parsimonious." He died on November 15, 1989, not long after he retired from the railroad for health reasons. This photograph appeared in the 1966 annual report of the KCSI.

to interchange points. The Holloway family moved out of the line-haul freight business, and L. B. Williams retired to Alexandria after more than sixty years in railroad service. The ferry operation at Natchez continued, serving primarily its owner, the Missouri Pacific, which had a branch line from the north to Ferriday and Vidalia.[4]

During the latter half of the 1960s Deramus made a valiant attempt to keep the passenger trains rolling—at least the flagship *Southern Belle*. Between 1955 and 1965 he acquired thirty-six light-weight passenger-train cars and had another thirty-five older cars refurbished by Pullman Standard. He cut fares, offered special inducements to both coach and sleeping-car patrons, and in the May 14, 1962, issue of *Railway Age* was quoted as saying, "We have no intention of going out of the passenger business." This statement was made shortly after the March 3, 1962, discontinuance of the Hope–Shreveport survivor of the *Shreveporter,* mentioned in the preceding chapter. The Deramus statement about the passenger business formed the title of an introspective article in the November 1967 issue of *Trains* magazine by Louis A. Marre. But with connecting trains of other roads disappearing rapidly, especially in Kansas City, Deramus was left with largely local patronage, and the losses, even on an out-of-pocket basis, began to mount.[5]

A significant blow was the withdrawal of the U.S. Post Office Department from the processing of mail on board trains (using Railway Post Office [RPO] cars) after January

A pileup on the Louisiana Midland in December 1962, just west of Georgetown. The train was eastbound and included loads of salt from mines in the Winnfield area; the salt is the white material on the ground. A KCS/L&A wrecker is doing the chores, the Midland wrecker having been blocked off on the east side. (Photograph courtesy of J. D. Oliver, Louisiana Midland Railroad)

1968. This caused a large reduction of income credited to passenger service. Even closed-pouch mail disappeared, moving from the baggage cars to trucks and airplanes. One result of this postal-service action was the elimination of trains 15 and 16 between Kansas City and Port Arthur, as well as trains 9 and 10, their connections between Shreveport and New Orleans, with last runs departing on May 10, 1968. The 1968 losses attributed to passenger trains were around $5 million.[6]

After May 10 only trains 1 and 2 remained, remnants of the once-glorious *Belle*, operating between Kansas City and New Orleans, and even their survival was greatly in question. By early 1969 it was clear that the flow of red ink on the profit/loss statement was intolerable, and with some misgivings the KCS/L&A applied to the ICC for permission to discontinue the trains. At the same time the *Belle* consist was reduced to a baggage car, a coach, and a café-lounge car. The ICC was reluctant to grant the discontinuance, and on May 6, 1969, ordered continued service for at least six months. Finally, on October 20, the ICC agreed that the trains could not possibly operate profitably, and on November 2, 1969, numbers 1 and 2 left Kansas City and New Orleans for the last time, completing their runs the next day. The *Southern Belle*, "The Sweetheart of American Trains," had been in service for more than twenty-nine years and, though still sprightly, was showing the wear and tear of time. Her countenance was wrinkled, and suitors in the form of interstate highways had lured away her friends. Her last runs were sad affairs for many admirers who lived along the line. And the sadness seemed to extend to physical structures: just three days after the last departures from the Union Station at Shreveport, the building burned. Soon thereafter, it was razed.[7]

As the 1970s arrived, it became obvious that a transformation of the KCS/L&A physical plant was taking place. The change was particularly evident in the roadway. At a time when most Class I railroads were eliminating rail joints and stabilizing track alignment by installing continuous welded rail (CWR) the KCS/L&A had only one test installation: 23.6

miles of 136-pound CWR laid in 1966 between Campti and Montgomery, Louisiana. Like an elderly human, the old rail was showing irregularities in its joints. The ballast was badly fouled in many places, with weeds growing rampant between heavy, but ancient, jointed rails. A sizable fraction of the wooden cross ties needed to be replaced, and their lack of support at the joints caused such rocking of cars that it seemed unsafe to stand close to a moving freight train. This instability was especially noticeable when covered hopper cars, with high centers of gravity, were being hauled: their bobbing up, down, and sideways reminded one of canal boats on rough waters. The trim and other painted surfaces of the depots looked dreadful. Even Deramus Yard, long a source of pride, began to look shabby, and problems with underground formations led to uneven yard tracks and derailments.[8]

The turning point for the railroad actually came in late 1972, when a series of derailments—most of them not on the L&A but in the mountainous territory of the KCS north of Shreveport—caught Deramus's attention. (It was later discovered that these mishaps were caused not only by poor track conditions but also by misplaced midtrain locomotives that appeared to push harder than they pulled.) According to Fred Frailey, writing for *Trains* magazine, by 1972 the railroad "set something of a national standard for dilapidation." *Forbes*

L. B. Williams went to work for William Edenborn's Shreveport and Red River Valley line in 1903, at the tender age of fifteen, and handled many key assignments for the railroad and its successors. After he retired, in 1945, he became general manager of the Louisiana Midland and remained there until the railroad was sold to the Illinois Central in 1967. He told the author a great deal about Edenborn and his river and rail operations on the south end of the L&A. Here he poses on the front porch of his home in Alexandria in August 1972, in his eighty-fifth year.

A KCS switcher works the cars for northbound train number 16 at the Shreveport Union Station on an afternoon in August 1964. At this point cars from Port Arthur and New Orleans were consolidated into an overnight train for Kansas City, with scheduled departure at 5:20 P.M. Illinois Central cars in the rear are for the Shreveport–Meridian, Mississippi, service. The view is to the southwest. (Photograph by J. Parker Lamb)

magazine published a KCS article on "The Little Railroad That Went Astray." And the bottom line was hit hard: George Kellogg, a KCS vice president, told *Railway Age* that "Our service went to hell, and that drove away many of our old, stable customers." To those who had always marveled at the attractiveness of the property, its appearance in the early 1970s was downright shameful.[9]

Another turning point was caused by an overseas influence: the Arab oil embargo that took place in late 1973. As crude petroleum prices, as well as those of natural gas, soared, it became evident to the utilities companies in the south, where oil or natural gas had been the traditional fuel for generating electric power, that coal could be substituted for these other fuels at substantial cost savings. But not just any coal would do—it needed to be western coal, with a low sulfur content, in order not to pollute the air with sulfur dioxide. This move reinforced the idea of unit trains hauling Wyoming coal to various power

plants in the South. The Burlington Northern served the Wyoming mines and did a large-scale promotion among utilities companies in Louisiana, Arkansas, Texas, and Oklahoma. As this development continued, the KCS/L&A convinced Southwestern Electric Power Company that it should locate a planned power plant along the Texas line. Such a plant would be served reliably and economically by the railroad, with the unit trains transferring to the KCS from the Burlington Northern at Kansas City and onto the L&A at Texas Junction, north of Deramus Yard. The plant was to be located at a new station designated Welsh, Texas, at milepost T91, some 42 miles west of Jefferson. And, importantly, the plant would need deliveries of coal beginning early 1978. This convinced Deramus, for he knew that his tracks simply could not carry the heavy coal trains. But he knew also that he did not have much time to restore his facilities to reasonable working condition.[10]

Fortunately, Deramus had relinquished the presidency to Thomas S. Carter in August 1973, retaining the titles of board chairman and chief executive officer of the railroad. Carter, a civil engineer by training, knew that the track and roadway were his major assignment. And he was able to sell Deramus and the other KCSI board members on the need for massive injections of capital to restore the road. It was Carter who discovered that the derailments had been caused in part by the misplaced midtrain diesel units, which were controlled from the front end of the train. He determined that the rebuilding of the KCS/L&A was a mammoth job that would take a number of years to accomplish. Some of the coal-train preparatory work was admittedly makeshift, but the deadline was met, and in 1978 some 154 coal trains of 100 cars each found their way to the Welsh plant with only minor mishaps. In that same year the coal business, which now included unit coal trains to two points on the KCS, accounted for 12 percent of the railroad's total revenues.[11]

The rebuilding of the lines over the next decade is ably described in a November 1992 article in *Railway Track and Structures*. Projections showed that, by the end of 1994, $500 million would have been spent on this undertaking. Earlier experiments with concrete cross ties were not completely successful because of cracking, but by 1970 this problem was corrected, and combinations of concrete and wood ties were used in the rehabilitation. CWR rail of 136-pound section became the standard on the main lines. Block signals and Centralized Traffic Control (CTC) were installed on the Texas line, to augment CTC in place between Kansas City and Port Arthur, as well as block signals between Baton Rouge and New Orleans (leaving the Shreveport–Baton Rouge and feeder lines radiating from Minden still "dark").[12]

As William Deramus III moved away from active administration of the KCS/L&A, it seems of interest to evaluate what had led him to abuse the railroad his father had loved so much. Before moving to the KCS in 1961 he treated MKT in the same manner, letting the physical plant go to near ruin while trying to

make a profit with slim revenues. John Barriger, a well-known and successful railroad executive, came out of semiretirement in 1965 to run the Katy and to deal with Deramus's legacy. Barriger never lost an opportunity to disparage Deramus's neglectful approach to property maintenance. When asked about the folly of his ways in 1978, Deramus's only response was, "Explanations are silly; God takes care of His own kind." For the present narrative, it can only be said that the L&A was spared most of the problems incurred by the KCS, partly because it had fewer grades and curves.[13]

At dusk in August 1973 a pair of SD-40s, with northbound freight train number 42, move down the western approach to the Mississippi River bridge at Baton Rouge. (Photograph courtesy of J. Parker Lamb)

At the west end of the L&A in Texas, the depot at Farmersville served both the Santa Fe and the L&A. This 1972 view is to the south, with the uneven rails of the L&A swinging in from the left, permitting L&A freight trains to use the Santa Fe tracks into Dallas. In 1992 the KCS purchased the Farmersville–Dallas trackage from the Santa Fe and completely upgraded the line with continuous rail and Centralized Traffic Control.

And so the 1970s witnessed a massive turnaround by the KCS/L&A. Profits were regained, and new businesses along the lines were developed. One sad occurrence, however, was the closing of the paper mill at Springhill, Louisiana, an operation that had been especially profitable for the L&A. In 1978 International Paper placed a new mill on stream near Texarkana, Texas (served jointly by the KCS and the MP) using state-of-the-art technology, and the thirty-year old Springhill operation was no longer competitive. Still, three new paper mills had been built along the L&A, at Campti, Pineville, and Baton Rouge; the petrochemicals business was excellent; and through freight service between New Orleans and California was being developed with the Santa Fe (the "Big D connection"). Deramus had finally delegated railroad responsibilities to Tom Carter, and in the midst of big mergers of big railroads, the KCS/L&A maintained both its profitability and its independence.[14]

By late 1992 the appearance of the railroad had changed significantly since the early 1970s, when research for the present work began. Without question, the primary line of the L&A was from Dallas to New Orleans,

and this line was challenging the KCS main line in traffic density. Completely upgraded, one could see 136-pound welded rail, clean crushed-stone ballast, new cross-ties, and plans for completing signaling by adding CTC to the Shreveport–Baton Rouge segment. Bridges had been strengthened or replaced, clearances had been increased to allow shipments of double-stacked containers, and coal trains of 110 cars each were traversing the Texas line regularly. Motive power was heavy, with Electro-Motive SD–60 (3,800 horsepower) locomotives becoming the standard. Truly, it was a first-class railroad.[15]

The other parts of the L&A system had not been upgraded on the same basis. The Hope branch was active only as far north as Cullen, where the remnants of the International Paper Company mill provided some carloads. (The old IP property was serving primarily as a distribution center for the company.) Interchange at Hope with the Kiamichi Railroad (formerly the Frisco) to Oklahoma was essentially nil, between Anthony (just south of Hope) and Cullen the line was embargoed, and a diesel switcher was kept at the Hope yard. Between Selby and Winnfield, the old high line had long been out of service and taken over by weeds. The line between Packton and Vidalia, sold by the LM to the Illinois Central Gulf in 1967, was sold back to a new company called Louisiana Midland, but the "new" LM had inadequate funding and limited business opportunities. It finally ended operations in 1982, when the loss of a bridge approach at Jonesville plus washouts near Zenoria provided the excuse it needed to shut down. Today the tracks are gone. In fact, Ferriday and Vidalia are without rail service, the Missouri Pacific having abandoned its branch line south of Tallulah in 1987. The ferry-transfer service between Vidalia and Natchez had ended in 1982.[16]

As with all main-line railroads, station agents had largely disappeared. Most of the depots had either been razed or moved off the property. A new yard and yard office had been built at Hughes Springs, Texas; and at Latanier, Louisiana, 20 miles south of Alexandria, a grass-roots classification yard had been built for the purpose of reblocking freight trains in and out of New Orleans. These were virtually the only operating facilities constructed in twenty years. In 1992, the only

open offices were at Hunt and Hughes Springs, on the Texas line, and at Shreveport (Deramus Yard), Baton Rouge, Latanier, and New Orleans (West yard).[17]

The business of the L&A in 1992 had settled down to the following. Through freight trains between California and New Orleans were instituted by the Santa Fe and L&A on November 1, 1980—the Big D Connection mentioned earlier. The roads touted five-day service between northern California and the Crescent City, and some run-through motive power could be observed on either side of Dallas. Coal trains continued to roll on the Texas line. Relatively new paper mills were in operation at Campti, Pineville, and Port Hudson. The sugar-mill business was good enough to warrant a switch engine stationed at Reserve. Petroleum products and derivatives provided a good business from such stations as Cotton Valley, Baton Rouge, and the area around Norco, Louisiana. Grain trains used part of the L&A rails, and there was a growing business with animal-feed distribution centers in Texas. Economic figures for the L&A were no longer separated from

The Foss Street station and office building in July 1975. This attractive structure opened in 1967 and saw only two years of passenger trains. The last train to use the station was the Southern Belle, *on November 3, 1967, its final southbound run.*

The KCS/L&A kept up-to-date on motive power if not in track maintenance, in the early 1970s. Here, in 1974 are two SD-40 3000 HP diesel-electric locomotives, not long received from General Motors. The third unit is not identified.

A quartet of GP-38 locomotives roaring through Winnsboro, Texas, headed for Shreveport with seventy-nine cars in tow, on March 10, 1980.

A westward-looking view of the new yard at Hughes Springs in January 1993. The yard serves classification needs regarding through traffic to and from Dallas. By this time the Texas line had Centralized Traffic Control and heavy, continuous welded rail.

No. 4000, a GP-38 dating back to May 1979, idles at Cullen, Louisiana, in January 1993. It has been relegated to local service between Shreveport and Cullen, a service which at this time is a mere shadow of its former might when the paper mill was in operation at Cullen.

those of the KCS, but for the entire system, coal accounted for about 12 percent of income and chemicals for about 10 percent.[18]

A longer-range concern of the railroad was the development of the U.S. Army Corps of Engineers' Red River Waterway between Shreveport and the Mississippi River. This $1.8 billion project precipitated a relocation of the L&A river crossing at Alexandria—which meant the end of the Edenborn Bridge that had served so well. The new crossing would be downriver from Alexandria and would facilitate the movement of trains through the area. Barge traffic on the new waterway would likely affect the business of the Union Pacific (formerly the T&P) and the L&A along the Red River Valley. To make things worse, plans called for extending the waterway into Texas, with a terminus near the town of Lone Star, just south of Daingerfield. The extension, which would parallel the L&A, was estimated to cost $680 million. It was opposed not only by the railroads but also by environmentalists, conservationists, and many local citizens, especially those with thriving businesses serving the Caddo Lake recreational areas. The first phase of the waterway (south of Shreveport) was targeted for completion in 1994–1995, though it was still far from completion at the time of this publication.[19]

The management of the KCS/L&A had undergone several changes over the past two decades. In February 1987 Kirke Couch, third son of Harvey Couch, retired from the KCSI Board of Directors. This was the first time in fifty years that a Couch had not been on the board, except for a brief period in the mid-1960s. On November 15, 1989, William Deramus III died; he had retired from active management of the railroad in 1986 but continued to serve on the board. He had seen to it that William IV found a good position with

the railroad, achieving its presidency in 1988. However, the youngest Deramus had little railroad-management experience, and resigned suddenly and mysteriously in October 1990. For the first time in perhaps sixty years no Deramus was active in the railroad management. The president and chief executive officer of KCSI, Landon Rowland, filled the position until George Edwards was brought in as railroad president and chief executive officer. These moves underscored the executive role played more and more by nonrailroad people.[20]

In 1992 several events occurred that affected the future of the railroad. First, arrangements were being made for the KCS to purchase the Farmersville–Dallas segment of the Santa Fe, which had been used by the L&A since 1937. By late in the year the railroads were awaiting ICC approval, but the KCS was not hesitating to begin a much-needed upgrading of the line. With this acquisition went a rearrangement of facilities in Dallas, occasioned by the decision of the Santa Fe to move its freight-classification yard to a new location on the north side of Fort Worth, near the station of Justin. This would call for freight train run-throughs over Santa Fe tracks to Fort Worth.[21]

Indeed, the L&A was surviving quite nicely in the early 1990s, but its days as a separate corporation were numbered. The KCS decided in 1992 to dissolve the subsidiary corporation and make legal what had been practiced for a number of years. For all intents and purposes there had not been an L&A during the KCSI era. Application for dissolution was duly filed with the ICC, which approved the demise of the L&A effective July 6, 1992.[22] And so, after almost a century of operation under the banner of the Louisiana and Arkansas Railway, the end had come.

T

he dissolution of the L&A as a corporate entity in July 1992 is a logical ending point for the present narrative. But a significant legacy of the L&A prevailed in 1996, mostly dealing with the railroad that Sarah Edenborn sold to the Harvey Couch syndicate. That railroad stretched from McKinney on the west to New Orleans on the east. Except for a short segment between McKinney and Farmersville in Texas, the line was intact, upgraded to high-density freight-traffic standards, and a genuine moneymaker for the KCS. Developments since 1992 have cemented the elevated status of this line.

In mid-1992 the KCS was negotiating with the Santa Fe to purchase about 90 route-miles of railroad in the Dallas–Fort Worth area. This addition to the west end of the Texas line would carry westbound KCS trains, on KCS rails, from Farmersville into Dallas at Zacha Junction, the location of Santa Fe's intermodal facilities. From Zacha Junction west to the north–south main line of the Santa Fe, at Dalton Junction, trains would move over rails that were built in 1955 to give the Santa Fe direct access to Dallas (and, incidentally, to handle the Dallas section of the flagship streamliner, the *Texas Chief*). Beginning at Dalton Junction, the westbound train would use Santa Fe rails southward a few miles to a new freight yard being developed by the Santa Fe just north of Fort Worth. Eastbound freights would reverse this sequence. This acquisition of trackage was consummated in late 1993, with the KCS dispatcher taking over the line on November 1. The extension to Fort Worth solidified the cooperation of Santa Fe and the KCS for New Orleans–West Coast through traffic, particularly of containerized freight and highway trailers on flatcars. Also included in this plan was the use of ex–Cotton Belt trackage to form a shortcut around Zacha Junction for through trains.

A larger development for the KCS, however, was its acquisition of MidSouth Industries, a holding company with four railroads, one of which was MidSouth Rail, owner of the former Illinois Central (earlier Vicksburg, Shreveport and Pacific) line between Shreveport and Meridian, Mississippi. The plan of merger was announced September 21, 1992, was approved by the ICC in June 1993, and became official on the last day of 1993. It gave the KCS the short line between Dallas–Fort Worth and Atlanta and the Southeast, in collaboration with the Norfolk Southern. The KCS lost no time in rehabilitating not only the Shreveport–Meridian segment but also a number of other properties of MidSouth. In 1996 three pairs of scheduled tonnage trains ran on the through route, adding to the Dallas–New Orleans trains and the coal trains on the ex-L&A Texas line. These trains were often longer than 6,000 feet and used heavy locomotive power.

The 1990s were marked by railroad-merger mania, but the KCS resisted becoming a part of a larger system. However, in July 1994 the KCS and the Illinois Central signed a letter of intent to merge. One reason why the parent company, KCSI, was agreeable to spinning off the railroad was that other KCSI investments were doing quite well, particularly the Janus Capital Corporation, with its assortment of mutual funds for private investors in the stock markets. But by October 1994 the KCS had lost interest in merger with IC, and the deal was called off.

Other developments along the ex-L&A may be noted. The line between Cullen, Louisiana, and Hope, Arkansas, was still embargoed in 1996, and the Kiamichi Railroad

AFTERWORD

was handling switching for the L&A at Hope. The new bridge over the Red River at Alexandria was placed in operation in early 1996, with the old, reliable Edenborn Bridge scheduled for dismantling. The future of the Minden–Shreveport line was in doubt, because it was essentially paralleled by the ex-MidSouth line between Sibley and Shreveport. Plans were in progress to build a 9-mile branch line from Gonzales, 21 miles south of Baton Rouge, to the Geismar industrial area along the Mississippi River. This would enable the KCS to tap the lucrative chemical business in that area. But objections were being raised by the Illinois Central, which had an exclusive at Geismar. In June 1995 Michael Haverty, formerly of the Santa Fe, replaced the retiring George Edwards as president and chief executive officer of the KCS. Landon Rowland continued in the equivalent position for the parent KCSI. One of Haverty's first jobs was to fight the pending merger of the Union Pacific and the Southern Pacific. Although interest in forming superrailroads through mergers continued, the KCS seemed to favor independence. The ex-L&A properties were making a strong contribution to the financial success of the railroad. Edenborn, Buchanan, and Couch had planned them well.

In planning for the new Union Passenger Station in New Orleans, a project that extended over a number of years and involved the elimination of a large number of grade crossings, the Terminal Board engaged a consulting firm, Godat and Heft, to make a study of train movements in the New Orleans area. The study of the L&A operations, conducted during 1943 and 1944, provides interesting insights into the methods by which freight trains and passenger trains were handled in carrying out normal business. The following is an adaptation of comments in the Godat and Heft report: New Orleans, Department of Public Utilities, *Proposed Railroad Grade Crossing Elimination and Terminal Improvement for New Orleans, Louisiana,* New Orleans, September 5, 1944.

The L&A entered New Orleans from the west. Its single-track main line paralleled and was about a quarter of a mile north of the Illinois Central main line. The L&A main crossed the New Orleans Terminal Company Outer Belt line at Shrewsbury. This L&A line came into the city parallel and immediately adjacent to the Airline Highway, up to South Carrollton Avenue. It crossed the New Basin Canal at Pontchartrain Boulevard and then continued down the northeastern side of the canal to a point near Gayoso Street (west of South Broad Avenue), where the main line diverged from Poydras Street immediately adjacent to the Yazoo and Mississippi Valley Poydras Yard. At Dorgenois Street the main line diverged from Poydras down Cypress Street to Liberty Street and then over private right-of-way to the passenger station on North Rampart Street at Girod Street.

The principal yard of the L&A in New Orleans was the Shrewsbury or West Wye Yard in Jefferson Parish, just beyond the Orleans Parish line and immediately adjacent to Southport Junction. This was a five-track yard with a capacity of approximately 500 cars. All road freight trains originated and terminated at this yard. It was used for all classification and makeup work. However, it had no engine terminal or car-repair facilities; these operations were handled at the Jefferson Davis Yard, which extended from Jefferson Davis Parkway to Gayoso Street. At this yard were a seven-stall roundhouse, a diesel pit, a machine shop, and car-repair and coach-cleaning facilities. At the Shrewsbury Yard a wye was extended to provide a connection with the Public Belt main line at Oak Street.

The L&A freight houses extended from South Claiborne Avenue to Liberty Street. Warehouse number 2, between Liberty and LaSalle Streets, was used to handle less-than-carload merchandise freight in both directions; number 5, between LaSalle and Freret Streets, was also used to handle some less-than-carload freight, as well as coffee. Warehouse number 1, at Liberty and Cypress Streets, was used to handle industrial freight. Warehouse number 4, between LaSalle and Freret Streets, was used by car-loading companies for merchandise freight. Five other warehouses were leased to various industries. The passenger station at Rampart and Girod Streets was a small, single-story brick structure, completed in 1923. It had only two station tracks.

Passenger service consisted of two trains each way daily. One of these was the streamliner *Southern Belle;* the other was a conventional steam train, the *Flying Crow.* The streamliner was handled around the wye at Shrewsbury and was backed into the station. After unloading it was moved to the Jefferson Davis Yard, cleaned and serviced, and then backed into the station in the evening for departure. The other train headed into the station. The total number of cars each way daily on these two trains varied from eighteen to twenty-four. The train arriving in the morning and departing in the evening carried three cars of less-than-carload freight, in addition to the regular passenger equipment. Mail and express cars were worked directly from trucks on the station tracks. Trains were handled from the station to the Jefferson Davis Yard by a switch engine, which also spotted the head-end cars carrying less-than-carload freight.

All freight trains were handled at the Shrewsbury Yard. Engines and cabooses were cut off and run into the Jefferson Davis Yard, where they were serviced. Traffic consisted of three scheduled freight trains each way daily, handling between 100 and 120 cars apiece. Of this total traffic, about 115–120 cars a day were oil traffic. There were about three or four transfer movements each way daily from the Shrewsbury Yard to the freight houses and industries of the city. Industrial business, coffee, and less-than-carload freight handled through the houses varied between twelve and fifteen cars daily. The industrial business in Orleans Parish varied between thirty-five and forty cars a day. A fairly substantial volume of industrial business was also handled in Jefferson Parish, with such industries as the American Creosote Works and the Shippers Compress. The team-track business varied between seven and ten cars a day.

Practically all of the freight handled by the L&A in New Orleans was for interchange. At the crossing of the New Orleans Terminal Company Outer Belt line were three interchange tracks, together with a long siding that was also used for interchange purposes. On these tracks the L&A interchanged with the New Orleans Terminal Company, the Illinois Central, and the Texas and New Orleans. Interchange with the T&NO averaged ten to fifteen cars a day; with the Illinois Central, twenty-five to thirty cars a day. Interchange with the IC at the Poydras Yard near Broad Avenue was for freight originating on or destined to industries between Broad Avenue and Rampart Street. This business was relatively small, averaging five to ten cars a day. Interchange with the New Orleans Terminal Company averaged 140 to 170 cars a day and included the entire then-abnormal oil movement, as well as the Louisville and Nashville–Gulf, Mobile and Ohio interchange. The connection with the Public Belt was made on an interchange track at Oak Street. That movement averaged between thirty and forty cars a day. Interchange with the T&P–MP was handled through the Public Belt as an intermediate switching line. Practically all traffic handled on the interchange tracks at the New Orleans Terminal Company–L&A crossing was through traffic, and only a small portion of it was destined for local delivery on the Terminal Company or connecting lines.

The total traffic handled through the Shrewsbury Yard averaged about 475 cars each way daily. About 350 cars were handled each way daily on road freight trains. The remainder of the traffic was received through connecting lines for local delivery or originated for delivery to connecting lines.

Locomotive historians have studied the locomotive rosters of the several L&A component companies and in general have made their results available in the published literature. It would seem redundant to reproduce their results here, so the references below will direct interested readers to the source materials. The exception to this situation is the steam-locomotive roster of the East Line and Red River Railroad, the narrow-gauge line that was the forerunner of the Texas line of the L&A. The roster for this railroad is given in chapter 4.

For the early L&A, the LR&N, and the later L&A, the steam-locomotive data are in William D. Edson, "Locomotives of the Louisiana and Arkansas Railway," *Railroad History*, no. 144 (Spring 1981): 60–75. *Railroad History* is published by the Railway and Locomotive Historical Society. A more complete, and possibly more accurate, steam-locomotive roster was compiled by Harold K. Vollrath, retired from the Kansas City Southern, on the basis of corporate records: Harold K. Vollrath, "All-Time Steam Roster of the Kansas City Southern," *Railroad Magazine,* January 1976, 56–59. Another source of steam-locomotive data for the overall L&A is A. E. Brown, *Locomotives and Trains of the L&A and KCS Railways* (Shreveport, La.: Privately published, 1953).

Data on the diesel locomotives of the L&A are in Sy Reich, "Diesel Power: Kansas City Southern and Louisiana & Arkansas," *Railroad Magazine,* January 1976, 59. By the time Reich's data were published, the parent railroad no longer identified ownership of the individual diesel units; instead, it consolidated all power into a KCS roster. Terry Lynch and W. D. Caileff Jr., *Route of the Southern Belle* (Boulder, Colo.: Pruett Publishing Co., 1987), is an excellent source of information on the KCS.

The L&A's interesting and varied steam locomotives have attracted the attention of historians. The author hopes that the corporate history revealed in the present work will serve as a satisfactory adjunct to the published information on the locomotives of the L&A.

APPENDIX B

Locomotives of the L&A

CHAPTER 1

William Edenborn, Steel Industry Captain

1. Archer Mayor, *Southern Timberman: The Legacy of William Buchanan* (Athens: University of Georgia Press, 1988); Winston P. Wilson, *Harvey Couch: The Master Builder* (Nashville: Broadman Press, 1947); Stephen Wilson, *Harvey Couch: An Entrepreneur Brings Electricity to Arkansas* (Little Rock: August House, 1986). After the present manuscript was completed, the author discovered a brief personal sketch of William Edenborn: Glen Coleman, *The Man Who Fenced the West* (St. Louis: Glen Coleman Co., 1984). A copy of the sketch is in the Louisiana State University–Shreveport Archives (hereafter cited as LSUS Archives).

2. *National Cyclopedia of American Biography* (New York: John T. White, 1922), vol. 18, 248–49.

3. *New Orleans Times-Picayune,* May 14, 1926; memoir by J. N. Campbell, in Maude H. O'Pry, *Chronicles of Shreveport and Caddo Parish* (Shreveport, La.: n.p., 1928), 349.

4. *National Cyclopedia of American Biography,* vol. 18, 248–49; James Cox, *Old and New St. Louis* (St. Louis: Central Biographical Publishing Co., 1894), 277–79; letter, William Edenborn to E. Boley of the American Steel and Wire Company, November 15, 1909, in the files of the USX (formerly United States Steel) Corporation, Pittsburgh, Pa. This letter gives a detailed account of Edenborn's early career as he remembered it and will hereafter be cited as Edenborn Recollections.

5. Herman Kayser, affidavit published in the *St. Louis Post Dispatch,* August 12, 1926; Edenborn Recollections.

6. Edenborn Recollections; Cox, *Old and New St. Louis;* Kayser, affidavit.

7. Testimonies of Augusta Brand, Alfred Clifford, and Dora Mattern, published in the *St. Louis Post Dispatch,* March 16, 17, and 31, 1927; marriage records of the City of St. Louis.

8. "The Magnates of the Wire Industry," *The Iron Age,* March 23, 1899, 16.

9. Edenborn Recollections.

10. Edenborn Recollections; Cox, *Old and New St. Louis.*

11. Edenborn Recollections.

12. Ibid.; Henry D. McCallum and Frances T. McCallum, *The Wire That Fenced the West* (Norman: University of Oklahoma Press, 1965).

13. Records, Office of the Missouri Secretary of State; USX Corporation files; Edenborn Recollections.

14. Lloyd Wendt and Herman Kogan, *Bet a Million! The Story of John W. Gates* (Indianapolis: Bobbs-Merrill Co., 1948); Robert Warshow, *Bet a Million Gates* (New York: Greenberg Press, 1932).

15. Edenborn Recollections.

16. Ibid.

17. U.S. Patent No. 250,795, "Machine for pointing wire," December 13, 1881; U.S. Patent No. 270,645, "Barb wire machine," January 16, 1883; U.S. Patent No. 270,646, "Barb wire machine," January 16, 1883; U.S. Patent No. 271,693, "Barbed fence machine," February 6, 1883; "Data concerning the history of sundry wire manufacturing plants in the Middle West," circa 1916 (unpublished manuscript in the files of the USX Corporation).

18. *The Iron Age,* December 1, 1892, 1060.

19. Ibid.; Wendt and Kogan, *Bet a Million!*

20. *The Iron Age,* August 29, 1895, 430; the date of Edenborn's move to Chicago is somewhat uncertain. Patent applications place the move between September 24, 1894, and January 27, 1896. *Gould's St. Louis Directory* (St. Louis: Gould Publishing Co., 1890–1892) indicates that the move was made in 1895. The St. Louis wire plant ceased operation in 1893 and was converted to a warehouse; the timing of Edenborn's move may have been based in part on this development.

21. Guy Forshey, "The Woman [Sarah Edenborn] $76,000,000 Could Not Change," *St. Louis Post Dispatch,* August 12, 1926; Cox, *Old and New St. Louis;* Kayser, affidavit; letter,

William Edenborn to Gustave Griesche, December 10, 1913, in the Edenborn Papers, LSUS Archives.

22. Letter, Edenborn to Griesche.

23. *The Iron Age,* March 24, 1898, 32; March 31, 1898, 8; and April 7, 1898, 21; letter, William Edenborn to W. B. Rose, Natchez, Miss., March 23, 1898; letter, William Edenborn to Clarence E. Ellerbe and Peter McIlvried, Shreveport, La., March 15, 1898. Copies of miscellaneous letters that Edenborn wrote to Ellerbe in 1898 were made available to the author by a descendent of Sarah Edenborn, Glen Coleman of St. Louis, Mo.

24. Frederick L. Allen, *The Great Pierpont Morgan* (New York: Harper and Bros., 1949), 165.

25. *Commercial and Financial Chronicle,* March 26, 1898, 615.

26. *The Iron Age,* January 12, 1899, 19; January 19, 1899, 18, 20; and March 23, 1899, 15.

27. U.S. Patent No. 653,339, "Wire fencing machine," July 10, 1900. Much later, Edenborn was granted one more patent (U.S. Patent No. 1,351,629, August 31, 1920), dealing with the extraction of resin from pine stumps (*Winnfield Enterprise/News-American,* December 5, 1957).

28. *The Iron Age,* April 11, 1901, 14; Horace L. Wilgus, *A Study of the United States Steel Corporation in Its Industrial and Legal Aspects* (Chicago: Callaghan & Co., 1901); Ida Tarbell, *The Life of Elbert H. Gary, The Story of Steel* (New York: D. Appleton, 1925); Wendt and Kogan, *Bet a Million!;* Allen, *The Great Pierpont Morgan;* J. K. Winkler, *Morgan the Magnificent* (Garden City, N.Y.: Garden City Publishing Co., 1930). According to Allen, the initial subscription of Edenborn to U.S. Steel stock was $3,275,000; that of Gates, $6,000,000 (292–93).

29. USX Corporation files; *The Iron Age,* December 9, 1909, 1787; Tarbell, *Life of Elbert H. Gary;* Edenborn Recollections.

30. O'Pry, *Chronicles;* files in the Office of the Louisiana Secretary of State, Baton Rouge; Interstate Commerce Commission, Valuation Docket 215 file, Washington, D.C., a summary of the commission's decision being given in ICC *Reports* 106 (1925): 46–66 (hereafter cited as ICC File, VD 215).

31. Keith L. Bryant, *Arthur E. Stilwell* (Nashville: Vanderbilt University Press, 1971); Kansas City Southern Railway Company, *Annual Report,* 1900; *Shreveport Times,* April 1, 1900;

Cox, *Old and New St. Louis; Who's Who in America, 1903–1905* (Chicago: Marquis Publishing Co., 1903); "Magnates of the Wire Industry."

32. Edenborn Recollections.

33. *National Cyclopedia of American Biography,* vol. 18, 248–49; Winkler, *Morgan the Magnificent;* Edenborn Recollections.

34. Tarbell, *Life of Elbert H. Gary.*

CHAPTER 2

Edenborn Builds His Personal Railroad

1. *Biographical Directory of the Railway Officials of America* (Chicago: Railway Age, 1901).

2. ICC File, VD 215; charter of the Shreveport and Red River Valley Railway Company, in the files of the Office of the Louisiana Secretary of State, Baton Rouge.

3. Files in the Office of the Louisiana Secretary of State, Baton Rouge; Letters, Edenborn to Ellerbe and McIlvried, 1898. The Fouke–Collins line between Shreveport and Texarkana was reorganized as the Texarkana, Shreveport and Natchez Railway Company on January 1, 1899, and shortly afterward went under control of the Texas and Pacific. Formal title transfer occurred on March 8, 1901 (*Shreveport Times,* March 9, 1901).

4. Files in the Office of the Louisiana Secretary of State, Baton Rouge; letters, Edenborn to Ellerbe and McIlvried, 1898. Perhaps the most famous (or infamous) construction company was The Credit Mobilier, formed for the building of the Union Pacific; see Charles E. Ames, *Pioneering the Union Pacific* (New York: Appleton-Century-Crofts, 1969).

5. *Railroad Gazette,* November 5, 1897, 791; *Railway Age,* October 29, 1897, 894, December 17, 1897, 1019; ICC File, VD 215. Rail weights are expressed in pounds per lineal yard; grades are expressed in net rise per length, as a percentage. Loggy Bayou connected Lake Bistineau with the Red River and was designated a navigable stream. Whenever possible, Edenborn had shipments of new rail loaded on purchased rolling stock, thus paying only a single tariff for the movements.

6. Harold K. Vollrath (Kansas City Southern Railway), private communication to the author, 1972; William D. Edson, "Locomotives of the Louisiana and Arkansas and Component Lines," *Railroad History,* no. 144 (Spring 1981): 60; *Shreveport Times,* April 15, 1898;

Railroad Gazette, April 22, 1898, 301; letters, Edenborn to Ellerbe, April 8 and July 13, 1898.

7. *Shreveport Times,* July 24, 1898.

8. Letter, William Edenborn to W. K. Bixby, June 23, 1898.

9. 51 *Louisiana Annual,* 814 (decided June 22, 1898); *Shreveport Times,* various news articles, May-June 1898; letters, Edenborn to Ellerbe, January 31 and June 13, 14, 16, and 24, 1898; ICC File, VD 215. The Union Station opened for service on August 1, 1897, and was owned by the Kansas City, Shreveport and Gulf Terminal Company, incorporated July 27, 1897. The *Shreveport Times,* August 2, 1897, called it a "Palace of Travel."

10. "Data concerning the History of Sundry Wire Manufacturing Plants in the Middle West," unpublished manuscript, circa 1916, in files of United States Steel Corporation, Pittsburgh, Pa.; letters, Edenborn to Ellerbe, March 22 and April 8, 1898; files in the Office of the Louisiana Secretary of State, Baton Rouge.

11. Letters, Edenborn to Ellerbe, November 17 and 21, 1898. The development of the Louisiana and Arkansas Railway by William Buchanan is detailed in chapter 5.

12. Shreveport and Red River Valley Railway, minutes of meeting and amended charter, in the files of the Office of the Louisiana Secretary of State, Baton Rouge; letters, Edenborn to Ellerbe, March 15, April 8, and July 4, 1898.

13. *Waterways Journal,* March 4, 1939; N. Philip Norman, "The Red River of the South," *Louisiana Historical Quarterly* 25 (April 1942): 397; steamboat service advertisements in the *Shreveport Times,* December 1898, passim; *Louisiana Reports,* 1901–1902, 568; Frederick Way, *Way's Packet Directory, 1848–1983* (Athens: Ohio University Press, 1983). According to H. B. Bozeman, the U&I made a special trip up Saline Bayou for a load of cotton—and the cotton caught fire (*Winnfield Enterprise/News-American,* September 8, 1960).

14. *Shreveport Times,* November 3, 1898; various Edenborn letters. A key connection would be with the Morgan's Louisiana and Texas line, a part of the Southern Pacific; this connection would permit consignment of freight all the way to New Orleans.

15. Dates of service are based on official timetables published in the *Shreveport Times* and on the *Railway Age,* June 30, 1899, 490; the name Machen was later changed to Montgomery.

16. *Shreveport Times,* March 9 and July 11, 1901; *Travelers' Official Guide of the Railways and Steam Navigation Lines in the United States and Canada* (hereafter cited as *Official Guide*), February 1901; T. Harry Williams, *Huey Long* (New York: Alfred A. Knopf, 1969), 45.

17. Williams, *Huey Long,* 159–60.

18. *Alexandria (La.) Daily Town Talk,* September 16, September 24, 1901, and October 1, 1901; *Shreveport Times,* July 10 and 11, 1900, January 9, 1901, August 5, 8, 24, and 31, 1901, and October 3, 1901; *Official Guide,* August 1901.

19. "The Red River Bridge at Alexandria," *Railroad Gazette,* September 20, 1901, 653–54; *Shreveport Times,* March 9, 1901; *New Orleans Daily Picayune,* April 27, 1902. The Cooper's rating takes into account both static and dynamic loads but is roughly equal to the axle loading of, say, a locomotive, in thousands of pounds. Edenborn's interest in bridges may well have stemmed from his earlier acquaintance with James B. Eads, known for his large bridge at St. Louis (Coleman, *The Man Who Fenced the West*). In the mid-1990s construction began on a new bridge downstream from Alexandria, to expedite freight movements and adhere to clearance requirements of a new waterway, not because of problems with the original bridge.

20. *New Orleans Daily Picayune,* April 27, 29, and 30, 1902.

21. ICC File, VD 215; files of the Kansas City Southern Railroad, Kansas City, Mo.; *Official Guide,* May 1902, June 1903; *New Orleans Daily Picayune,* July 6, 1902; ICC *Reports* 106 (1925): 47–66. Locally, the Southern Pacific operated as Morgan's Louisiana & Texas. Its line between Alexandria and New Orleans was circuitous and certainly not the direct route that Edenborn desired. One wonders whether he would have been much better off to stop at Alexandria and enter into a more formal haulage agreement with the ML&T.

22. ICC *Reports* 99 (1925): 731–35; *Railroad Gazette,* April 10, 1903, 274; *Railway Age,* April 27, 1929, 959.

23. Rachael E. Norgress, "The History of the Cypress Lumber Industry in Louisiana," *Louisiana Historical Quarterly* 30 (1947): 982–83; ICC File, VD 215; charter, in the files of the Office of the Louisiana Secretary of State, Baton Rouge (also published in the *Shreveport Times,* July 1, 1901); *Official Guide,* January 1904.

24. Charter, in the files of the Office of the Louisiana Secretary of State, Baton Rouge; ICC *Reports* 106 (1925): 47–66; *Commercial*

and Financial Chronicle, May 16, 1903, 1085, and July 4, 1903, 36.

25. *Railway Age*, April 3, 1903, 691; *Official Guide*, January 1904; interview with L. B. Williams, former telegraph operator, station agent, and trainmaster for the LR&N, in Alexandria, La., August 26, 1972, plus a taped interview with Williams by an unknown person, a transcription of which was provided to the author by Harold K. Vollrath of Kansas City, Mo. (hereafter cited as Williams interview). One of the cuts was about fifty feet deep, according to Williams, and was said to be one of the deepest in the United States. The old river landing was known as Angola Plantation; the LR&N station was designated as Angola.

26. *Railroad Gazette,* April 15, 1904, 293; Williams interview.

27. ICC *Reports* 97 (1925): 406–17; *Railroad Gazette,* April 15, 1904, 298, February 17, 1905, 56, March 10, 1905, 79; *New Orleans Daily Picayune,* November 7, 1906. The new vessel was not the first to be named *William Edenborn;* an ore boat belonging to U. S. Steel Corp. was christened with the same name. Built in 1900 at West Bay City, Michigan, that boat was 478 feet long and moved about the Great Lakes until it was scrapped in 1962 (Edenborn Papers, LSUS Archives).

28. Manuscript of recollections of Paul Sippel, dated August 1, 1968, and deposited in the LSUS Archives (hereafter cited as Sippel Recollections). Mr. Sippel, now deceased, was for many years an officer of the LR&N and L&A roads.

29. *Railroad Gazette,* May 26, 1905, 175, July 28, 1905, 31, June 1, 1906, 161.

30. *Official Guide,* July 1906; ICC *Reports* 97 (1925): 406–17; *New Orleans Daily Picayune,* October 26, October 28, and December 13, 1906; files in the Office of the Louisiana Secretary of State, Baton Rouge.

31. *Commercial and Financial Chronicle,* September 26, 1903, 769; *Railroad Gazette,* September 18, 1903, 680.

32. Information on locomotives is taken from several sources: Edson, "Locomotives"; A. E. Brown, *Locomotives and Trains of the L&A and KCS Railways* (Shreveport, La., [1953]); Harold K. Vollrath, unpublished roster of the LR&N; mechanical department records of the railroad.

33. *New Orleans Daily Picayune,* February 8 and April 15, 1907; *Railroad Gazette,* March 8, 1907, 321, April 19, 1907, 565; *Com-mercial and Financial Chronicle,* September 26, 1903, 769.

34. Forshey, "The Woman"; *New Orleans Times-Picayune,* May 15, 1926.

35. Edenborn Recollections; *The Iron Age,* December 9, 1909, 1787; Forshey, "The Woman."

CHAPTER 3

Operation of the LR&N

1. ICC *Reports* 106 (1925): 47; Floyd Mundy, *The Earning Power of Railroads* (New York: Jas. H. Oliphant & Co., 1913); ICC *Reports* 97 (1925): 406.

2. Control of the Katy by the Gould interests ended in 1890. For background on this control, see Maury Klein, *The Life and Legend of Jay Gould* (Baltimore: Johns Hopkins University Press, 1986); Julius Grodinsky, *Jay Gould: His Business Career, 1867–1892* (Philadelphia: University of Pennsylvania Press, 1957). A much more detailed discussion is given in W. J. Burton, "History of the Missouri Pacific Railroad" (unpublished manuscript in the corporate files of the Union Pacific Railroad, St. Louis, Mo.).

3. *Official Guide,* May 1907; ICC *Reports* 75 (Kansas City Shreveport and Gulf Terminal Company, 1919): 425; *Shreveport Times,* August 1 and 4, 1897; ICC *Reports* 106 (1925): 47; *New Orleans Daily Picayune,* April 13, 1907; Vicksburg, Shreveport and Pacific Railway, *Annual Reports,* 1901–1910. The Cotton Belt bridge was located about a mile downstream from the VS&P bridge and was operated by the Shreveport Bridge & Terminal Company, a subsidiary of the Cotton Belt; the bridge was placed in service on March 25, 1907 (VS&P Railway, *Annual Report,* 1908).

4. *New Orleans Daily Picayune,* April 20, 1907; the bids for construction were opened May 1, 1907. See also *Commercial and Financial Chronicle,* March 21, 1908, 721; Thomas S. Hines, *Burnham of Chicago: Architect and Planner* (New York: Oxford University Press, 1974); Louis C. Hennick and E. Harper Charlton, *Louisiana: Its Street and Interurban Railways,* vol. 2, *The Streetcars of New Orleans, 1831–1965* (Shreveport, La.: L. C. Hennick, 1965); ICC *Valuation Reports* 37 (1931): 895. In its annual report to the ICC dated June 30, 1909, the LR&N stated that the contract with the New Orleans Terminal called for $500 per day for

two trains and $750 per day for four trains, plus 45 cents per train mile for trackage (Louisiana Railway and Navigation Company, *Annual Report*, 1909).

5. *Official Guide*, February 1909, March 1909.

6. "Edenborn Line Rapidly Expanding: Brings New Business to the Port," *The Trade Index* [Journal of the New Orleans Board of Trade] 28 (September 1916): 24. Two of the warehouses were destroyed by fire on March 14, 1914, with $200,000 damage and the loss of 4,000 bales of cotton (*New Orleans Daily Picayune*, March 15, 1914). The warehouses were soon rebuilt.

7. *Shreveport Times*, January 24, 1899; Engineering Report in file of Valuation Docket 215, ICC, (hereafter cited as LR&N Engineering Report), a summary of which was published in ICC *Reports* 106 (1925): 47–66; Louis C. Hennick and E. Harper Charlton, *Louisiana: Its Street and Interurban Railways*, vol. 1, (Shreveport, La.: L. C. Hennick, 1963); Charlton and Hennick, *The Streetcars of New Orleans, 1831–1965*, 106.

8. *Official Guide*, 1910–1914, passim.

9. *New Orleans States*, April 29, 1923.

10. R. W. Hidy and M. E. Hidy, *History of Standard Oil Company (New Jersey): Pioneering in Big Business, 1882–1911* (New York: Harper & Brothers, 1955), 420; Carl C. Rister, *Oil! Titan of the Southwest* (Norman: University of Oklahoma Press, 1949), 102–3; John L. Loos, *Oil on Stream! A History of Interstate Oil Pipe Line Company, 1909–1959* (Baton Rouge: Louisiana State University Press, 1959), 30–32; "Refinery Celebrates 50th Anniversary," *Esso News* (Baton Rouge Refinery, Esso Standard Oil Company, Baton Rouge, La., November 6, 1959): 3–23.

11. Hodding Carter, *John Law Wasn't So Wrong: The Story of Louisiana's Horn of Plenty* (Baton Rouge: Esso Standard Oil Co., 1952); H. B. Helm, "Edenborn Line: Louisiana Railway and Navigation Company," *The Trade Index* [Journal of the New Orleans Board of Trade] 27 [1915] (the exact date and page are not identified). In later years the volume of traffic in and out of the refineries justified retaining a switch engine at Gramercy-Reserve.

12. Robert E. Caudle, "History of the Missouri Pacific Lines: Gulf Coast Lines and Subsidiaries and International Great Northern," September 1949 (unpublished manuscript in the corporate files of the Union Pacific Railroad,

St. Louis, Mo.), 92–95; *Official Guide*, 1909–1910, passim; St. Louis and San Francisco Railroad Company, *Annual Report*, 1909. The Missouri Pacific ferry at Baton Rouge would continue until 1947, when trackage rights over the L&A into Baton Rouge were obtained.

13. *Railway Age*, May 26, 1905, 175; ICC *Reports* 23 (1912): 277, 549; *Railroad Gazette*, August 20, 1909, 340; abandonment order No. 2049, Louisiana Public Service Commission, October 17, 1916 [Tioga branch].

14. St. Louis and San Francisco Railroad Company, *Annual Report*, 1915; LR&N Engineering Report, 1915; ICC *Reports* 106 (1925): 47; Caudle, "History of the Missouri Pacific Lines," 92–95; ICC File, VD 215; Williams interview. Annual reports by the LR&N to the ICC showed payments received from the Gulf Coast Lines of around $60,000 each year.

15. LR&N Engineering Report.

16. Williams interview; *Biographical Directory of Railroad Officials of America*, 1913 [Helm]; *Co-Operative News*, December-January 1931–1932 (the employee magazine of the L&A, hereafter cited as *Co-Op News*). Ellerbe remained in Shreveport and became a cotton farmer and part owner of the large Huron Plantation (KCS *Current Events* No. 49, November 1914; information in Shreve Memorial Library, Shreveport, La.). He died in 1937.

17. Franks and Lambert, *Early Louisiana and Arkansas Oil*, 43, 69; Helm, "Edenborn Line"; K. Beaton, *Enterprise in Oil* (New York: Appleton-Century-Crofts, 1957), 141, 344–47; Henry E. Yoes III, *A History of St. Charles Parish to 1973* (Norco, La.: St. Charles Herald Publishers, 1973).

18. ICC *Reports* 106 (1925): 47 (LR&N valuation).

19. Walker D. Hines, *War History of American Railroads* (New Haven: Yale University Press, 1928); *Railway Age*, August 23, 1918, 364; *Moody's Manual—Railroad Section* (New York: Moody's Investors Service, 1919) (this manual has been published annually since 1909, under varying titles [currently *Moody's Transportation Manual*] and will hereafter be cited as *Moody's Manual*); Henry V. Poor, ed. *Manual of the Railroads of the United States* (New York: H. V. and H. W. Poor, published annually, 1876–1921), years 1920 and 1921. The LR&N was paid $300,000 by the USRA, which included an excess of about $33,000 that had to be repaid later. The L&A was not returned to its owners until March 1, 1920.

20. Augusto P. Miceli, *The Pickwick Club of New Orleans* (New Orleans: Pickwick Press, 1964), 154; *Who's Who in Louisiana and Mississippi* (New Orleans: Times-Picayune, 1918), 80.

21. Williams, *Huey Long*, 43.

22. "State Railroad Commission Fines L. R. & N.," *Railway Age*, May 14, 1920, 1428. The quoted material is an excerpt from a statement by R. E. Milling; Louisiana Railroad Commission Order 2255, March 25, 1919.

23. Public Service Commission of Louisiana, Order No. 2379, January 26, 1921, and Order No. 2822, March 7, 1922.

24. Hennick and Charlton, *Louisiana*, vol. 1; annual reports of the Louisiana Railroad and Public Service Commissions. The Yazoo & Mississippi Valley offered competing service; see *Railway Age*, July 3, 1926, 13; Public Service Commission Order No. 449, April 16, 1927.

25. Letters, Huey Long to LR&N, May 8, May 12, May 22, 1924; letter, Huey Long to William Edenborn, May 27, 1924. In Long papers, Louisiana Public Service Commission; quoted in Williams, *Huey Long*, 159.

26. Files in the Office of the Louisiana Secretary of State, Baton Rouge. The Angola Transfer Company was organized November 9, 1906, but its state charter was not filed until October 13, 1921; LR&N, "Corporate Chart," ICC File, VD 215.

27. I. P. Rutherford, "Across the Wide Mississippi," *The Eagle* 4 (February 1977): 3.

28. Williams interview; Vollrath, personal communication, 1972; Baton Rouge *State-Times,* August 9, 1940.

29. Williams interview; Rutherford, "Across the Wide Mississippi." Edenborn patronized the Howard Ship Yards at Jeffersonville, Indiana. In his book on this enterprise, *From Paddle Wheels to Propellers* (Indianapolis: Indiana Historical Society, 1970), Charles Fishbaugh shows $12,835 as the cost of the *William.* No cost information is given for the *Sarah* or the *William II.* Costs in the table, taken from the ICC files, appear excessively high.

30. *Railway Age,* January 28, 1922, 303, February 25, 1922, 502, March 4, 1922, 548, February 10, 1923, 402, July 7, 1923, 47; *New Orleans Times-Picayune,* May 1, 1954.

31. *Official Guide,* June 1924; Ralph Wafer, "Railroad Stations of the City of New Orleans," September 30, 1970 (manuscript in the Howard-Tilton Library, Tulane University).

32. *Moody's Manual,* 1925; ICC *Reports* 76 (1923): 651; Engineering Report on Missouri, Kansas and Texas Railroad of Texas, in file of Valuation Docket 814, ICC, a summary of which was published in ICC *Valuation Reports* 34 (1930).

33. ICC *Reports* 99 (1925): 357; "Deed of sale, M K & T Rwy *et al.* to William Edenborn," filed for record in the Collin County, Texas, courthouse, April 3, 1923.

34. *Railway Age,* April 7, 1923, 934. The fate of this magazine is not known; the author has been unable to locate copies.

35. This line was laid entirely with secondhand rail of what was considered light. The heaviest was sixty-six-pound rail, but about two-thirds of the line had rail even lighter (Engineering Report, M K & T of Texas).

36. *New Orleans States,* April 29, 1923. Guy Forshey ("The Woman") describes the willing efforts of Sarah Edenborn in the kitchen of the *William Edenborn* during the transfer of the party across the river.

37. *Railway Age,* July 25, 1925, 205, reported the application to the Public Service Commission; *Railway Age,* August 1, 1925, 1, reported approval by that body. Approval by the ICC came in October (ICC *Reports* 99 [1925]: 731); Williams interview.

38. R. E. Milling, testimony in file of Finance Docket (FD) 7076, ICC (hereafter cited as Milling Testimony); Williams interview.

39. *Railway Age,* July 25, 1925, 205, August 1, 1925, 249, October 10, 1925, 686.

40. "Float 300-ft. Span into Place in a Swift Current," ibid., April 27, 1929, 959; Percy F. Lyons, "New Railway in Louisiana Cuts Off Long Ferry Transfer," *Engineering News-Record,* October 6, 1927, 540; Williams interview.

41. The Mississippi River flood of 1927 caused $125,000 damage to the LR&N (*Railway Age,* September 17, 1927, 511), plus considerable lost revenue. Much of the line from Mansura to Naples was under water; flooding of the Red was also a problem in the East Point area. For popular reports on the flood, see Frederick Simpich, "The Great Mississippi Flood of 1927," *National Geographic Magazine,* September 1927, 243; and Pete Daniel, *Deep'n as It Come: The 1927 Mississippi River Flood* (New York: Oxford University Press, 1977).

42. A crevasse that occurred near Sarto on May 14, 1927, rapidly led to severe flooding from the Bayou des Glaises. Kleinwood, a station on the LR&N 1.7 miles west of Sarto, had sixteen feet of water by 5:00 P.M. the same day

(Isaac Monroe Cline, *Storms, Floods and Sunshine,* 2d ed. [New Orleans: Pelican Publishing Co., 1945], 204); Daniel, *Deep'n as It Come,* 38–39.

43. Sippel Recollections; "Float 300-ft. Span into Place in a Swift Current," *Railway Age,* April 27, 1929, 959.

44. Williams interview. The *Kellogg* was left behind to handle ferry needs between Naples and Angola. Its fate was described by Williams:

> We had another steamer there, the *Kellogg,* which was a sidewheeler we used to pump sand and gravel and sometimes [to] make commercial trips. While these two boats [*William* and *Sarah*] were at Simmesport the *Kellogg* was our only means of transportation and she was making the trips. The second night I was called shortly after midnight and was told that they could not hear anything further from the *Kellogg*—that they thought they heard a distress signal, so I got up and in a few minutes they called me again and said the *Kellogg* had sunk. Apparently they had left a hatch open at the front of the boat, had run the boat pretty fast (they had 13 loads on her, not shoved back too far) and the boat sank. We got the crew safely put away, having to buy some of them clothes . . . .

45. Way, *Way's Packet Directory;* Williams interview.

46. Williams interview; *New Orleans Times-Picayune,* May 14, 1926.

47. *New Orleans Times-Picayune,* May 15, 1926. In his last years, Edenborn spent much of his time at the Emden farm, where he conducted agricultural research, and he had a laboratory in which he studied methods for recovering turpentine and tars from pine stumps. For the latter effort he was awarded his last patent, as mentioned in chapter 1, note 27 (*Winnfield Enterprise/News-American,* December 5, 1957).

48. "Resolution Passed by the Board of Directors of the Louisiana Railway & Navigation Company, May 19th, 1926, In memoriam—William Edenborn," LSUS Archives.

49. *New Orleans Times-Picayune,* May 16, 1926.

50. Milling Testimony; *Shreveport Times,* May 17, 1926.

51. Milling Testimony; Franks and Lambert, *Early Louisiana and Arkansas Oil,* 75–76.

52. *Co-Op News,* December–January 1931–1932; Sippel Recollections. Henry Helm moved to the Shreveport and Red River Valley in 1901 and rose to a vice president–treasurer position with the LR&N. Edward Staman joined the LR&N in 1914 and later became a vice president; he stayed with the L&A as treasurer and assistant secretary. Business in 1927 was hampered by boll weevil damage to cotton crops along the LR&N (Sippel Recollections).

53. Indeed, this flow was bolstered nicely in 1925 and 1926 by oil and gas royalties from the well-known Urania Lumber Company in LaSalle Parish. Years earlier, at the same time William had invested in 65,000 acres of timberlands near the railroad, he had also become a major and early investor in the Urania Lumber Company, some distance from the railroad. Kenny Franks and Paul F. Lambert, *Early Louisiana and Arkansas Oil* (College Station: Texas A&M University Press, 1982), 75–76; John D. Klorer, ed., *The New Louisiana: The Story of the Greatest State of the Nation* (Baton Rouge: Louisiana Governor's Office, 1936); Coleman, *The Man Who Fenced the West.*

54. *New Orleans Times-Picayune,* April 14 and 16, 1928; *Railway Age,* April 27, 1929, 959; Lyons, "New Railway in Louisiana"; Carmine L. Saucier, *History of Avoyelles Parish, Louisiana* (New Orleans: Pelican Publishing Co., 1943). According to the testimony of E. A. Staman during the October 16, 1928, ICC hearings, the total cost of the bridge plus relocation was $2,156,631 (FD 7076).

55. For biographical data on Couch, see chapter 6.

56. Winston Wilson, *Harvey Couch, Master Builder;* Poor, *Manual,* 1930.

57. FD 7076.

58. Ibid.

59. ICC *Reports* 150 (1929): 477 (FD 7076); letter, Huey Long to ICC, September 20, 1928 (FD 7076).

60. Guy Forshey, "The Woman"; New Orleans *Times-Picayune,* June 19, 1926; May 10, 1929.

61. St. Louis *Post-Dispatch,* July 22, 1926; July 29, 1926; August 11, 1926; August 12, 1926; October 7, 1926; April 25, 1928; New Orleans *Times-Picayune,* August 12, 1926.

62. St. Louis *Post-Dispatch,* December 8, 1934.

63. St. Louis *Post-Dispatch,* August 9, 1944; November 26, 1944; November 27, 1944. One of Edgar's grandchildren, Glen

Coleman, later published a laudatory book about Edenborn's career.

CHAPTER 4

The Earliest L&A Antecedent

	Standard	Narrow
Flatcars	20,000	19,000
Boxcars	20,000	17,600
Coal cars	30,000	20,000
Cattle cars	19,600	12,600

1. D. White and T. C. Richardson, eds. *East Texas: Its History and Its Makers* (New York: Lewis Historical Publishing Co., 1940), 1109.

2. Charles S. Potts, *Railroad Transportation in Texas,* University of Texas Bulletin no. 119 (Austin, 1909), 20; *From Ox-Teams to Eagles* (Dallas: Texas and Pacific Railway Co., [1946]), 6–7; J. Fair Hardin, "An Outline of Shreveport and Caddo Parish History," *Louisiana Historical Quarterly* 18 (October 1935): 759–871. The Shreveport–Marshall line was part of a projected railroad to the Pacific, known as "the 32nd parallel route."

3. United States, *Statutes at Large 16,* 573–579; Virginia H. Taylor, *The Franco-Texan Land Company* (Austin: University of Texas Press, 1969), 76–78.

4. H. P. N. Gammel, ed., *The Laws of Texas, 1822–1897,* 10 vols. (Austin: Gammel Book Co., 1898), 6:1188.

5. *Railroad Gazette,* April 21, 1876, 178, May 26, 1876, 234, June 23, 1876, 282, September 15, 1876, 409, November 3, 1876, 487, December 1, 1876, 529, February 16, 1877, 78, July 13, 1877, 321, November 9, 1877, 502, March 1, 1878, 116, August 23, 1878, 419, February 7, 1879, 75, April 25, 1879, 227; ICC *Valuation Reports* 34 (1930): 625, 628; Poor, *Manual,* 1879; *Galveston Daily News,* October 26, 1876, September 15, 1878.

6. ICC *Valuation Reports* 34 (1930): 552, 630; White and Richardson, *East Texas;* Gammel, *Laws of Texas* 7:1133; Fred Tarpley, *Jefferson: Riverport to the Southwest* (Austin: Eakin Press, 1983).

7. *Proceedings of the National Narrow-Gauge Railway Convention,* held at St, Louis, Mo., June 19, 1872; Howard Fleming, *Narrow Gauge Railways in America,* 2d ed. (Philadelphia: n.p., 1876); George Hilton, *American Narrow Gauge Railroads* (Stanford: Stanford University Press, 1990).

8. Hilton, *American Narrow Guage Railroads.* Some comparative capacities (in pounds) of freight cars, according to Fleming (*Narrow Gauge Railways in America,* 54–56), are:

9. *Galveston Daily News,* June 9, 1876; *Dallas Daily Herald,* June 11, 1876; *American Railroad Journal,* April 6, 1878, 398; East Line and Red River Railroad, minutes of the meetings of the Board of Directors, 1876–1881 (hereafter cited as Minute Book) (DeGolyer Library, Southern Methodist University, Dallas, Texas).

10. Minute Book, June 19, 1876, August 7, 1876, September 11, 1876. The steam locomotive cost $4,985.40, delivered to Jefferson.

11. Texas, Office of the State Engineer, *State Engineer's Report of the Inspection of the First Section of Twenty Miles of the Road* [East Line and Red River Railroad], Jefferson, Tex., December 2, 1876 (prepared by E. A. Blanch); *Galveston Daily News,* September 15, 1878.

12. Minute Book, May 21, 1877, June 15, 1877; Taylor, *Franco-Texan Land Company; Galveston Daily News,* September 15, 1878; *Texas Railroad Gazetteer for Distribution on Railways, Steamships and Stages* (Galveston: O. C. Moore and Co., 1878).

13. *Railway Age,* December 18, 1879, 610.

14. *Official Guide,* January 1880; *Railroad Gazette,* January 9, 1880, 23, May 28, 1880, 295, October 15, 1880, 549, December 24, 1880, 693, March 18, 1881, 162, June 17, 1881, 339.

15. Minute Book, October 11, 1881, November 28, 1881. In November 1881 Jay Gould owned 6,065 of the 6,130 outstanding shares of East Line capital stock.

16. Poor, *Manual,* 1881; V. V. Masterson, *The Katy Railroad and the Last Frontier* (Norman: University of Oklahoma Press, 1952), 223; ICC *Valuation Reports* 34 (1930): 629; *Dallas Herald,* March 4, March 30, and April 21, 1882.

17. *Dallas Herald,* May 18, 1882.

18. ICC *Valuation Reports* 34 (1930): 629.

19. T. R. Fehrenbach, *Lone Star: A History of Texas and the Texans* (New York: Macmillan Co., 1968), 619.

20. ICC *Valuation Reports* 34 (1930): 625.

21. Robert C. Cotner, *Addresses and State Papers of James Stephen Hogg* (Austin: University of Texas Press, 1951), 190–91.

22. ICC *Valuation Reports* 34 (1930): 625; *Texas Reports* 65 (1885): 167–73; *Railway Age,* July 12, 1883, 416; *Railroad Gazette,* September 30, 1892, 736; *Dallas Morning News,* September 11, 1892. The date of gauge change, Greenville to McKinney, is not certain, but is known to be between late 1886 and early 1888 (*Texas Reports* 69 (1887): 306–18; E. C. M. Rand, *Findings in the Investigation of Matters Relating to the Missouri, Kansas and Texas Railway Co.* (New York: Devinne Press, 1888).

23. *Indenture by and between Sherman, Shreveport and Southern Railway Co. and Central Trust Co.,* New York, June 1, 1893 (copy on file, Association of American Railroads, Washington, D.C.); *Railway Age,* February 3, 1893, 101; Masterson, *Katy Railroad,* 248. To comply with state law, the Katy lines in Texas were deeded to the Missouri, Kansas and Texas Railway of Texas, organized October 28, 1891.

24. Texas, Railroad Commission, *Annual Report,* 1893, 140–42, 1893; *Railway Age,* June 16, 1893, 483; Poor, *Manual,* 1901. Rumors of an extension west from McKinney persisted until 1927 (*Railway Age,* April 2, 1927, 1090).

25. Texas, Railroad Commission, *Annual Reports,* 1894–1897; Interstate Commerce Commission, *Statistics of Railways in the United States,* 1894–1899 (Washington, D.C.: Government Printing Office, 1894, 1899.).

26. *Railway Age,* July 28, 1893, 588, January 12, 1894, 24, March 2, 1895, 144, April 5, 1895, 173, July 26, 1895, 368; *New Orleans Daily Picayune,* January 5, 1898.

27. *Railway Age,* March 10, 1899, 162, May 19, 1899, 382; St. Clair G. Reed, *A History of the Texas Railroads and of Transportation Conditions under Spain and Mexico and the Republic of Texas and the State* (Houston: St. Clair Publishing Co., 1941), 384; *Shreveport Times,* December 13, 1898, and May 20, 1899.

28. *Railroad Gazette,* January 19, 1900, 30, January 26, 1900, 64; Poor, *Manual,* 1901; *Commercial and Financial Chronicle,* February 17, 1900, 329, November 3, 1900, 911, December 1, 1900, 1115; *Shreveport Times,* December 4, 1898, December 31, 1899, and January 9, April 4, June 23, and July 28, 1900. Newton Crain Blanchard, a former U.S. Senator from Louisiana, was serving as an associate justice of the Supreme Court of Louisiana; later he would be elected governor of the state.

29. *Shreveport Times,* July 30, 1900.

30. Interstate Commerce Commission, *Statistics of Railways in the United States,* Washington, 1900, 1901; VS&P Railroad, *Annual Report,* 1900. As noted in chapter 3, the Shreveport Union Station had opened in August 1897.

31. Missouri, Kansas and Texas Railroad, public timetables for the 1904–1910 period (in author's collection); VS&P Railway, *Annual Report,* 1901.

32. Reed, *Texas Railroads,* 439, 459; ICC *Reports* 76 (1923): 158, 230, 771–73.

33. "Deed of Sale, MK&T Rwy *et al.*"

34. Texas, Railroad Commission, *Annual Report,* 1895, 252; ICC Valuation Docket 814 (Missouri, Kansas and Texas Railroad of Texas; engineering report in docket file, Washington, D.C.).

CHAPTER 5

William Buchanan and the Original L&A

1. ICC *Reports* 133 (1927): 704.

2. C. J. Corliss, *Main Line of Mid-America* (New York: Creative Age Press, 1950), 399; *Railroad Gazette,* July 10, 1885, 447, December 25, 1885, 830; Poor, *Manual,* 1886; B. S. Atkinson, "The Development of the American Railroads," address before the New Orleans Traffic Club, June 1932.

3. Jacob E. Anderson, *A Short History of the St. Louis Southwestern Railway Lines* (St. Louis: St. Louis Southwestern Railway, 1947). The bridge over the Red River at Garland City, Arkansas, was not opened until May 16, 1883 (*Arkansas Gazette,* May 17, 1883; *Arkansas Democrat,* September 7, 1952 [magazine section]).

4. Files in the Office of the Arkansas Secretary of State, Little Rock; Mayor, *Southern Timberman,* 15.

5. Barbara O. Chandler and J. Ed Howe, *History of Texarkana and Bowie and Miller Counties, Texas-Arkansas* (Texarkana: J. Ed Howe), 247–48; Mayor, *Southern Timberman.*

6. James W. Mosley, "A Legacy Greater than Wealth: An Appreciative Appraisal of the W. C. Brown Family," *Proc. Presbyterian Hist. Soc. Southwest* (March 1989): 15–20.

7. Files in the Office of the Arkansas Secretary of State, Little Rock.

8. Clifton Johnson, *Highways and Byways of the Mississippi Valley* (New York: Macmillan Co., 1906). The account is based on Johnson's travels in southern Arkansas in the early part of the century.

9. Correspondence between the L&A and

the Interstate Commerce Commission, 1896–1898, obtained from the KCS files, courtesy H. K. Vollrath.

10. Charles A. Roach, "Boomers," *Railroad Magazine,* July 1950, 102–3.

11. Mayor, *Southern Timberman,* 18; *Louisiana & Arkansas Railway: Its Territory, Industries and Financial Condition* (New York and Boston: Fisk and Robinson Co., 1904), 59. Capacities of mills in board feet of lumber were commonly based on a ten-hour-per-day operation. For a discussion of preferential rates for lumber companies, see L. A. Dew, "The Arkansas Tap Line Cases: A Study in Commerce Regulation," *Arkansas Historical Quarterly* 29 (1940): 327–44; and ICC *Reports* 23 (1912): 277–344, 549–651.

12. KCS files; files in the Office of the Arkansas Secretary of State, Little Rock; ICC *Reports* 133 (1927): 704; *Shreveport Times,* September 30 and October 4, 1898; L&A operating timetable, July 12, 1900.

13. Files in the Office of the Arkansas Secretary of State, Little Rock; *Railway Age,* October 14, 1898, 758, April 7, 1899, 246, July 14, 1899, 524, September 15, 1899, 686, December 29, 1899, 976; KCS files; ICC *Reports* 133 (1927): 704; *Shreveport Times,* January 1 and September 6, 1899. The AL&S was purchased for $132,218 (L&A, *Annual Report to the Railroad Commission of Louisiana, June 30, 1900*). Gus Knobel had located much of the Iron Mountain line through Arkansas; the Arkansas town of Knobel was named in his honor. The quotation is from the *Shreveport Times,* January 3, 1900.

14. Arkansas, Railroad Commission, *First Annual Report, 1899-1900,* 369–73.

15. *Railroad Gazette,* April 11, 1902; KCS files.

16. For more on the Buchanan-Edenborn rivalry, see chapter 2.

17. ICC *Reports* 133 (1927): 704; L&A, *Annual Report to Stockholders,* 1902 (see *Commercial and Financial Chronicle,* December 13, 1902, 1306–7); Roach, "Boomers."

18. L&A, *Annual Report, 1902.* A detailed roster of L&A steam locomotives may be found in Edson, "Locomotives"; less complete roster data are given in Brown, *Locomotives and Trains.* Trackage maps in the LSUS Archives for circa 1901 form a basis for comparison of the Stamps trackage with that shown in later maps obtained by the author from KCS files.

19. O'Pry, *Chronicles;* Coleman, *The Man Who Fenced the West.*

20. *Co-Op News,* August 1931, 15–16; Poor, *Manual,* 1908, 359; ICC *Reports* 23 (1912): 277 (Tap Line case; see note 11 above).

21. L&A, *Annual Report,* 1903; *Commercial and Financial Chronicle,* November 21, 1903, 2044–45.

22. L&A, *Annual Reports,* 1903–1905; *Commercial and Financial Chronicle,* November 5, 1904, 2096–97, and September 30, 1905, 1050–51; Mayor, *Southern Timberman;* Writers' Program, Works Progress Administration, *Louisiana: A Guide to the State* (New York: Hastings House, 1941).

23. *Louisiana and Arkansas Railway;* Louisiana, Railroad Commission, *Annual Report,* 1905.

24. L&A, *Annual Reports,* 1906–1907.

25. Ibid., 1907. The L&A started using the Edenborn bridge after being consolidated with the LR&N in 1928. The Rock Island, Arkansas and Louisiana Railroad was formed by the consolidation of three rail lines on October 31, 1905; on January 31, 1906, it was leased to the Rock Island system (CRI&P, *Annual Report,* 1906) The Rock Island later abandoned its Winnfield–Packton route and began to use L&A tracks on June 1, 1925 (CRI&P, *Annual Report,* 1925).

26. ICC *Reports* 133 (1927): 723; L&A, *Annual Reports,* 1909–1910; *Official Guide,* July 1910; *Webster Signal,* August 18, 1905, March 12, 1909. The bridge over the Red River was owned by the Shreveport Bridge and Terminal Company, a Cotton Belt subsidiary.

27. L&A, *Annual Report,* 1911; *Official Guide,* 1911, passim.

28. L&A, *Annual Reports,* 1911–1914; J. A. L. Waddell, *Memoirs and Addresses of Two Decades,* ed. F. W. Skinner (Easton, Pa: Mack Printing Co., 1928) [steel bridges on the Jena extension]; Brian Thompson, *Narrow Gauge Railways in America* (Oakland, Calif.: Grahame Hardy, 1949). See also Hilton, *American Narrow Gauge Railroads.* The Natchez, Red River and Western was built as a narrow-gauge (3'0") connection between traffic on the Black River and Vidalia, opposite Natchez on the Mississippi.

29. ICC *Reports* 133 (1927): 687 (L&A Valuation Docket); Poor, *Manual,* 1917–1921.

30. Poor, *Manual,* 1922. By this time the L&A had leased the Iron Mountain line between Wildsville Junction and Vidalia. Ferry transfer at Natchez was provided by the Natchez and Louisiana Transfer Company (later Natchez and Southern Railway Company), see David S.

Price and Louis R. Saillard, *Natchez Route: A Mississippi Central Railroad Album* (Hattiesburg: Mississippi Great Southern Chapter, National Railway Historical Society, 1975).

31. O'Pry, *Chronicles;* Stephen E. Shoup, *The KCS—L&A: Report and Recommendations on Merger of the Properties* (Kansas City: Kansas City Southern, December 1946); KCS files.

32. Atkinson, "American Railroads."

33. Mayor, *Southern Timberman,* 106–10.

34. Ibid., 115.

35. ICC *Reports* 131 (1927): 180; Edson, "Locomotives"; undated clipping in KCS files; *Railway Age,* May 7, 1927, 1389, September 17, 1927, 511. Between Rhinehart and Concordia Junction the railroad sank wooden posts at each rail joint on the north side of the track, before the water rose to track level. The rails were lashed to the posts and after the waters receded it was found that there was essentially no movement of the track. For more on the effects of the flood on the ultimate L&A system, see chapter 3.

CHAPTER 6

Harvey Couch and the New L&A

1. Franks and Lambert, *Early Louisiana and Arkansas Oil;* Rister, *Oil!;* Moody's Manual, 1925–1940.

2. *Moody's Manual,* 1925–1940; the Vicksburg, Shreveport and Pacific was part of the Queen and Crescent system, which extended to Cincinnati, Ohio, on the north.

3. The biographical information on Harvey Couch given in this chapter was obtained from a number of sources, including Winston Wilson, *Harvey Couch: Master Builder,* and Stephen Wilson, *Harvey Couch: Entrepreneur,* neither of which offers source documentation and both of which provide little coverage of Couch's railroad activities. A wealth of data on Couch were provided in a collection of newspaper articles written at the time of his death (and loaned to the author by H. K. Vollrath). Couch's railroad career up to the time of the KCS acquisition is outlined in *Railway Age,* June 3, 1939, 950, 953. Some supplementation of the published information was provided by personal interviews with C. Hamilton Moses, lawyer and long-time business associate of Harvey Couch, and Pratt Remmel, son-in-law of Couch.

4. The Louisiana and North West Railroad was a new road supported to a large degree by logging and by lumber shipments. Chartered on

January 1, 1895, it was opened from Magnolia, Arkansas, to Natchitoches, Louisiana, in November 1898; a branch of the Cotton Belt between McNeil and Magnolia was leased by the L&NW (Poor, *Manual,* 1908). Regular service between McNeil and Gibsland began on October 1, 1898 (*Shreveport Times,* September 30, 1898).

5. *Arkansas Gazette,* July 31, 1941.

6. Information on McCain was obtained from *Co-Op News,* October 1931. Additional biographical data on McCain may be found in the *New York Times,* December 14, 1957 (obituary), and *Who's Who in Railroading,* 11th ed. (New York: Simmons-Boardman, 1946), 449.

7. Winston Wilson, *Harvey Couch: Master Builder;* KCS files, courtesy H. K. Vollrath; ICC *Reports* 150 (1929): 477 (FD 7076). E. A. Frost was identified earlier as one of the purchasers of the Bodcaw mill at Stamps, Ark.

8. *Arkansas Gazette,* July 31, 1941; Stephen Wilson, *Harvey Couch: Entrepreneur,* 70–72. Arkansas Power and Light was chartered on October 3, 1926.

9. KCS files; ICC *Reports* 150 (1929): 477 (FD 7076).

10. ICC *Reports* 150 (1929): 477 (FD 7076).

11. Ibid.

12. L&A operating timetables; KCS files; Price and Saillard, *Natchez Route.* The mileage given includes trackage rights, Shreveport–Waskom, Wildsville Junction–Vidalia, Hamburg–Simmesport. Later, trackage rights would be obtained for Farmersville–Dallas and Torras Junction–Baton Rouge.

13. A. E. Brown, "The Louisiana & Arkansas Railway: Structure and Operation in the Age of Steam," *Railroad History,* no. 144 (Summer 1981): 50–59; Brown, *Locomotives and Trains; Official Guide,* 1928, passim. On December 14, 1934, the ICC approved liquidation of the LR&N, and the property was taken over by the L&A on December 31, 1934 (*Moody's Manual,* 1936).

14. Brown, *Locomotives and Trains;* letter, C. E. Johnston to W. A. Van Hook, February 26, 1938 (courtesy K. K. Vollrath). Contemporary photographs show the rather deplorable condition of the Texas line trackage.

15. *Co-Op News,* various issues; LR&N Engineering Report; FD 7076; *Railway Age,* June 30, 1928, 1532.

16. *Co-Op News,* December 1928, January 1929.

17. The café-parlor car was Missouri

Pacific No. 10501 and after the inaugural run was renumbered 609 by the L&A; a wooden car with steel underframe added later, it survived until streamlined equipment came to the railroad in 1940. The sleeper was Pullman *Uruguay,* and the baggage-mail was L&A 45; the coach is not identified (*Co-Op News,* January 1929).

18. Ibid.

19. Ibid.; Brown, *Locomotives and Trains;* Edson, "Locomotives"; contemporary photographs available to the author.

20. These cars were painted blue and nicknamed "Bluebird." A trailer car was also purchased. Trials on the Texas line were evidently unsuccessful, possibly because of the heavy grades (*Co-Op News,* November 1928). Various issues of *Co-Op News* document events during 1929 and 1930 and provide useful information on the period covered. The political gatherings at Baton Rouge are described in Williams, *Huey Long,* 450.

21. The work projects are described in FD 7076, ICC, Washington.

22. A lengthy biographical sketch on C. P. Couch may be found in *Co-Op News,* July 1932. Other biographical data may be found in *Who's Who in Railroading,* 11th ed., 1946, 142; the *Baton Rouge State-Times,* August 9, 1940; and a number of trade sources.

23. *Co-Op News,* May 1930; Mayor, *Southern Timberman.* The "cradle" was used to connect the incline rails with the barge rails.

24. *Co-Op News,* March 1931; *Kansas City Southern Magazine,* February-April 1932. Barksdale Field was to be the new home of the Third Attack Group; the site covered some 22,000 acres. For details, see *The History of Barksdale Air Force Base, 1933–1970* (N.p.: [U.S. Air Force], n.d.).

25. Kansas City Southern Industries, Inc., Office of the Vice President and Secretary, *Manual No. 63,* July 1, 1975, 34.

26. ICC *Reports* 162 (1930): 184, 199, 766; *Moody's Manual,* 1931; KCS files.

27. *Moody's Manual,* 1931.

28. "Louisiana and Arkansas Railway Company Emergency Board Report," *Machinists' Monthly Journal,* 1931, 460–64, 510.

29. *Co-Op News,* March 1931, October 1931.

30. Progress on the south end was reported regularly in *Co-Op News;* and the author inspected the property. Operating ratio is the total cost of operation divided by total revenues, expressed as a percentage.

31. Fon W. Boardman, *The Thirties: America and the Great Depression* (New York: Henry Walck, 1967); Walter F., *History of the Brotherhood of Railroad Trainmen* (New York: Albert and Charles Boni, 1936), 164–70. For a discussion of railroad wages during this period, see Harry E. Jones, *Railroad Wages and Labor Relations, 1900–1952* (New York: Bureau of Information, Eastern Railways, 1953).

32. Jesse H. Jones, with Edward Angly, *Fifty Billion Dollars: My Thirteen Years with the RFC (1932–1945)* (New York: Macmillan Co., 1951); *Arkansas Gazette,* January 26, 1932; personal files of John W. Barriger III, now in Mercantile Library, St. Louis. For the role of Herbert Hoover in the 1927 flood, see chapter 3.

33. *Co-Op News,* March-April 1932.

34. Advertisements in local press; issues of the *Official Guide; Co-Op News,* July 1932; public timetables in the author's possession. The comment on coffee service is taken from the *National Railway Historical Society Quarterly,* April 1938, 15.

35. "To Build Long Bridges over Bonnet Carre Floodway," *Railway Age,* July 21, 1934, 67. The Illinois Central and the Yazoo & Mississippi Valley also had to build new trestles.

36. The Huey Long Bridge was the first structure to span the Mississippi south of Vicksburg; it was completed and dedicated on December 16, 1935, slightly more than three months after Long's assassination on September 8. Planning of the Baton Rouge bridge is discussed in ibid., February 7, 1931, 322, and June 29, 1940, 1172.

37. ICC *Reports* 217 (1936): 489. This branch of the T&P was originally intended to be part of a Jay Gould line down the west side of the Mississippi from St. Louis and Memphis to New Orleans. It was lightly built, and in 1936 much of the original sixty-three-pound rail was still in place (ICC *Reports* 244 [1941]: 235).

38. *Railway Age,* February 7, 1931, 322.

39. *History of Barksdale Air Force Base;* Vollrath, personal communication, 1972; *Shreveport Times,* February 2, 1933.

40. L&A, *Annual Reports,* 1932–1934. The payment for the Bonnet Carre bridge did not come without an argument. Negotiations, which began in 1929, led to a suit filed in the federal district court in June 1930. The settlement yielded a total of $4,332,736 to the three railroads building bridges (Illinois Central, Yazoo & Mississippi Valley, L&A) in January 1934 (*Railway Age,* January 27, 1934, 175). The

spillway was fully complete in early 1936 and had its first use in January 1937, when floodwaters were diverted from the river to the lake (Yoes, *St. Charles Parish*).

41. Motive-power information from KCS files; tonnage ratings may be found in operating timetables of the L&A for the period under discussion; bridge ratings are given in Brown, *Locomotives and Trains*. Tonnage ratings south of Angola took into account the availability of a switch engine helper to boost southbound freights over Tunica Hill.

42. L&A, *Annual Report*, 1936; clippings on file, St. Louis *Post-Dispatch*. A comprehensive article on the strike was published in the November 15, 1936, issue of the *Post-Dispatch*.

43. Contemporary clippings in the *St. Louis Post-Dispatch* archives.

44. Ibid., November 15, 1936; "Settle Strike of L. & A. Train Service Employees," *Railway Age*, November 28, 1936, 808.

45. L&A, *Annual Reports*, 1935–1936; Jones, *Fifty Billion Dollars*; *Kansas City Star*, March 22, May 25, May 26, 1937.

46. L&A, *Annual Report*, 1937; "Springhill, La.—Prosperity from the Piney Woods," *KCS Newsfolder*, July 1952, 3–11. Construction of the mill began in September 1937 in the community of Clifford, Louisiana, 2.6 miles south of the Springhill station. In 1939 the station name was changed from Clifford to Cullen, in honor of the president of International Paper ("A Birthday for Springhill and International Paper Company," *Springhill Digester* 19 (Summer 1973): 8–9; International Paper Company, *International Paper Company after Fifty Years* (n.p., 1948).

47. The Rock Island reorganization plan is described in ICC *Reports* 242 (1937): 298. The application of the L&A to the ICC was dated February 2, 1937. The ICC set rules that were similar to those imposed on the L&A when acquiring the LA&T; adequate provisions would be made for displaced employees of the L&A and RIA&L (*Railway Age*, November 12, 1938, 717). A lengthy article by E. B. Chestnutt on the implications of the possible merger of RIA&L and L&A, "Couch Seen as Seeking Great Rail System," was published in the *Arkansas Gazette*, February 27, 1937.

48. ICC *Reports* 224 (1937): 22; letter, R. R. Farmer to C. P. Couch, September 2, 1936; letter, N. Johnson to R. R. Farmer, September 4, 1936.

49. Brown, *Locomotives and Trains*; Voll-

rath, personal communication, 1972.

50. L&A, *Annual Reports*, 1934–1937; Mundy, *Earning Power of Railroads*, 1934–1937.

51. *Kansas City Star*, December 16, 1936, May 25, 1937.

52. Kansas City, Pittsburg and Gulf Railroad, *Annual Report*, 1898; KCS, *Annual Reports*, 1936–1937.

53. Letter, C. E. Johnston to W. A. Van Hook, February 26, 1938 (courtesy H. K. Vollrath).

54. ICC *Reports* 230 (1938): 156; ICC *Reports* 233 (1939): 123, 299; "Forging a Major Link Between the 'Heart of America' and the South and Southwest," *Kansas City Southern Magazine*, Oct.–Dec., 1938.

55. KCS *Newsfolder*, July 1952, 3–11. Even though not yet in full operation, the paper mill was the largest L&A shipper for 1938. The following list details the carloads of freight (inbound plus outbound) for the largest customers in 1938 (Shoup, *Report and Recommendations*):

International Paper

Springhill	30,365
Standard Oil Baton Rouge	30,000
Colonial Sugars Gramercy	15,000
Arkansas Fuel Oil Shreveport	15,000
Godchaux Sugar Reserve	15,000

56. ICC *Reports* 230 (1938): 156; ICC *Reports* 233 (1939): 123; KCS, *Annual Report*, 1939; L&A, *Annual Report*, 1939; *Railway Age*, October 5, 1940, 469; Reed, *Texas Railroads*, 440. Details of the conditions for the merger of the L&A and the LA&T may be found in *Railway Age*, November 12, 1938, 717.

57. L&A, *Annual Report*, 1940; KCS, *Annual Report*, 1940; "KCS–L&A Streamliner 'Southern Belle,'" *Railway Age*, October 5, 1940, 469.

58. L&A, *Annual Report*, 1940; KCS, *Annual Report*, 1940.

59. Interviews with L. B. Williams and H. K. Vollrath; internal memoranda, KCS/L&A; "KCS–L&A Streamliner 'Southern Belle,'" *Railway Age*, October 5, 1940, 469.

60. Internal memoranda, KCS/L&A; Wayne Kuchinsky, "Miss Belle and the Crow," *Passenger Train Journal* (April 1986): 17–31.

61. ICC *Reports* 236 (1940): 759; file, Finance Docket 12306, ICC Washington; Kansas City Southern Industries, *Manual No.*

63, 32; *Railway Age,* June 26, 1937, 1060.

62. Internal memorandum, KCS/L&A, dated May 21, 1940 giving details of May 26 schedule changes; public timetable for May 26, 1940.

63. Kansas City Southern Railway Company, "Southern Belle," calendar for 1995.

64. L&A, *Annual Report,* 1940; KCS, *Annual Report,* 1940; *Kansas City Star,* November 25, 1969; "Another Streamliner for the South," *National Railway Historical Society Bulletin* (Issue no. 4, 1940): 18; *Railway Age,* November 16, 1940, 731.

65. "Unusual Features of Design and Construction Mark New Bridge over the Mississippi," *Railway Age,* June 29, 1940, 1172–78; *Railway Age,* August 10, 1940, 228; Williams interview. The grade for the bridge approach from the east was nearly as bad as that from the west, measuring 1.07 to 1.13 percent. A special "bridge edition" of the Baton Rouge *State-Times,* published on Friday, August 9, 1940, included biographical sketches of principal L&A officers.

66. L&A, *Annual Reports,* 1938–1941; Williams interview; KCS files.

67. ICC *Reports* 242 (1940): 298.

68. *Arkansas Gazette,* July 31 and August 1, 1941; Winston Wilson, *Harvey Couch: Master Builder;* Stephen Wilson, *Harvey Couch: Entrepreneur;* interview with Pratt C. Remmel, son-in-law of Harvey Couch, 1972.

CHAPTER 7

A Big Little Railroad

1. L&A, *Annual Reports,* 1940–1941; locomotive assignments obtained from the L&A via H. K. Vollrath; Sippel Recollections; ICC *Reports* 217 (1936): 235, 244, 489. The L&A spent more than $300,000 on the Torras–Lobdell segment after finding that minor upgrading did not prevent numerous derailments.

2. L&A, *Annual Reports,* 1941–1942; *The Handbook of Texas* (Austin: The Texas State Historical Assn., 1952), Vol. II, 79 (Longhorn Ordnance Works); Clipping file, LSUS Archives; *Webster, 1871–1971* (Minden, La.: Webster Parish Centennial, Inc., 1971).

3. Williams interview; Mayor, *Southern Timberman;* L&A, *Annual Reports,* 1941–1942; ICC *Reports* 254 (1943): 817, 820. The mill at Trout was sold to Delta Hardwood Products, Inc., in 1929 and continued in operation until

1955 (Alexandria *Daily Town Talk,* July 15, 1957).

4. *Official Guide,* 1941–1942; official roster data, KCS/L&A; *EMD Reference Data,* Service Dept., Electromotive Division, General Motors, January 1, 1959; Sy Reich, "Diesel Power: Kansas City Southern and Louisiana & Arkansas," *Railroad Magazine,* January 1976, 59. Diesel locomotives of the KCS were operating over L&A tracks before 1948; for example, a Fairbanks-Morse two-unit, 4,000 horsepower locomotive began regular operations on the Texas line, where grades were severe, in 1947 ("Diesels Chief Tool in Road's Improvement," *Railway Age,* April 3, 1948, 41). The T&P line was shorter between Shreveport and Dallas, 188 miles versus 223 miles for the L&A/Santa Fe.

5. Observations of the author, who worked at the plant in 1942–1943.

6. L&A, *Annual Reports,* 1942–1943; ICC *Reports* 254 (1943): 817, 820; a portion of the line to Paloma [Maryland–Port Hudson] was later repurchased by the L&A to provide service to an expanding industrial base north of Baton Rouge.

7. *Kansas City Star,* September 22, 1941; *Kansas City Times,* October 2, 1941; *Who's Who in Railroading,* 1946, 175.

8. *Business Week,* March 18, 1944, 20, April 8, 1944, 104–5; KCS, *Annual Reports,* 1944–1946.

9. KCS, *Annual Reports,* 1944–1946.

10. Interview, Pratt Remmel, 1972; C. Peter Couch died on June 2, 1955, in Little Rock, Ark. (KCS *Newsletter,* August 1955, 22). Harvey Couch Jr. became the family representative on the KCS board in May 1959, serving until his death on May 21, 1963 (KCS, *Annual Report,* 1963).

11. *New Orleans Times-Picayune,* April 5, 1944; Edward A. Lewis, *American Short Line Railway Guide* (Strasburg, Pa.: Baggage Car, 1975). The West Feliciana Railway was incorporated under the laws of Louisiana on December 10, 1943, for the purpose of purchasing the Angola–St. Francisville branch of the L&A; it was abandoned June 30, 1948.

12. L&A, *Annual Report,* 1943; Baton Rouge *State-Times,* October 4, 5, and 8, 1943, December 3, 1943; KCS/L&A, *Annual Report,* 1945; ICC *Reports* 261 (1945): 820, 846; Louisiana Midland Railway Company, *History and Operation* (n.p.: n.d., obtained from J. D. Oliver, Baton Rouge, 1972).

13. Vollrath, unpublished roster of the L&A Railway.

14. *Louisiana Midland Railway History;* Williams interview. The executive offices of the Midland were in Baton Rouge.

15. Notes in L&A file, DeGolyer Library, submitted by a trainwatcher in Dallas during the war years; *The Handbook of Texas,* Vol. III, 988.

16. Joseph C. Goulden, *The Best Years, 1945–1950* (New York: Atheneum, 1976); KCS/L&A, *Annual Report,* 1946.

17. KCS/L&A, *Annual Reports,* 1947–1950; "Order from Chaos," *Business Week,* April 6, 1946, 32; "Five Stations Combine into One," *Business Week,* August 12, 1946, 36–37; ICC *Reports* 267 (1948): 763.

18. Edward F. Haas, *DeLesseps S. Morrison and the Image of Reform: New Orleans Politics, 1946–1961* (Baton Rouge: Louisiana State University Press, 1974); *Railway Age,* December 17, 1951, 45; "Kansas City Southern Lines Maintain Progressive Tradition," *Modern Railroads* 6 (December 1951): 35; New Orleans, Department of Public Utilities, *Proposed Railroad Grade Crossing Elimination and Terminal Improvement for New Orleans, Louisiana* (New Orleans, September 5, 1944).

19. Arthur E. Tuckerman, "The Southern Belle Goes South," *Wheels* 5 (1949): 10; "The New Southern Belle," KCS *Newsfolder,* June 1949, 3; KCS/L&A, *Annual Report,* 1949; Kuchinsky, "Miss Belle and the Crow."

20. *Official Guides,* 1948–1956; KCS/L&A public and employee timetables in author's possession; Kuchinsky, "Miss Belle and the Crow."

21. "Traffic Strangulation: And What New Orleans Did About It," *Railway Age,* April 26, 1954, 22; "Union Passenger Terminal," *Trains* 14 (September 1954): 14; *New Orleans Times-Picayune,* May 1, 1954; Haas, *DeLesseps S. Morrison.*

22. "New Orleans Cures a Headache," KCS *Newsfolder,* August 1954, 3.

23. "Springhill, Louisiana: Prosperity in the Piney Woods," KCS *Newsfolder,* July 1952, 3.

24. "Down to the Sea with 77," KCS *Newsfolder,* November 1950, 3.

25. Sippel Recollections. The Morganza Spillway was designed to move Mississippi River overflow southeastward to the Atchafalaya River.

26. KCS/L&A, *Annual Reports,* 1952–1953; tonnage ratings from L&A employee timetables; profile chart from KCS files; ICC *Reports* 282 (1953): 817.

27. ICC Accident Investigation Report No. 3419, October 4, 1951; Sippel Recollections; contemporary newspaper reports.

28. KCS *Newsfolder,* April 1955, 28; "Deramus Yard Opens!" KCS *Newsfolder,* June 1956, 3–16; KCS/L&A, *Annual Report,* 1956; "Not Just a Yard. . . It's a Terminal," *Railway Age,* May 7, 1956, 52–54, 63.

29. ICC *Reports* 290 (1954): 434; "New Techniques Used on Fox–Blanchard Line," KCS *Newsfolder,* March 1957, 10.

30. KCS/L&A, *Annual Reports,* 1955–1956; KCS *Newsfolder,* October 1956, 10.

31. *Railway Age,* November 13, 1961, 26; H. Roger Grant, *The Corn Belt Route* (DeKalb: Northern Illinois University Press, 1984), 139–42; *Wall Street Journal,* November 3, 1961; personal communication, John W. Barriger III, 1965 (Barriger became president of the Katy in 1965). It is interesting that KCS, *Annual Report,* 1961, makes no mention of the assumption of the presidency by the younger Deramus.

32. ICC *Reports* 317 (1962): 155.

CHAPTER 8

Submerged in the Holding Company

1. KCSI, *Annual Reports,* various years.

2. Fred W. Frailey, "The Railroad that Unraveled," *Trains* 39 (August 1979): 22–29; Vollrath, personal communication, 1972.

3. Louis Saillard, "Louisiana Midland: From Backwoods Hauler to Bridge Road," *Trains* 51 (September 1991): 32–37; Louis Saillard, "Louisiana Midland Finale," *Trains* 51 (October 1991): 58–65; Louisiana Midland *History; Illinois Central Magazine,* September 1966, 2, June 1967, 2; ICC *Reports* 334 (1969): 282.

4. Saillard, "Louisiana Midland Finale"; "The Natchez and Southern," *Missouri Pacific Lines Magazine,* August-September 1959, 10; "Natchez Ferry: Mo-Pac's Navy on the Mississippi," *Mo-Pac News,* May 1978, 7.

5. Louis Marre, "About the Railroad Whose President Says, 'We Have No Intention of Going Out of the Passenger Business,'" *Trains* 28 (November 1967): 40–49; *Railway Age,* May 14, 1962, 41; Michael Palmieri, "The

Ghosts of the Southern Belle," *The Belle* [Kansas City Southern Historical Society] 14 (Nos. 3–4), 3–5; ICC *Reports* 331 (1968): 51 and 334 (1969): 807. A rather poignant photographic report on the demise of trains 15 and 16 was provided later by Philip R. Hastings, "Twilight of the Flying Crow," *Passenger Train Journal* 9 (September 1977): 18.

6. Marre, "About the Railroad"; with regard to discontinuance of all passenger service, a "we deeply regret" message to "patrons and friends" by Deramus, made in late 1967, stated that the railroad earned $680,000 from mail revenues in 1966, and he had been notified that the last two Railway Post Office cars would be removed on January 12, 1968 (statement reproduced in *The Belle* 13 [Nos. 3–4], 14–15).

7. Wayne Kuchinsky, "Miss Belle and the Crow," *Passenger Train Journal* 17 (April 1986): 17–31; "Southern Belle Ends 29 Year Service Today," *Shreveport Times,* November 2, 1969; "Fire Destroys Union Station," *Shreveport Times,* November 6, 1969.

8. Frailey, "The Railroad That Unraveled"; James O'Hanlon, "The Little Railroad That Went Astray," *Forbes,* July 24, 1978, 66; KCSI *Annual Report,* 1967; personal observations of the author.

9. Harold Vollrath, personal communication, 1973; Frailey, "The Railroad That Unraveled"; Frank W. Bryan, "KCS Stages a Quiet Turnaround," *Modern Railroads* 45 (September 1990): 84; O'Hanlon, "The Little Railroad"; Frank Malone, "A Lean Little Railroad with a PIP of a Program," *Railway Age,* June 25, 1979, 22.

10. Fred W. Frailey, "President Carter (Tom, That Is) Puts a Railroad Back Together," *Trains* 39 (September 1979): 22–32.

11. KCSI, *Annual Reports,* 1973–1976; Frailey, "President Carter."

12. Frailey, "President Carter"; "Rebuild-ing the Kansas City Southern," *Railway Track and Structures* 88 (November 1992): 13–14; O'Hanlon, "Little Railroad."

13. KCSI, *Annual Reports,* 1970–1991; O'Hanlon, "Little Railroad"; interviews with John W. Barriger III, St. Louis, Mo., 1965–1968.

14. International Paper Company, *Annual Report,* 1978; KCSI, *Annual Reports,* 1970–1991.

15. "KCS Sets New Growth Goals," *Railway Age,* September 1992, 37; *Railway Track and Structures,* November 1992, 13; field observations of the author; KCSI, *Annual Report,* 1991, which notes that by the end of the year 46 SD–60 locomotives were on hand.

16. Saillard, "Louisiana Midland Finale," 59; *Mo-Pac News,* "Natchez Ferry"; ICC *Reports* 5 (1989, second series): 542; Lowell McManus, Leesville, La., personal communication (Hope activity); field observations of the author.

17. Various issues of *The Crow,* newsletter of the Kansas City Southern Historical Society; field observations of the author.

18. KCSI *Annual Report,* 1980; *The Crow,* various issues; *Moody's Manual,* 1980–1990; Bryan, "Quiet Turnaround."

19. David Matustik, "Channel Plan Runs into Criticism," *Austin American-Statesman,* June 22, 1992; *The Crow,* various issues.

20. KCSI, *Annual Reports,* 1988–1991; *The Crow,* various issues. Kirke Couch followed his older brothers Johnson and Harvey Jr. as a board member representing the Couch family interests; he served for 22 years.

21. Field observations of the author; *The Crow,* various issues.

22. Personal communications from Gerald A. Hook, Baton Rouge, La. and Lowell McManus, Leesville, La. (regarding the official date of dissolution).

REPORTS, MANUSCRIPTS, AND GOVERNMENT PUBLICATIONS

Arkansas, Railroad Commission. *First Annual Report, 1899–1900.*

Atkinson, B. S. "The Development of the American Railroads." Address given before the New Orleans Traffic Club, June 1932.

Britton, J. H. "Report of the State Engineer on the Physical Condition of the Railways." Austin, Texas, 1884.

Burton, W. J. "History of the Missouri Pacific Railroad." 1956. Unpublished manuscript in the corporate files of Union Pacific Railroad, St. Louis, Mo.

Caudle, Robert E. "History of the Missouri Pacific Lines: Gulf Coast Lines and Subsidiaries; International Great Northern." September 1949. Unpublished manuscript in the corporate files of Union Pacific Railroad, St. Louis, Mo.

East Line and Red River Railroad. Minutes of the meetings of the Board of Directors, 1876–1881. DeGolyer Library, Southern Methodist University, Dallas, Texas.

———. *Report of the President and Charter.* Jefferson, Texas: Jimplecute Press, 1877. University of Texas Archives, Austin, Texas.

Edenborn, William E. Papers. Louisiana State University—Shreveport Archives, Shreveport, Louisiana.

Epperson, Benjamin H. Papers. University of Texas Archives, Austin, Texas.

Indenture by and between Sherman, Shreveport and Southern Railway Co. and Central Trust Co., New York, June 1, 1893.

Interstate Commerce Commission. *Statistics of Railways in the United States.* Washington: Government Printing Office, 1894, 1899.

Interstate Commerce Commission Reports for Valuation and Finance Dockets. (The ICC *Reports* are identified separately in the notes, with the dates being those of the ICC decisions.)

Kansas City Southern Industries, Inc. *Annual Report* to stockholders, 1963–1991.

———. *Manual* No. 63, July 1, 1975.

Kansas City Southern Railway Company. *Annual Report* to stockholders, 1902–1907, 1909–1914, 1928–1962.

Louisiana and Arkansas Railway Company. *Annual Report* to stockholders, 1901–1916, 1934–1943 [consolidated with KCS reports after 1943].

Louisiana Midland Railway Company—History and Operation. Undated typescript, obtained from J. D. Oliver, Baton Rouge, 1972.

Louisiana Public Service Commission. *Annual Report,* 1921–1927, Baton Rouge.

Mosley, James W. "A Legacy Greater Than Wealth: An Appreciative Appraisal of the W. C. Brown Family." In *Proceedings, Presbyterian Historical Society of the Southwest,* 11th Annual Meeting, Little Rock, Arkansas, March 10–11, 1989, 15–45.

New Orleans Department of Public Utilities. *Proposed Railroad Grade Crossing Elimination and Terminal Improvement for New Orleans, Louisiana.* New Orleans, September 5, 1944. Prepared for the New Orleans Terminal Board by Godat and Heft, Consulting Engineers.

Potts, Charles S. *Railroad Transportation in Texas.* University of Texas Bulletin No. 119. Austin, 1909.

"Proceedings of the National Narrow-Gauge Railway Convention." St. Louis, June 19, 1872.

Rand, E. C. M. *Findings in the Investigation of Matters Relating to the Missouri, Kansas and Texas Railway Co.* New York: The Devinne Press, 1888.

Shoup, Stephen E. *The KCS–L&A: Report and Recommendations on Merger of the Properties.* Kansas City, Mo.: Kansas City Southern, December 1946.

Sippel, Paul. Recollections set forth in 40-page typescript dated August 1, 1968. Louisiana State University—Shreveport archives.

Texas, Office of State Engineer. *State Engineer's Report of the Inspection of the First Section of Twenty Miles of the Road* (East Line and Red River Railroad). Jefferson, Texas, Dec. 2, 1876. Prepared by E. A. Blanch.

Texas, Railroad Commission. *Annual Report,* 1893–1897.

United States. *Statutes at Large 16,* 573.

Vicksburg, Shreveport and Pacific Railroad Company. *Annual Report and Statement of Accounts,* 1900.

Vicksburg, Shreveport and Pacific Railway Company. *Annual Report and Statement of Accounts,* 1901, 1907.

Wafer, Ralph. "Railroad Stations of the City of New Orleans," September 30, 1970. Manuscript in the Howard-Tilton Library, Tulane University.

BOOKS, PAMPHLETS, ARTICLES

Allen, Frederick L. *The Great Pierpont Morgan.* New York: Harper & Bros., 1949.

Ames, Charles E. *Pioneering the Union Pacific.* New York: Appleton-Century-Crofts, 1969.

"An Opportunity for Growth." *Railway Age,* July 1993, 43–46.

Anderson, Jacob E. *A Short History of the St. Louis Southwestern Railway Lines.* St.Louis: St. Louis Southwestern Railway, 1947.

Beaton, K. *Enterprise in Oil.* New York: Appleton-Century-Crofts, 1957.

Biographical Directory of the Railway Officials of America. Chicago: Railway Age, 1901, 1913.

"A Birthday for Springhill and International Paper Company." *The Springhill Digester,* Summer 1973, 8–9.

Boardman, Fon W. *The Thirties: America and the Great Depression.* New York: Henry Walck, 1967.

Brown, A. E. *Locomotives and Trains of the L&A and KCS Railways.* Shreveport, La.: Privately published, Shreveport, 1953.

———. "Louisiana & Arkansas: A Young System's Power." *Locomotive Quarterly* 5 (Summer 1982): 2–19.

Bryan, Frank W. "KCS Stages a Quiet Turnaround." *Modern Railroads,* September 1990, 84, 88, 90, 93.

Bryant, Keith L. *Arthur E. Stilwell.* Nashville: Vanderbilt University Press, 1971.

Carter, Hodding. *John Law Wasn't so Wrong: The Story of Louisiana's Horn of Plenty.* Baton Rouge: Esso Standard Oil Co., 1952.

Chandler, Barbara. O., and J. Ed Howe. *History of Texarkana and Bowie and Miller Counties, Texas-Arkansas.* Texarkana: J. Ed Howe, 1939.

Chestnutt, Edgar B. "Couch Seen as Seeking Great Rail System." *Arkansas Gazette,* February 27, 1937.

Cline, Isaac Monroe. *Storms, Floods and Sunshine.* 2d ed. New Orleans: Pelican Publishing Co., 1945.

Coleman, Glen. *The Man Who Fenced the West.* St. Louis: Glen Coleman Co., 1984.

Corliss, C. J. *Main Line of Mid-America.* New York: Creative Age Press, 1950.

Cotner, Robert C. *Addresses and State Papers of James Stephen Hogg.* Austin: University of Texas Press, 1951.

Cox, James. *Old and New St. Louis.* St. Louis: Central Biographical Publishing Co., 1894.

Daniel, Pete. *Deep'n as It Come: The 1927 Mississippi River Flood.* New York: Oxford University Press, 1977.

"Deramus Yard Opens!" KCS *Newsfolder,* June 1956, 3–11.

Dew, Lee A. "The Arkansas Tap Line Cases: A Study in Commerce Regulation." *Arkansas Historical Quarterly* 29 (1970): 327–44.

"Diesels Chief Tools in Road's Improvement." *Railway Age,* April 3, 1948, 41–44.

"Edenborn Line Rapidly Expanding: Brings New Business to the Port." *The Trade Index* [Journal of the New Orleans Board of Trade] 28 (September 1916): 24–25.

Edson, William D. "Locomotives of the Louisiana and Arkansas Railway and Component Lines." *Railroad History,* no. 144 (Spring 1981): 60–75.

Fehrenbach, T. R. *Lone Star: A History of Texas and the Texans.* New York: Macmillan Co., 1968.

"First, KCS—MidSouth, Now. . .?" *Railway Age,* June 1994, 64–66.

Fishbaugh, Charles P. *From Paddle Wheels to Propellers.* Indianapolis: Indiana Historical Society, 1970.

Fleming, Howard. *Narrow Gauge Railways in America,* 2d. ed. Philadelphia: 1876. [Reprint with additions by Grahame Hardy, Oakland, California, 1949.]

"Float 300-ft. Span into Place in a Swift Current." *Railway Age,* April 27, 1929, 959.

"Forging a Major Link Between the 'Heart of America' and the South and Southwest." *Kansas City Southern Magazine,* October-December 1938, 3–5.

Frailey, Fred W. "The Railroad That Unraveled." *Trains* 39 (August 1979): 22–29.

————. "President Carter (Tom, That Is) Puts a Railroad Back Together." *Trains* 39 (September 1979): 22–32.

Franks, Kenny, and Paul F. Lambert. *Early Louisiana and Arkansas Oil.* College Station: Texas A&M University Press, 1982.

From Ox-Teams to Eagles. Dallas: The Texas and Pacific Railway Co. [194?].

Frost, Meigs O. "Who's This Man Bill Edenborn Anyhow?" *New Orleans States,* April 29, 1923.

Gammel, H. P. N., ed. *The Laws of Texas, 1822–1897.* 10 vols. Austin: Gammel Book Co., 1898.

Gould's St. Louis Directory. St. Louis: Gould Publishing Co., 1890–1892.

Goulden, Joseph C. *The Best Years, 1945–1950.* New York: Atheneum, 1976.

Grant, H. Roger. *The Corn Belt Route.* DeKalb: Northern Illinois University Press, 1984.

Grodinsky, Julius. *Jay Gould: His Business Career, 1867–1892.* Philadelphia: University of Pennsylvania Press, 1957.

Haas, Edward F. *DeLesseps S. Morrison and the Image of Reform: New Orleans Politics, 1946–1961.* Baton Rouge: Louisiana State University Press, 1974.

Hardin, J. Fair. "An Outline of Shreveport and Caddo Parish History." *Louisiana Historical Quarterly* 18 (October 1935): 759–851.

Hastings, Philip R. "Twilight Flight of the Flying Crow." *Passenger Train Journal* 9 (September 1977): 18–22.

Helm, H. B. "Edenborn Line: Louisiana Railway and Navigation Company." *The Trade Index* [Journal of the New Orleans Board of Trade] 27 [1915]. (The exact date and page are not identified.)

Hennick, Louis C., and E. Harper Charlton. *Louisiana: Its Street and Interurban Railways,* Vol. 1. Shreveport: L. C. Hennick, 1963.

————. *Louisiana: Its Street and Interurban Railways,* Vol. 2. *The Streetcars of New Orleans, 1831–1965.* Shreveport: L. C. Hennick, 1965.

Hidy, R. W., and M. E. Hidy. *History of Standard Oil Company (New Jersey): Pioneering in Big Business, 1882–1911.* New York: Harper & Bros., 1955.

Hilton, George. *American Narrow Gauge Railroads.* Stanford, Calif.: Stanford University Press, 1990.

Hines, Thomas S. *Burnham of Chicago: Architect and Planner.* New York: Oxford University Press, 1974.

Hines, Walker D. *War History of American Railroads.* New Haven: Yale University Press, 1928.

The History of Barksdale Field, 1933–1970. N.p.: [U.S. Air Force], n.d.

International Paper Co. *International Paper Company after Fifty Years, 1898–1948.* N.p., 1948.

Johnson, Clifton. *Highways and Byways of the Mississippi Valley.* New York: Macmillan Co., 1906.

Jones, Harry E. *Railroad Wages and Labor Relations, 1900–1952.* New York: Bureau of Information, Eastern Railways, 1953.

Jones, Jesse H., with Edward Angly. *Fifty Billion Dollars: My Thirteen Years with the RFC (1932–1945).* New York: Macmillan Co., 1951.

"K.C.S.–L.& A. Streamliner 'Southern Belle.'" *Railway Age,* October 5, 1940, 469–74.

"KCS Sets New Growth Goals." *Railway Age,* September 1992, 17.

Klein, Maury. *The Life and Legend of Jay Gould.* Baltimore: Johns Hopkins University Press, 1986.

Klorer, John D., ed. *The New Louisiana: The Story of the Greatest State in the Nation.* Baton Rouge: Office of the Governor of Louisiana, 1936.

Kuchinsky, Wayne. "Miss Belle and the Crow." *Passenger Train Journal* 17 (April 1986): 17–31.

Lewis, Edward A. *American Short Line Railway Guide.* Strasburg, Pa.: Baggage Car, 1975.

"Locomotives of the Louisiana & Arkansas." *Railroad Magazine,* May 1941, 48–51.

Loos, John L. *Oil on Stream! A History of Interstate Oil Pipe Line Company, 1909–1959.* Baton Rouge: Louisiana State University Press, 1959.

Louisiana and Arkansas Railway: Its Territory, Industries and Financial Condition. New York: Fisk and Robinson Co., 1904.

"Louisiana and Arkansas Railway Company

Emergency Board Report." *Machinists'
Monthly Journal,* August 1931, 460–64,
510.

Lynch, Terry, and W. D. Caileff, Jr. *Route of the
Southern Belle.* Boulder, Colo.: Pruett
Publ. Co., 1987.

Lyons, Percy F. "New Railway in Louisiana Cuts
Off Long Ferry Transfer." *Engineering
News-Record,* October 6, 1927, 540–54.

"M. P. and L.& A. Joint Trackage Rights."
Railway Age, February 7, 1931, 322–23.

"The Magnates of the Wire Industry." *The Iron
Age,* March 23, 1899, 15.

Malone, Frank. "A Lean Little Road with a PIP
of a Program." *Railway Age,* June 25,
1979, 22–26, 28.

Marre, Louis A. "About the Railroad Whose
President Says, 'We Have No Intention of
Going out of the Passenger Business.'"
Trains 28 (November 1967): 40–49.

Masterson, V. V. *The Katy Railroad and the Last
Frontier.* Norman: University of Oklahoma Press, 1952.

Matustik, David. "Channel Plan Runs into Criticism." *Austin American-Statesman,* June
22, 1992.

Mayor, Archer. *Southern Timberman: The
Legacy of William Buchanan.* Athens:
University of Georgia Press, 1988

McCaleb, Walter F. *History of the Brotherhood of
Railroad Trainmen.* New York: Albert
and Charles Boni, 1936.

McCallum, Henry D., and Frances T. McCallum. *The Wire that Fenced the West.* Norman: University of Oklahoma Press,
1965.

Miceli, Augusto P. *The Pickwick Club of New
Orleans.* New Orleans: Pickwick Press,
1964.

Moody's Manual: Railroad Section. New York:
Moody's Investors Service, 1909–. Pub-
lished annually. Title varies; currently
Moody's Transportation Manual.

Mundy, Floyd. *The Earning Power of Railroads.*
New York: Jas. H. Oliphant & Co.,
1906–1946.

"The Natchez and Southern." *Missouri Pacific
Lines Magazine,* August-September 1959,
10–11.

"Natchez Ferry: Mo-Pac's Navy on the Mississippi." *Mo-Pac News,* May 1978, 7.

National Cyclopedia of American Biography,
Vol. 18: 248–49. New York: John T.
White, 1922.

"New Orleans Cures a Headache." KCS *Newsfolder,* August 1954, 3–8.

"New Station Facilities Provided at Baton
Rouge, La." *Railway Age,* July 3, 1926,
13–16.

"New Techniques Used on Fox–Blanchard
Line." KCS *Newsfolder,* March 1957,
10–12.

Norgress, Rachael E. "The History of the Cypress Lumber Industry in Louisiana."
Louisiana Historical Quarterly 30
(1947): 982–83.

"Not Just a Yard . . . It's a Terminal." *Railway
Age,* May 7, 1956, 52–54, 63.

O'Hanlon, James. "The Little Railroad that Went
Astray." *Forbes,* July 24, 1978, 66, 68.

O'Pry, Maude H. *Chronicles of Shreveport and
Caddo Parish.* Privately published,
Shreveport, Louisiana, 1928.

Palmieri, Michael. "The Ghosts of the Southern
Belle." *The Belle* 14, 3–4 (1995): 3–5.

Poor, Henry V., ed. *Manual of the Railroads of
the United States, 1876–1915.* New York:
H.V. and H.W. Poor, 1876–1915.

Price, David S., and Louis R. Saillard. *Natchez
Route: A Mississippi Central Railroad Album.* Hattiesburg: Mississippi Great
Southern Chapter, National Railway Historical Society, 1975.

"Railroads Complete Long Bridges over Bonnet
Carre Floodway." *Railway Age,* July 8,
1935, 3–7.

"Rebuilding the Kansas City Southern." *Railway Track and Structures* 88 (November
1992): 13–14.

"The Red River Bridge at Alexandria." *Railroad Gazette,* September 20, 1901,
653–54.

Reed, St. Clair G. *A History of the Texas Railroads and of Transportation Conditions
under Spain and Mexico and the Republic
of Texas and the State.* Houston: St. Clair
Publ. Co., 1941.

"Refinery Celebrates 50th Birthday." *Esso News*
[Baton Rouge Refinery], November 6,
1959, 3–23.

Reich, Sy. "Diesel Power: Kansas City Southern
and Louisiana & Arkansas." *Railroad
Magazine,* January 1976, 59.

Rister, Carl C. *Oil! Titan of the Southwest.* Norman: University of Oklahoma Press,
1949.

Roach, Charles A. "Boomers." *Railroad Magazine,* July 1950, 102–113.

Rutherford, I. P. "Across the Wide Mississippi."
The Eagle 4 (February 1977): 3.

"Saga of the Kansas City Southern." *Brotherhood of Locomotive Firemen and Enginemen's Magazine,* December 1949, 346–51.

Saillard, Louis R. "Louisiana Midland: From Backwoods Hauler to Bridge Road." *Trains* 51 (September 1991): 32–37.

———. "Louisiana Midland Finale." *Trains* 51 (October 1991): 58–65.

Saucier, Carmine L. *History of Avoyelles Parish, Louisiana.* New Orleans: Pelican Publishing Co., 1943.

"Settle Strike of L. & A. Train Service Employees." *Railway Age,* November 28, 1936, 808.

"Shreveport Gets Largest Airport." *Kansas City Southern Magazine,* February–April 1932, 3.

Simpich, Frederick. "The Great Mississippi Flood of 1927." *National Geographic Magazine,* September 1927, 243–.

"Springhill, La.: Prosperity from the Piney Woods." KCS *Newsfolder,* July 1952, 3–11.

Tarbell, Ida M. *The Life of Elbert H. Gary, The Story of Steel.* New York: D. Appleton, 1925.

Tarpley, Fred. *Jefferson: Riverport to the Southwest.* Austin: Eakin Press, 1983.

Taylor, Virginia H. *The Franco-Texan Land Company.* Austin: University of Texas Press, 1969.

The Texas Business Diretory, 1878–1879.

Texas Railroad Gazetteer for Distribution on Railways, Steamships and Stages. Galveston: O. C. Moore and Co., 1878.

Thompson, Brian. *Narrow Gauge Railways in America.* Oakland, Calif.: Grahame Hardy, 1949.

"To Build Long Bridges over Bonnet Carre Floodway." *Railway Age,* July 21, 1934, 67–68.

"Traffic Strangulation: What New Orleans Did About It." *Railway Age,* April 26, 1954, 22–34.

Tuckerman, Arthur. "The Southern Belle Goes South." *Wheels* 5 (1949): 10–15.

"Unusual Features of Design and Construction Mark New Bridge over the Mississippi." *Railway Age,* June 29, 1940, 1172–78.

Vollrath, Harold K. "All-Time Steam Roster of the Kansas City Southern." *Railroad Magazine,* January 1976, 56–59.

Warshow, Robert. *Bet a Million Gates.* New York: Greenberg Press, 1932.

Way, Frederick. *Way's Packet Directory, 1848–1983.* Athens: Ohio University Press, 1983.

Webb, Walter P., ed. *The Handbook of Texas.* Austin: Texas State Historical Association, 1952. In 3 volumes.

Webster, 1871–1971. Minden, La.: Webster Parish Centennial, Inc., 1971.

Wendt, Lloyd, and Herman Kogan. *Bet a Million! The Story of John W. Gates.* Indianapolis: Bobbs-Merrill Co., 1948.

White, D., and T. C. Richardson, eds. *East Texas: Its History and Its Makers.* New York: Lewis Historical Publ. Co., 1940.

Who's Who in America, 1903–1905. Chicago: Marquis Publ. Co., 1903.

Who's Who in Louisiana and Mississippi. New Orleans: Times-Picayune, 1918.

Who's Who in Railroading, 9th ed. New York: Simmons-Boardman, 1930.

———, 11th ed. New York: Simmons-Boardman, 1946.

Wilgus, Horace L. *A Study of the United States Steel Corporation in its Industrial and Legal Aspects.* Chicago: Callaghan & Co., 1901.

Williams, T. Harry. *Huey Long.* New York: Alfred A. Knopf, 1969.

Wilson, Stephen. *Harvey Couch: An Entrepreneur Brings Electricity to Arkansas.* Little Rock, Arkansas: August House, 1986.

Wilson, Winston P. *Harvey Couch: The Master Builder.* Nashville, Tenn.: Broadman Press, 1947.

Winkler, J. K. *Morgan the Magnificent.* Garden City, N.Y.: Garden City Publishing Co., 1930.

Writers' Program, Works Progress Administration. *Louisiana: A Guide to the State.* New York: Hastings House, 1941.

Yoes, Henry E. III. *A History of St. Charles Parish to 1973.* Norco, La.: St. Charles Herald Publishers, 1973.

MAGAZINES AND NEWSPAPERS

Alexandria (La.) *Daily Town Talk*
Arkansas Democrat
Arkansas Gazette
Baton Rouge (La.) *State-Times*
The Belle [Kansas City Southern Historical Society]
Business Week
Commercial and Financial Chronicle
The Crow [Kansas City Southern Historical Society]

Dallas Daily Herald
Dallas Morning News
Enterprise/News-American (Winnfield, La.)
The Iron Age
KCS *Newsfolder*
Kansas City Southern Magazine
Kansas City Star
Kansas City Times
L & A Cooperative News
New Orleans Daily Picayune
New Orleans States
New Orleans Times-Picayune
New York Times

Railroad Gazette
Railroad Magazine
Railroad Man's Magazine
Railway Age
St. Louis Post-Dispatch
Shreveport Times
Travelers' Official Guide of the Railways and Steam Navigation Lines in the United States and Canada
Wall Street Journal
Waterways Journal
Webster Signal (Minden, La.)
Wheels

A number in bold type refers to caption material located on that page.

Adams, W. N., 70
Alexandria, La., 11, 13–16, 24, 35, 57, 60, 63–64, 70, 71, 75–76, 87; bridge at, 15, 16, 122; extension of L&A to, 60, 62; Iron Mountain/T&P depot, 62; map of railroads, 64
Allen, Frederick, 8
Alvord, E. M., 49
American Steel & Wire Co., 8, 9
Angola, La., 16–20, 23–24, 39, 71, 77, 86–87, 99, 102; penal farm at, 100, 102
Angola Plantation, La., 16
Angola Transfer Co., 18, 29–30
Arab oil embargo, 116
Arkansas, Louisiana & Southern Railway, 57
Arkansas & Choctaw Railroad, 61
Arkansas Light & Power Co., 70
Arkansas Power & Light Co., 70, 87, 98
Arkansas Southern Railroad, 13, 17
Ashland, La., 57–58, 103
Atchafalaya River, 16, 34; bridge at Simmesport, 16, 34–37, 38; and first train across bridge, 38
Atchison, Topeka & Santa Fe Railway, 88, 118–19, 122–23
Atkinson, B. S., 58, 67
Atlanta, La., 17

Baker, James A., 44
Baker Wire Co., 7
Baldwin Locomotive Works, 19, 60
Bankers Trust Co., 70
Barksdale Field, La., 77, 79–80, 82–83
Barriger, John W., 117
Baton Rouge, La., 17, 21, 24–25, 29, 35, 71, 82, 112, 119; branch to Angola, 100, 102–3; bridge at, 30, 82, 94–95, 97, **111, 117**; oil refinery at, 24, 28; L&A yard at, 104
Bayou des Glaises, 17, 35
Beardsley, J. D., 13, 14
Beardsley Road (Louisiana & North West Railroad), 13

Beaumont, Miss., 66
Bienville, La., 69, 70
Big Cypress Bayou, 41
"Big D connection," 119
Big Steel. *See* United States Steel Corp.
Black River, 64, 103; bridge across, 64, **65**
Black River, La., 64
Blanch, E. A., 43
Blanchard, La., 108, 110
Blanchard, Newton, 50
Blanchard cut-off, 109, **110,** 112
Bodcaw Lumber Co., 53, 55–56, **62;** mill closed, 77; railroad, 56; store, 56
Bonnet Carre spillway/trestle, 81, 83, **84, 91**
Bossier City, La., 12, 77, 108
Bottoms, G. W., 53
Boydston, B. F., 50
Braddock Wire Co., 9
Brill, J. G., Co., 75
Brown, Joseph D., 101
Brown, Thomas A., 55
Brown, William C., 55
Buchanan, James A., 55–57, 67
Buchanan, Robert, 57
Buchanan, W. J. (son of William), 67
Buchanan, William, 3, 11, 13–14, 16, 18, 24, 38, 53, 56–57, 59–63, **66,** 68, 70, 103, 124; death of, 67; heirs of, 69; and private car of, 67
Buchanan, William T., 53
Buchanan mill, at Trout, La., 99
Burlington Northern Railroad, 116; unit coal trains, 116
Burnham, D. H., 22
Bush, B. F., 66

Caddo Lake, Tex., 41, 122
Cairo & Fulton Railroad, 53
Caldwell, Rogers, 71
Calhoun, Ark., 69
Campti, La., 14–15, 115
Carnegie Steel Co., 9
Carter, Thomas S., 117–18; leads KCS rehabilitation, 117
Catahoula Parish, La., 18
Central Trust Co., New York, 47, 50

Centralized Traffic Control, 117, 121
Chase National Bank, 10
Chicago, Rock Island & Pacific Railway, 16–17, 63, 83, 87
Chicago Great Western Railroad, 112, 113
Clifford, Alfred, 7
Coal trains, 116–17, 119, 123
Colfax, La., 15
Colfax & Northern Railway, 15
Collins, Ben, 11
Colonial Sugars Co., 24
Colorado Southern, New Orleans & Pacific Railroad, 24; trackage rights on LR&N, 24
Concordia Jct., La., 103
Confederate States of America, 42
Consolidated Steel & Wire Co., 7–9
Cook, George, 86
Coolidge, Calvin, 35
Co-Operative Club of L&A, 79
Co-Operative News, 73–74
Cotton Belt line. See St. Louis Southwestern Railway
Cotton Pool of Shreveport, 14
Cotton Valley, La., 57, 74, 104, 119
Couch, Charles Peter, 76, 78–80, 86, 88, 91, 98, 100–101; leads employee excursions, 79, 80; ousted from management, 101; president of both L&A and KCS, 91
Couch, Harvey, 3, 38, 67–68, 70–71, 73–74, 82, 87–88, **89**, 91, 98–100, 103, 107–8, 122, 124; appointed to RFC Board, 80; death of, 98; early history of, 69; elected to KCS Board, 88; forms telephone company, 70; moves from telephones to electric utilities, 70; and private car, 80; as railway mail clerk, 69; retreat, "Couchwood," 87, 98
Couch, Johnson, 102
Couch, Kirke, 122
Couch investment group, 38–40, 123
Coushatta, La., 11–14, 76; first train to, 13
Coverdale & Colpitts Co., 71
Crichton, La., area oil, 25
Crowell, Caleb, 53
Cullen, La., 91, 99, 107, 118, **121**; new depot, 104

Daingerfield, Tex., 43, 97, 99, 103, 108, 122; steel mill at, 97, 99, 103
Dallas, Tex., 23, 41, 78, 119; changes in trackage at, 122; Santa Fe yards/shops at, 103; service to, 88
Decatur, Tex., 49
Derailments. See Wrecks
Deramus, William, 101–2, 108, 112–13, 116–18; becomes president of KCS, 101; death of, 112

Deramus, William III, 111–16; becomes president of KCS/L&A, 111; death of, 114, 122; organizes Kansas City Southern Industries, 112; president of Chicago Great Western Railroad, 112; president of Missouri-Kansas-Texas Railway, 113
Deramus, William IV, 122
Deramus Yard, Shreveport, La., 109, 115–16, 119
Dettly, Fida, 4, 39
Dillon, Read & Co., 71
Dippel, William, 30, 33
Doyline, La., 99
Drain, Edgar, 11, 40
Drain, Henrietta, 40
Drain, John, 4
Drain, Malvina, 40
Drain, Sarah, 5 (see also Edenborn, Sarah); marries William Edenborn, 4
Drake, F. H., 53, 57, 63

East Line & Red River Railroad, 41, 95; charter of, forfeited, 45; construction of, 43; decision for narrow gauge for, 42; special excursion of, 43; first locomotive of, 42; gauge change of, 47; groundbreaking ceremony for, 42; incorporated, 41; land grant for, 42; locomotive roster for, 46; physical characteristics of, 45; schedule for, 43; sold, 47
Edenborn, Antoinette, 8
Edenborn, Lena, 3, 8, 40
Edenborn, Lilly, 3
Edenborn, Sarah, **5**, 11, 19, 36–40, 71, 73, 99, 123; death of, 40; retirement of, 39; settles lawsuit with Meiers, 39; settles husband's estate, 39; settles with Couch group, 73; and value of her property in Louisiana, 40
Edenborn, William, 3, **5**, 8, 11, 14, 16, 51, 57–58, 60, 62, 71, 79, 82, 88, 99, 103, 124; appearance of, 32; and association of with Fida Dettly, 4; and association of with John Gates, 6; at American Steel & Wire Co., 8, 10; becomes member of United States Steel Board, 9; charters Shreveport & Red River Valley Railroad, 8; children of, 8; death and burial of, 36; and difficulties with Huey Long, 15, 26–29, 32; and diversification of interests, 9; early history of, 3; forms American Steel & Wire Co., 8; forms Consolidated Steel & Wire Co., 7; and "Goodwill Special" to Texas, 32; home in New Orleans of, 19, 20; home in St. Louis of, 8; influences oil refinery location at Baton Rouge, 24; institutes shuttle service at Baton Rouge, 28; and introduction to

wire-making of, 3; leaves United States Steel Corp., 24; marries Sarah Drain, 4; moves to Chicago, 8; moves to St. Louis, 4; as official of KCS, 10; opens office at Shreveport, 9; patents of, 7; private car of, 32; purchases Sherman, Shreveport & Southern Railroad, 31, 51
Edenborn brake of cypress, 17
Edenborn bridge at Alexandria, 60, 62–63
Edenborn Lines (publication), 31
Edwards, George, 122
El Dorado, Ark., 87
Electro-Motive Corp., 93, 99
Ellerbe, Clarence, 12–15, 17–18; background, 11; president of Louisiana Central Construction Co., 11; leaves railroad, 25
Ellwood, Isaac, 6, 9
Emden, La., 36
Employees' Benefit & Insurance Assn., 10
Ems, La., 18, 24
Epperson, Ben W., 43
Eunice, La., 87
Ewing, John D., 101
Exxon Corp., 24

Faker, Tex., 52
Farmer, Robert R., 31–32, 37, 88, 92
Farmersville, Tex., 88, 95, **118,** 122–23
Ferguson, Hannah, 53
Ferguson, Joseph, 53, 55
Ferguson, W. T., 53
Ferriday, La., 114
Filston, La., 35, 39, 40, 77, 82, 95, 99; terminal layout at, 34
Fitch, Thomas W., 6, 7
Florida East Coast Railroad, 75, **82**
Flying Crow, 97, 99, 105, 107
Fomby branch of L&A, 57
Ford, Edward, 50
Fort Worth & Denver City Railway, 49
Fouke, George, 11
Frailey, Fred, 115
Frankstown, Pa., 4
Fratt, F. W., 49
Frisco railroad. *See* St. Louis & San Francisco Railroad
Frost, E. A., 53, 70

Gardner, James, 109
Gary, Elbert, 8–9
Gates, John W., 6–10
Geismar, La., 124
Georgetown, La., 62, 103
Gibbsland, La., 13, 70
Gilinsky, S. E., 101

Glidden, Joseph, 6
Globe Rolling Mill Co., 4
Godchaux Sugars, Inc., 24
Goldonna, La., 58
Gonzales, La., 19, 124
Good Hope Refinery, 25
Good Pine, La., 77
Gould, Jay, 44–47; purchases East Line & Red River Railroad, 44
Goulden, Joseph, 104
Grande Ecore, La., 35
Great Depression of the 1930s, 78–80
Greenville, Tex., 31–32, 42, 44, 47, 49–51, 73, 78, 88, 99; Dallas connection at, 77; offices closed, 92
Guess, C. M., 36
Gulf, Mobile & Northern Railroad, 66
Gulf Coast Lines, 24–25, 82

Harahan swamp, 18
Harper, C. R., 47
Harrison, W. M., 43
Harrison Wire Company of St. Louis, 6
Hattiesburg, Miss., 66
Hattiesburg & Bonhommie Railroad, 66
Haverty, Michael, 124
Hedrick & Frost Engineers, 34
Helm, Henry B., 25, 37
Henderson-Brown road, 13
Hessmer, La., 35
Hibernia Bank Building, New Orleans, 20
Hickory Hill, Tex., 42
Hogg, James S., 45–47
Holloway, Hamric, 102–3; family interests of, 102, 114
Holloway, Hamric, Jr., 103
Homer, La., 70
Hoover, Herbert, 35, 80
Hope, Ark., 59, 61, 64, 71, 74, 111, 118; extension of L&A to, 59–61
Houston & Texas Central Railroad, 44–45
Huey Long Bridge, New Orleans, 81
Hughes Springs, Tex., 51, 73, 100, 119, **121**
Hunt (Greenville), Tex., 119
Hustler, 80–81, 95, 97; schedule of, 81

Illinois Central Gulf Railroad, 119
Illinois Central Railroad, 31, 109, 113, 123–24; purchases Louisiana Midland, 113
Illinois Steel Co., 8
International Paper Co., 118; mill at Springhill, La., 87, **92,** 95, 97, 107, 118; closes mill, 118
International Railway Improvement Co., 44
Interstate Commerce Commission, 21, 25, 34,

37, 39, 56, 66, 71, 77–78, 82, 91, 99, 102–3, 115, 122; decides against L&A acquiring Rock Island properties, 98; gives Illinois Central permission to purchase Louisiana Midland, 113
Iowa Barb Wire Co., 7
Iron Mountain line. *See* St. Louis, Iron Mountain & Southern Railway

J. B. Lewis (steamboat), 23
Jackson, La., 100
James Y. Lockwood (steamboat), 103
Jefferson, Tex., 41–43, 47, 49, 99
Jena, La., 18, 59–60, 62; extension of L&A to, 60, 62; as Louisiana Midland headquarters, 103
Johnson, Clifton, 55
Johnson, N., 88
Johnston, C. E., **89,** 90–91
Jones's Commercial College, St. Louis, 4
Jonesville, La., **65,** 67, 86, 103, 119
Junction City, Ark.-La., 13

Kansas City, Mo., 117
Kansas City, Pittsburg & Gulf Railroad, 10, 90
Kansas City Southern Industries, Inc., 112–13, 123
Kansas City Southern Railway, 3, 10, 15, 34, 37, 83, 87, 90–91, 94, 99, 104, 113; acquires control of L&A, 91; locomotives of, 127; management changes within, 100–101; physical plant of, 113, 115, 118; purchases line into Dallas, 122–23; purchases MidSouth Industries, 123; rebuilt in the 1970s, 117; signaling by, 117; track conditions of, 115
Karnack, Tex., 99, 100, 110
Katy Railroad. *See* Missouri, Kansas & Texas Railway
Kayser, Herman, 3, 8
KCS Skyways, 105
Kellogg, George, 116
Kellogg (steamboat) 30, 36; sinks, 36
Kemper, R. Crosby, 100
Kemper group of Kansas City, 100–101
Kennon, Robert, 35
Kentucky Town, Tex., 41
Kiamichi Railroad, 123
Knobel, Gus, 57
Korean War, 104, 107

Lake Pontchartrain, 81
Lambert & Bishop Wire Fence Co., 5
Landa Motor Lines, 78, 95
Landry, Margaret, 95, **96**
Latanier, La., 119

Lettsworth, La., 108
Lima Locomotive Works, 86
Lipton, W. T., 19
Litchfield Car Co., 42
Little Rock, Ark., 74, 87
Lobdell, La., 97, 99, 108
Lockhart, Tex., 49
Loggy Bayou, La., 12
Lone Star, Tex., 122
Lone Star Steel Co., 103
Long, Huey, Jr., 15, 26–29, 39, 75, 77; becomes governor of Louisiana, 28
Long, Huey, Sr., 15, 26
Long-Bell Lumber Co., 61
Longhorn Ordnance Works, 99, 100
Longino, H. A., 69–70
Loree, L. F., 68, 90
Louisiana, Arkansas & Texas Railway, 78, 90; chartered, 78; line profile of, 51; merged into L&A, 88
Louisiana, Arkansas & Texas Transportation Co., 78
Louisiana & Arkansas Railway (Arkansas), 16, 18, 24, 38–39, 52; incorporated, 59; first annual report of, 59; forms Natchez Route with Mississippi Central, 66; locomotives of, 67; shops of, 67; sold to Couch group, 67–68; taken over by U. S. Railroad Administration, 66
Louisiana & Arkansas Railway (Delaware): begins to lose identity, 112; chartered, 71; last steam locomotive of, 111; locomotive assignments of, 85; locomotives of, **59,** 71, 78, 84–88, 93, 95, 127; map of system, 72; and new diesel-electric locomotives, 92–94, 99; shops of, 73; and strike in 1936, 86
Louisiana & North West Railroad, 13, 69–70, 88, 98
Louisiana Central Construction Co., 11
Louisiana Development Association, 36
Louisiana Midland Railway, 102, **103,** 113–14, 119; buys Vidalia branch, 103; purchased by Illinois Central, 113; steam locomotives of, 103
Louisiana Ordnance Plant, 99
Louisiana Power & Light Co., 70
Louisiana Public Service Commission, 28–29, 33–34
Louisiana Railroad Commission, 25, 27, 62; fines LR&N, 27
Louisiana Railway & Navigation Co., 17, 19–21, 51, 62–64, 67, 71, 90, 99; applies to New Orleans for entrance, 31; begins using Terminal Station in New Orleans, 22–23; chartered, 17; discontinues

overnight train, 29; dissolution of corporation, 71; early financial results of, 26; locomotives of, 71; locomotives change to burning oil, 25; map of system, 20; moves from Terminal Station to Rampart Street Station, New Orleans, 31; and new depot at New Orleans, 31; purchased by Couch group, 69; recovers from government control, 26; sales offices of, 23; schedules of, 28; shop facilities of, 23, 73; valuation by government, 39; watercraft of, 29
Louisiana Railway & Navigation Co. of Texas, 71, 73, 78; business car of, **37**
Ludlow, F. M., 4, 10
Ludlow-Saylor Wire Co., 4
Lynn, James J., 100–101

Machen, La., 15
Maestri, Robert, 104
Magnolia, Ark., 69, 79–80, 98
Malinkrodt (Mallin), La., 16
Malvern, Ark., 70
Mann, Frederick, 8
Mansura, La., 16–17, 35, 77
Marre, Louis, 114
Marshall, Tex., 41
Maryland, La., 100
Mayor, Archer, 67
Maxwell, J. W., 50
McCain, Charles, 70–71, 101
McCants, S. L., 19
McClelland, William, 19, 30
McComb, William, 77
McElroy swamp, 18
McIlvried, Peter, 13–15; leaves LR&N, 17
McKinley, William, 15
McKinney, Tex., 44–45, 47, 123
McKinney branch, 44, 47, 51; abandoned, 95
McNeil, Ark., 69, 98
Meier, Sophie, 39
Meier, William, 39
Memphis, El Paso & Pacific Railroad, 43
Memphis, Tenn., 16, 69
Metairie, La., 104
Meyers, Louis, 70
MidSouth Rail, Inc., 123
Milling, Robert, 31, 37
Minden, La., 13, 58, 63, 67, 71, 74–76, 85, 99, 100, 105; hurt by 1936 strike, 86; north yard of, 107
Minden East & West Railway, 63
Minden Lumber Co., **61**
Minden Railroad & Compress Co., 53, **54**, 57
"Minden Tap." *See* Minden Railroad & Compress Co.

Mississippi Central Railroad, 66, 71, 113; bought by Illinois Central, 113
Mississippi River, 16, 81; levee, 108; flood of 1927, 35, 67, 80–81
Missouri, Kansas & Texas Railway, 21, 23, 33, 41, 45, 47, 49–51, 88, 95, 113; map of system, 48
Missouri Barbed Fence Co., 6
Missouri Car & Foundry Co., 13
Missouri-Illinois Railroad, 30
Missouri Pacific Railway, 14, 21, 24, 66, 82–83, 103, 114, 118; *Sunshine Special,* 74; *Texan,* 74
Mobile, Ala., 66
Moffett, J. A., 71
Monroe, La., 53
Montgomery, La., 115
Moore, Randle T.: director of KCS, 101; director of L&A, 70
Moreauville, La., 35
Morgan, J. Pierpont, 8, 9
Morrison, DeLesseps, 107; daughter Corrine, 107
Moses, Hamilton, 39, 70, 98
Mount Pleasant, Tex., 41
Munson, W. Ben, 49

Naples, La., 17, 20, 23–24, 30
Natchez, Miss., 14, 24, 35, 57, 59–60, **103;** extension to, 64
Natchez, Red River & Texas Railway, 64
Natchez & Western Railway, 64
Natchez ferry, 103, 114, 119
"Natchez Route," 66, 71, 103, 113; discontinued, 113
National Park Bank, 71
Neff, Pat, 69
New Orleans, La., 14, 16–18, 21–22, 25–26, 60, 71, 79, 86, 99, 106, 108, 111, 123; Carrollton Ave. Station, 19, 31–32; celebration for *Southern Belle,* 95, 97; City Council, 19; Country Club, 26; and first passenger train, 19; German Old Folks Home, 26; German Protestant Orphan's Home, 26; Hagan Ave. shops, 23, **30;** line to Baton Rouge, 76; L&A operations in 1944, 125–26; New Basin Canal, 19, 23; new shops/yards of, 104; and rail lines, 106; Rampart St. Station, 31, 97, 104, **105,** 106, 125–26; Terminal Station, 22, **23;** Tulane Ave. trolley, 19; Union Passenger Terminal, 31, 104–7, 125–26; warehouses of LR&N, 23, 31, 76, 125; West Yard (*see* Shrewsbury, La.)
New Orleans, Texas & Mexico Railway, 24

New Orleans Refining Co., 25
New Orleans Terminal Co., 22, 125–26
New Roads, La., 108
Norco, La., 25, 119
Norfolk Southern Railway, 123
Norgress, Rachael, 17
North Baton Rouge, La., 27, 100
Northcutt, Marshall, 57
North Louisiana Telephone Co., 70

Old River, 16, 21, 30, 34

Pack, Randolph, 70–71
Packton, La., 103, 113
Paine, Webber & Co., 87, 90
Paloma, La., 100
Paper mills: Campti, La., 118–19; Cullen
    (Springhill), La., 118–19; Pineville, La.,
    118–19; Port Hudson, La., 119;
    Texarkana, Tex., 118
Patterson, F. E., 7
Phillipston, La. *See* Filston, La.
Pickwick Club of New Orleans, 26
Pine Bluff, Ark., 53, 98
Pineville, La., 15, 18, 62–63, 118
Pittsburg, Kan., 112
Pittsburg, Tex., 43
Plettenberg, Germany, 3
Polk, L. U., 42
Poor, Henry W., 47
Port Arthur, Tex., 9, 117
Port Hudson, La., 17, 118
Porter, Bell & Co., 42
Pressed Brick Co., 10
Princeton, Tex., 95
Pullman-Standard Car Co., 93

Queen & Crescent Route. *See* Vicksburg,
    Shreveport & Pacific Railway

Railway Post Office cars, 115
Reconstruction Finance Corporation, 80, 87;
    Harvey Couch joins RFC Board; loan to
    L&A, 87
Red River, 9, 12, 15–16, 41, 57–58, 122
Red River Landing, La., 16
Red River raft, 41-42
Red River (steamboat) Line, 14
Red River Waterway, 122
Republic of Texas, 42
Reserve, La., 24, 119
Roach, Charles, 56
Rock Island, Arkansas & Louisiana Railroad, 63,
    87
Rock Island-Frisco System, 24

Rock Island line. *See* Chicago, Rock Island &
    Pacific Railway
Rogers, H. H., 24
Rookery Building, Chicago, 7
Rowland, Landon, 122

St. Charles (La.) swamp, 18
St. Francisville, La., 100
St. Louis, Iron Mountain & Southern Railway,
    16, 61–62, 64, 69
St. Louis, Mo., 74
St. Louis & San Francisco Railroad, 83
St. Louis Iron & Machine Works, 8
St. Louis Southwestern Railway, 13, 53, 55,
    77–78, 83, 98
St. Louis Wire Mills Co., 4, 6–7
St. Maurice, La., 15
Ste. Genevieve, Mo., 30
Salem Methodist Church, St. Louis, 4
San Marcos, Tex., 49
Santa Fe Railroad. *See* Atchison, Topeka & Santa
    Fe Railway
Sarah Edenborn (steamboat), 30, **33,** 35–37, 39
Sarto, La., 17, 35
Sayers, J. D., 49
Saylor, Oliver P., 4
Schwab, Charles, 9
Sellers, La., 25
Sheffield Coal & Iron Co., 10
Shell Oil Co., 25
Sherman, Shreveport & Southern Railroad, 31,
    47, 49–50; chartered, 47; extended to
    Shreveport, 49; merged into the Katy Rail-
    road, 50; sold to Edenborn, 31, 51–52
Sherman, Tex., 41
Shreveport, La., 9–11, 15, 19–22, 26, 41,
    49–50, 53, 58, 63–64, 68, 71, 73–75, 79,
    88, 95, 106, 108, 110–11, 116; Central
    Station, 63, **65,** 73, 75, **76,** 80, 83, **84,**
    109; Cotton Belt bridge, 22, 63, 108; cot-
    ton pool, 14; Deramus Yard, 109, 115–16,
    119; extension of L&A to, 63; extension of
    Texas line to, 49–50; first S&RRV depot in,
    15, 22; and first train on Texas extension,
    50; L&A shops, 67, **108;** LR&N shops,
    23; Silver Lake yards/shops, 73, 108;
    Union Station, 13, 22, 50, 95, 108, **116**
Shreveport & Red River Valley Railroad, 9–13,
    15, 17, 58, 60, 62; first locomotive of, 12
Shreveporter, 74–75, 77, 82, 112, 114; maiden
    run of, 74–75, 77; schedule for, 81, 85;
    stops operation, 112
Shrewsbury, La., 22, 104, 125–26; West Yard,
    105, 119, 125–26
Sibley, La., 11, 53, 57, 61, 105, 124

Sibley, Lake Bistineau & Southern Railway, 61
Silver Lake Junction, La., 108
Simmesport, La., 35, 71, 82, 108; LR&N bridge, 36
Simmesport-Lettsworth construction, 108
Sippel, Paul, 25, 35, 37, 108–9
Southern Barbed Wire Co., 7
Southern Belle, 93, 95–97, 99, 105–8, 114–15; in Harvey Couch funeral, 98; inaugural celebration of, 95, 97; faster schedule for, 105; last run of, 115; maiden run of, 97; new equipment for, 105; wreck at Lettsworth, La., 109
Southern Ice & Utilities Co., 76
Southern Pacific Railroad, 16, 22, 31, 60, 81
Southern Railway, 22
South Shore Railway (La.), 100, 103
Southwestern Electric Power Co., 116
Springhill, La., 118; mill at (International Paper Co.), 87, 91, 92, 95, 97, 107, 118; new depot at, 104
Staman, Edward, 37
Stamps, Ark., 53, 56–58, 61, 67, 74; mill at, 53, 62; trackage, 56
Stamps Construction Co., 62–63
Standard Oil Co. of Louisiana, 24, 26, 99
Stauffer, Grant, 100–101
Steel mill at Daingerfield, Tex., 99
Steere, Kenneth, 89, 90
Stilwell, Arthur, 90
Stonegap Colliery Co., 10
Sulphur Springs, Tex., 43, 51, 53

Tap-line case of ICC, 61
Taylor, Ark., 57
Taylor, E. W., 43
Taylor, W. F., 11
Tetro, L. N., 47
Texarkana, Ark.-Tex., 41, 53, 61, 66, 69; L&A offices closed, 73
Texas & Northern Railway, 103
Texas & Pacific Railway, 21–22, 34, 41–43, 50–51, 53, 62, 64, 81–82, 97–98, 110, 122; chartered, 51; line rehabilitation, 99; Shreveport-Dallas service, 99; Torras-Lobdell line, 108
Texas & St. Louis Railway, 53
Texas Junction, La., 110, 116
Texas line of L&A, 39–40, 41, 71, 78, 86, 88, 117; connections for, 51; curvature of, 52; line profile of, 51–52; passenger service ends, 99; rehabilitated, 103
Texas Press Association, 42
Tioga, La., 24, 62
Tioga Jct., La., 24

Tioga Southeastern Railroad, 24
Torras, La., 97, 108
Torras Junction, La., 99
Torras-Lobdell line of T&P, 108
Trout, La., 77, 99
Tunica Hills (La.), 17
Turnbull's Island (La.), 34

U & I (steamboat), 14
Unit coal trains, 116–17, 119, 123
United States Engineers, 36
United States Post Office Department: eliminates railway post office cars, 114–15
United States Railroad Administration, 26, 66; returns L&A to owners, 66
United States Steel Corp., 8–10, 20
Urania Lumber Co., 37

Valley Line. see Shreveport & Red River Valley Railroad
Veals, Tex., 52, 103, 108
Vicksburg, Shreveport & Pacific Railway, 13, 23, 31, 49–51, 53–54, 61, 73, 109, 123; bridge at Shreveport, 22; terminal facilities at Shreveport, 50
Vidalia, La., 67, 102–3, 113
Vidalia branch, 86, 102–3
Vulcan Iron Works, 42

Waskom, Tex., 49–51, 52, 73, 99, 109–10
Water Valley (Sarto), La., 16
Waycott, A. T., 19
Webster Parish, La., 53
Welch, F. M., 14, 16
Welch, Tex., power plant, 116–17
Western Union Barbed Wire Fence Co., 6–7
West Feliciana Railroad, 102
Westphalia, Germany, 3
White Cliffs Cement Co., 10
Whitesboro, Tex., 49
Winnsboro, Tex., 47
Wildsville Junction, La., 64, 103
William II (steamboat), 30, 33, 35–36
William Edenborn (steamboat), 18–19, 22, 24, 30, 33
William Scovell (steamboat), 14
Williams, C. T., 112
Williams, L. B., 35–36, 103, 114, 115
Williams, T. Harry, 27
Winnfield, La., 13–15, 57–58, 63, 86–87, 102, 105; quarry at, 77, 79
Winnfield branch, 14, 17, 26, 36, 76; abandoned, 76
Winn Parish, La., 58
Winnsboro, Tex., 47, 100, 120

World War I, 26
World War II, 99, 104
Wrecks: Georgetown, La., 86; Lettsworth, La.,
    108–9; Louisiana Midland, 114
Wright, Daniel T., 4
Wyandotte, Kansas City & Northwestern Rail-
    road, 47

Yazoo & Mississippi Valley Railroad, 18, 24–25,
    82, 100
Yellow Pine, La., 61

Zacha Junction (Dallas), Tex., 123